PRAISE FOR
Refusing Compulsory Sexuality

"Highly educational, expertly researched, and easy to digest, *Refusing Compulsory Sexuality* eloquently reframes our understanding of asexuality, Blackness, and how the two intersect, providing an essential contribution to a discussion that is often dominated by white voices and perspectives."

—YASMIN BENOIT, asexual activist and model

"Sherronda's writings continue to be a gift to the reader. With *Refusing Compulsory Sexuality*, they expand our understanding of gender, sexuality, and (anti-) Blackness with deftness and precision while also pushing us to rethink our understanding of asexuality and our relationships with ourselves and others. Without any doubt, people will find themselves in this book after spending years trying to find themselves elsewhere, and for those readers, this book will be home."

—LARA WITT, writer and editorial director of *Prism*

"A gloriously honest examination of asexual history and Blackness. Brown's words traverse binaries, exude care, and act as radical archive for those marked by the violence of cisheteropatriarchy. Rarely is a book this rich with history this capable of integrity. It captures the gaps and lives of those deemed unworthy of remembering. *Refusing Compulsory Sexuality* will change you and encourage you to reignite a world worthy of it."

—AMBER BUTTS, author, editor, and organizer

"With *Refusing Compulsory Sexuality*, Sherronda continues to introduce us all to a new and/or deeper perspective on (a)sexuality, queerness, and desire with razor-sharp racial analysis, limpid prose, and incredible research. She is keenly aware of the ways that Black folks have often been removed from conversations specific to asexuality; the ways that the hypersexualization of queer identity has played a significant role in the subjugation of folks on (and outside of) the ace spectrum; and the ways that the hypersexualization of Black flesh is a particular form of anti-Blackness that has been employed by white and non-Black people for centuries—across political lines—to hurt, harm, and abuse Black(ened) subjects.... Sherronda proves with *Refusing Compulsory Sexuality* that they are a leading thinker in asexuality scholarship; gender and sexuality studies will never be the same."

—DA'SHAUN L. HARRISON, author of *Belly of the Beast*

"*Refusing Compulsory Sexuality* is an accessible primer for anyone in the general public looking to understand asexuality; Sherronda J. Brown illustrates the intellectual and lived ramifications for Black asexual possibility by synthesizing a wide range of personal experiences, academic, and activist sources for a sustained and loving look at this critical intersection. The deeper into the book you move, the more grateful you become that they have taken on this project and shared it with us, the world."

—IANNA HAWKINS OWEN, assistant professor
of English and African American studies, Boston
University

Refusing Compulsory Sexuality

Refusing Compulsory Sexuality

A Black Asexual Lens on Our Sex-Obsessed Culture

Sherronda J. Brown

Foreword by HESS LOVE
Afterword by GRACE B FREEDOM

North Atlantic Books
Huichin, unceded Ohlone land
aka Berkeley, California

Published by
North Atlantic Books
Huichin, unceded Ohlone land
aka Berkeley, California

Cover design by Amanda Weiss
Book design by Happenstance Type-O-Rama

Printed in Canada

Refusing Compulsory Sexuality: A Black Asexual Lens on Our Sex-Obsessed Culture is sponsored and published by North Atlantic Books, an educational nonprofit based in the unceded Ohlone land Huichin (*aka* Berkeley, CA) that collaborates with partners to develop cross-cultural perspectives; nurture holistic views of art, science, the humanities, and healing; and seed personal and global transformation by publishing work on the relationship of body, spirit, and nature.

North Atlantic Books' publications are distributed to the US trade and internationally by Penguin Random House Publisher Services. For further information, visit our website at www.northatlanticbooks.com.

ISBN 978-1-62317-710-2 (pbk.) — ISBN 978-1-62317-711-9 (ebook)

Library of Congress Cataloging-in-Publication data
is available from the publisher upon request.

1 2 3 4 5 6 7 8 9 MARQUIS 26 25 24 23 22

This book includes recycled material and material from well-managed forests. North Atlantic Books is committed to the protection of our environment. We print on recycled paper whenever possible and partner with printers who strive to use environmentally responsible practices.

for the impossibles

Contents

FOREWORD BY HESS LOVE xi
INTRODUCTION 1

1 ACEPHOBIA 17
2 GATEKEEPING 29
3 NEVERLAND 43
4 PRODUCTIVITY 55
5 DESIRE 69
6 FRIGIDITY 83
7 UNFIT 95
8 UNHUMAN 109
9 UTILITY 123
10 REFUSAL 137
11 HISTORIES 151
12 POSSIBILITIES 167

BLACK ASEXUAL INSIGHTS 173
AFTERWORD BY GRACE B FREEDOM 177
NOTES 181
INDEX 205
ABOUT THE AUTHOR 225

Foreword

MAYBE SHERRONDA WOULDN'T CLASSIFY herself as a conjurer, but I would. We needed someone to create an understanding of Black asexuality. In response, Sherronda coaxed together research and analysis of Black asexuality in long form. We haven't seen that exist until right now, with this book. All the will, intention, and magic that it takes to conjure something that doesn't yet exist into the world is found here. What you have in your hands is not only a declaration of time, space, and embodiment; what you have in this book is a grimoire on how to cast yourself and folks like you into the world in a way that won't be denied.

Who are we to name ourselves, to declare ourselves as intergalactic territory that isn't colonized in Genesis? Who are we to declare that parts of our most honest, unadulterated personhood aren't up for collaboration, not even for reasons that the collective deem as "good"?

Sherronda does something in this book that I want to stress to you, dear reader. They declare that asexuality can exist, does exist, and should exist in such a way that we don't need to make utility of it. Asexuality just, is. As a society, we have a hard time reckoning with that. There must be "usefulness" somewhere in this gray space. Then, when discussing Black relationships, Black love, Black romance, and Black sex, we often see the relationship as something that functions and reproduces within the larger family, then within the larger community, and finally within the larger society. All toward reproduction, consumption, subjugation, or pleasure. All of it a "utility" to keep the lights on in this machine. All of them we need to step away from when talking about sexuality. Sherronda has helped me learn that parts of my identity don't have to be in service to others. This book is an extension of that: a long, lingering medicine.

I looked at my own asexuality as a model of self-fulfillment, as if it was only valid if I could paint it as something that elevated me spiritually and intrapersonally. What some spiritual traditions will tell you is that queer folk (intentionally inclusive of asexuality) were once prized in their assumed ability to hold certain foresight and wisdom; it was seen as a spiritual rendering of self. In that way, I manufactured and romanticized the usefulness of my own asexuality. That made me feel less misunderstood. Stepping out of centering usefulness helped me shape and reshape my own sexuality.

Sexuality is a flight of the senses; within sexuality is the asexual experience—also a flight of the senses. We believe that if another entity or person is not there to partake, or witness us partake, then it's not sensual. It is. Sense of the self, the abyss, the space where there is no giver and no taker—just being. A divine place that is just as misunderstood as "balance" is. Where Blackness intersects on the realm of sexuality is simultaneously spiritual, political, social, and physical. We don't *have* to perfectly understand Black asexuality to make way for it. Asexuality is already valid. We can know this about ourselves, and we can have trouble with understanding it, unpacking it, and feeling secure within it. Knowing is a way of being in the world. It's an act that can take many forms, even conflicting ones. Conflict doesn't negate knowing.

Black asexuality reminds me of that Kwanzaa tenet—you know, the one that talks about self-determination (Kujichagulia). Kujichagulia—"too expresses itself as both commitment and practice. It demands that we as an African people define, defend, and develop ourselves instead of allowing or encouraging others to do this."

I don't celebrate Kwanzaa, but I define Kujichagulia as having a self-determined attitude about things that you do of yourself, through yourself. To then have the audacity to embody that work and stand on it, whether it adds to the collective in ways we deem valid—or not. There's no surprise that people don't value or see what asexuals add to the collective because they flatten our existence, an experience that doesn't always neatly fit within the binary of consumption and reproduction. So, what does the asexual add to the collective? What *do* Black asexuals add to the collective? We could say that our existence is a reminder to each other that there are parts of ourselves that get to exist outside of the chattel chain reaction to be evoked. We also could say that we don't have to be duty-bound to be useful.

Medicine is not always bitter. Regularly, and without always knowing it, Sherronda has given us necessary pills to swallow. We needed someone to give us the groundwork of Black asexuality, and I couldn't have thought of a better person to do so. Receipts? Sherronda got it. Nuance? They won't renege on it. If all the Black asexuals were to meet on an island, this book would be its shore with warm, clear waters of life and understanding to meet us at our feet. Welcome to the journey.

HESS LOVE

Introduction

If there's a book that you want to read, but it hasn't been written yet, then you must write it.

—TONI MORRISON

COFFEE, ICE CREAM, AND ALCOHOL. These are three things that always elicit a look of shock, horror, and disbelief or even an audible gasp whenever someone learns that I do not enjoy them. *How can you not like coffee? But everyone likes ice cream, it's delicious! So you don't like any kind of alcohol?* They either instantly pity me or become irrationally angry about my aversions—which I did not consciously choose to have. They try to convince me that I simply haven't tried coffee, ice cream, or alcohol in the **correct** way, that I should just try it the way **they** like it. Then, they often pressure me to say that I will commit to trying it again at some undetermined point in the future. Sometimes, I lie and say I will.

Sometimes what they display feels a lot like moral outrage, and maybe it is. People tend to attach morality to peculiar things. They instantly take offense, and in turn become defensive, because they either assume that I am insulting something that brings them great pleasure, comfort, and joy or because they think I am judging them for their indulgence in it. Neither assumption is true. I have simply tried these things—on multiple occasions, with different flavors, and in various situations—and I have determined that I do not like them, and I currently have no interest in trying them again, in any iteration. This is apparently a difficult thing for many people to grasp when it comes to coffee, ice cream, and alcohol—a few of our society's favorite things that we are all encouraged to love, to one extent or another—and I have experienced and witnessed similar reactions when people learn about the existence of asexuality.

This is not a book about sex and food and the connections between social attitudes toward them. Although, the connection is worth mentioning, as examples continue to show up in our everyday lives. Not the least of which is the widely held belief that Black people are given to excess and have poor impulse control concerning both sex and food, a myth that continues to inform anti-Black and anti-fat attitudes and policies. In this way, and many others, purity culture and diet culture are indeed siblings. They are the offspring of colonialism and capitalism, and shame is integral to them both. Diet culture attaches morality to food as a way to police the way people eat and to bring bodies under colonial and capitalist control. Purity culture attaches morality to sex to do the same. Beneath it is the assumption that sex will inevitably occur and that everyone desires it. In fact, that assumption is an essential part of purity culture—the idea that we are all "sinners" continually battling sexual urges, and resisting those urges until we are bound in heterosexual marriage "ordained by God" is what makes us pure. It doesn't seek to hinder people from ever having sex at all; it seeks to control the conditions under which people do have sex. But I digress.

This is a book about compulsory sexuality and asexual experience. People on the asexuality spectrum, also called ace, **experience little to no sexual attraction and/or little to no sexual desire, and these things are not evidenced by either the presence or absence of sexual arousal or activity.** Even though "lacking sexual attraction and/or desire" is the widely accepted general definition, I do not understand asexuality to be defined by this "lack." It is not about being without sexuality, though some may choose to describe themselves this way. I believe it is more true to say that asexuality is defined by a relationship to sex that is atypical to what has been decided on by society at large to be normative, and that atypical nature is marked by varying degrees of sexual attraction and desire. Asexual experiences stand outside what has been accepted and approved of as "normal" sexual experiences for both the queer and the heterosexual communities.

Here are just a few things people "know" about sex, attraction, and desire:

- Sexual attraction and desire, whether queer or heterosexual, are universal; everyone experiences them and should experience them in the same way.
- Sex is a necessary, unavoidable part of life and inherent to human nature.
- Everyone is allosexual—experiencing sexual attraction and desire in normative ways. Anyone who does not have sex is merely celibate or abstinent, suppressing their sexual urges for moral, spiritual, or religious

2

reasons, and people who claim not to want sex are disordered or stunted in some way.

- Sex occurs because sexual attraction and desire signal that we actively want to have sex with someone.
- Desire for sexual contact is sustained, especially within committed romantic relationships.
- Partnered sex is more important, more valuable, and more mature than solo sex.
- These ideas are immovable and not influenced by societal expectations, permissions, or other environmental factors.

This book will challenge every one of these, and more. Asexuality itself—the utmost "abnormal" sexuality, according to many—is already a challenge to these "truths," as it recognizes that we do not experience sexual attraction and desire universally or uniformly precisely because some of us do not experience them at all. It acknowledges that desire for sexual contact with others will not always be sustained, that it is possible for desire to never even be present, and more importantly, that boundaries should always be honored when desire is not present. The asexual lens reveals that sex can and does occur in the wake of mutual sexual attraction, but that it also occurs for a myriad of other reasons, and there are a whole host of negotiations, rationalities, and compromises that take place— sometimes in a split second—when we decide to have sex. It understands that sex can be technically consensual, but still unwanted. Asexual consciousness recognizes that none of the things we "know" to be true about sex are immovable, and they are **always** influenced by societal expectations, permissions, or other environmental factors.

What we call asexuality is only one type of multifaceted experience along a vast spectrum of experiences with sex, attraction, and desire; it is simply another way of being. To be asexual in a world that privileges normative sexual partnership is to be atypical, Other, queer. It is to exist in such a way that many allosexuals perceive us to be lacking because asexual relationships to sex do not align with theirs, with what we have always been told is "normal" and right and required. In their eyes, seeing the world through the prism of compulsory sexuality, asexuals must be lacking in joy and satisfaction, intimacy and connection, emotional intelligence, maturity, sanity, morality, and humanity.

Asexual Realities

As a diverse group, asexuals have varying experiences with asexuality, as well as varying ways of defining and talking about those experiences. *Asexual* is an umbrella term for those who exist on a spectrum, with a myriad of observations, perspectives, and conclusions about asexuality itself, how we relate to it, and how it fits—or refuses to fit—into the existing world. It is not always synonymous with having rare or absent sexual attraction, nor is it always synonymous with having rare or absent sexual desire. Whether or not aces choose to participate in sex and masturbation, and to what degree, is also not the defining factor. Asexual queerness is always transgressive of normative sexuality, in one way or another, but that transgression is not so clearly demarcated that it can be universally applied to the entirety of the spectrum. That being said—even if one might resonate with one or multiple descriptions of asexuality and asexual experience, there is never any obligation to label oneself as asexual if it does not feel comfortable or ring true.

Asexual is a descriptor that has been adopted by many people who identify with the definition of "having little to no sexual attraction and/or desire" while others might gravitate toward "varying levels of sexual attraction and/or desire" and others might find themselves "experiencing only secondary sexual attraction and/or desire" in acutely specific contexts or only with specific people only after forming emotional bonds. Meanwhile, others might describe themselves as someone who "experiences sexual desire but has little to no inclination to ever act upon it (with another person)" or they might say that they simply "prefer not to have sex, have opted out of sex, never want to have anything to do with sex, just never cared about sex, or like the idea of sex more than sex itself." Some may not have pinned down the best language to describe or talk about their personal relationship to sex, attraction, and desire, but they find a home in asexuality nonetheless because they recognize their experience as being atypical, as outside the "normativity" of allosexuality.

People on the ace spectrum can also fluctuate in their feelings toward sex as a characteristic of their asexuality. While some remain firmly in the position of either sex-repulsed, sex-indifferent, or sex-favorable, there are aces who are more fluid between two or all three. Fluctuation can also take place between asexuality and allosexuality, with some people finding themselves falling somewhere in a gray area with a notable amount of flexibility or neutrality. In other respects, ace people can and do experience other types of attraction, and some seek out relationships and partnerships based on those attractions. Regardless of how we might come into asexuality and claim the term as something that describes how we relate to sexual attraction and desire—whether it be absent, rare, secondary, or contextual—it's all valid.

"The Asexual Manifesto" was published by Lisa Orlando in 1972. In it, she offers this definition:

> "Asexual," as we use it, does not mean "without sex" but "relating sexually to no one." This does not of course exclude masturbation but implies that if one has sexual feelings, they do not require another person for their expression. Asexuality is, simply, self-contained sexuality.[1]

For the purposes of this book, I follow Orlando's lead, understanding asexuality to be "relating sexually to no one" and a "self-contained sexuality." Though I recognize and honor all asexual experiences, my discussion here will center an asexuality characterized by rare or absent desire for sexual activity with others as I interrogate compulsory sexuality—the enduring belief that sex is desired by everyone. Discourse and educational resources about asexuality often work to reassure readers that some asexuals still engage in "normal" amounts of sex for an array of reasons, regardless of their actual relationship with sexual attraction and desire, and many of those reasons are not about the asexual's needs but their sexual partner's gratification and comfort.

There will be no such reassurances here. I find them often to be more harmful than helpful, especially when these reassurances are presented as a means to make asexuality more palatable—or at least more tolerable—and more legible to allosexuals. Not only does it demarcate a hard separation between sex-repulsed and sex-favorable/sex-indifferent asexuals, painting the former as true deviance and the latter as a more acceptable form of asexuality, but it also presents even further opportunity for people to misunderstand asexuality as a binary rather than a spectrum. When there is a constant, urgent cry for it to be known that "some asexuals still have sex"—while this is a fact—there must also be an equally urgent accompanying affirmation for those who prefer not to. Here, I want to make sure to affirm those who rarely or never desire sex with others. I

5

also refuse the idea that asexuality is not a normal way to experience sexuality. I name allosexuality as **normative**—as in embodying what society has merely deemed "normal" sexual interest—only as a means to juxtapose it against the distinct ways that asexual queerness has been determined to be "abnormal."

Additionally, many of the things discussed here will also be applicable to aromantic people—those who experience little to no romantic attraction and/or desire—as aromanticism and asexuality often overlap, with many people being both asexual and aromantic. This, too, is a spectrum of people who resist societal expectations and demands surrounding intimacy and kinship. Aros, like aces, are relational misfits. Therefore, there will be moments throughout this work on compulsory sexuality and asexual experience that will also be relevant to compulsory romance and aromantic experience.

This book is not concerned with proving whether or not asexuality is a real orientation and identity. That is not up for debate. Nor is its aim to definitively name what asexuality is, to make it unassailable to detractors and rebuttals. As with other orientations, asexuality carries multiple meanings outside of its dictionary definition or the generally held consensus. Across the spectrum, asexuals articulate their own meaning and make their own determinations about what their asexuality signifies for and about themselves. Every one of us possesses that right, regardless of identity.

In "Asexual and Autoerotic Women: Two Invisible Groups"—one of the earliest academic texts to explore asexuality, published in 1977—Myra T. Johnson asserts that a significant challenge to asexuals has been the lack of available language to talk about our asexuality, which contributes to our invisibility. She writes,

> There appear to be few really appropriate words in the English language to describe the individual who, regardless of physical or emotional condition, actual sexual history, and marital status or ideological orientation, seems to prefer not to engage in sexual activity. Oppressed by the consensus that they are nonexistent, these are the "unnoticed."[2]

As with other identity labels, *asexual* is not prescriptive of behavior; it is a tool. People are free to use the term to help better understand themselves and find community with others who also find the label to be accurate. It is unfortunately quite true that labels can sometimes feel as carceral as they do liberating. But labels don't put us in a box. Ideas do. For so many of us, it is in asexuality that we find the affirmation we have always needed but were never afforded by any other language. We have taken hold of the part of our being, or our becoming, that has long been nameless, and we have given it a name.

Compulsory Sexuality

Content note: sexual violation, coercion, r*pe and r*pe culture

Compulsory sexuality is the idea that sex is universally desired as a feature of human nature, that we are essentially obligated to participate in sex at some point in life, and that there is something fundamentally wrong with anyone who does not want to—whether it be perceived as a defect of morality, psychology, or physiology. Therefore, it creates barriers to seeing asexuality as a valid existence. As Kristina Gupta asserts in "Compulsory Sexuality: Evaluating an Emerging Concept," it is an "assumption that all people are sexual and [describes] the social norms and practices that both marginalize various forms of nonsexuality, such as a lack of sexual desire or behavior, and compel people to experience themselves as desiring subjects, take up sexual identities, and engage in sexual activity."[3] And this ideology "regulates the behavior of all people, not just those who identify as asexual."[4]

When sex is compulsory, it fosters the sense that we are each duty-bound to consistently engage in a certain arbitrary amount of sexual activity—regarding it as something that should be weighed, measured, and quantified, rather than an experience that people should engage in only when all involved have the desire and ability to do so, regardless of how frequent or infrequent that may be. Removing it from the center and the pedestal in our relationships—or, in some cases, our mere existence—would better serve everyone, not only asexuals.

The many "rules" compulsory sexuality generates keep many people committed to (sometimes willfully) misunderstanding asexuality, and also often keep many asexuals from recognizing or honoring our own asexuality. Compulsory sexuality allows for a tacit refusal or inability to accept the idea that we all have the inherent right to govern our own bodies and make our own decisions about whether or not to engage in sex, and that we can do this based on whatever criteria we deem fit. This right to total sexual autonomy is central to consent, and society's inability to properly honor consent and interrogate rape culture—and the ways it is upheld by misogyny and racism—is central to the denial of asexuality.

This book will take a particular focus on people socialized as women—those assigned female or perceived to be women regardless of their actual gender identity, alongside cis women. While the writers I quote here speak only of (presumably) cis women, when I speak of people socialized as women in this work, I am referring both to people who are self-affirmed as women and those merely assumed to be women through a cisnormative lens. This includes those who are nonbinary, trans, intersex, genderqueer, or genderfree; who may consider themselves to be woman-aligned, woman-adjacent, or to have no connection to womanhood at all, but who are nevertheless marginalized by and experience the oppressive effects of misogyny, patriarchy, male supremacy, and the gender binary. I write with this focus in order to emphasize how compulsory sexuality and cisheteropatriarchy both impact our (a)sexual experience as marginalized genders or genderfree people, namely through the expectations of "dutiful sex" and sociosexual submission to men, both of which uphold rape culture. Within rape culture, sexual violation becomes trivialized and normalized, victims are made to carry the weight of the blame, and those who commit these violations are not held accountable. People who are socialized as and perceived to be women are often especially vulnerable to being victimized in this way; we too often have our entire lives undone by rape culture and the abuses it permits.

It's important to understand that asexual experience is not monolithic. However, sexual violation is a common reality for people on the asexuality spectrum. For that reason, this book must discuss sexual violence and coercion at various points. Some of the pages that follow explore the ways compulsory sexuality promotes rape culture and how this, in turn, creates barriers to understanding and respecting asexuality. Compulsory sexuality and rape culture result in people being pressured into sexual situations because of the assumption that they should want to have sex and that there is something wrong, unnatural, and inhuman about not wanting it to the extent that others expect or not wanting it at all. Sex is so often regarded as a property and a "right" owed, as a demand that we are obligated to fulfill, that many people feel entitled to sex—and not just the men we easily recognize as incels, or "involuntary celibates." These are male supremacists who fail to form romantic and sexual relationships or connections, blame others for their social and sexual ineptitude, and believe that women should be required or forced to have sex with them. Several have even become mass killers because of their frustrations and misogyny. Violent, angry men inhabiting incel circles, perhaps more than any other subset of people, demonstrate how dangerous compulsory sexuality fused with rape culture can be.

Under compulsory sexuality, the desires of those with normative sexual urges are prioritized. It's a belief system that eschews consent and preaches instant gratification for people who want sex, but cares not for the safety, comfort, health, or autonomy of people who do not. It doesn't just ask us to comply. It makes way for others to demand, manipulate, coerce, and force us into situations in which we are expected to disregard our own well-being for the sake of "normality." It keeps far too many people tethered to an existence wherein having sex when they would rather not or enduring sex they do not enjoy is a common and normalized occurrence. We have to acknowledge the damage that is done when we don't admit that our society views sex as compulsory, as an inescapable obligation, largely because it is viewed as something owed to men. We have to contend with how that contributes to both rape culture and asexual discrimination, which are often one and the same.

Throughout this book, I often name how cisheteronormativity and cisheteropatriarchy inform compulsory sexuality and asexual discrimination. As queer theorist Cathy J. Cohen writes in "Punks, Bulldaggers and Welfare Queens: The Radical Potential of Queer Politics," heteronormativity is "both those localized practices and those centralized institutions which legitimize and privilege heterosexuality and heterosexual relationships as fundamental and 'natural' within society."[5] I make the addition of cis—to say cisheteronormativity—to acknowledge how these practices and institutions also legitimize and privilege people who are cis while oppressing trans, nonbinary, and otherwise genderqueer identities as well as intersex people who "fail" to perform their assigned gender according to societal standards. Meanwhile, I use cisheteropatriarchy to refer to the political-social system that provides institutional power to cisheterosexual men through the exploitation and subjugation of women and other marginalized genders, as well as people of sexualities that do not align with heterosexuality.

When our society largely accepts sex as a mandatory practice—and also remains deeply invested in cisheteronormativity, cisheteropatriarchy, white supremacy, capitalism, healthism, ableism, fatphobia, anti-Blackness, rape culture, and more—it is imperative to examine how compulsory sexuality impacts the most marginalized. For this work, it is also necessary to examine how various power dynamics work to paint asexuality either as an impossibility, or as not queer (enough), or as somehow both at the same time. Cohen states that she is "interested in examining the concept of 'queer' in order to think about how we might construct a new political identity that is truly liberating, transformative, and inclusive of all those who stand on the outside of the dominant constructed norm of state-sanctioned white middle- and upper-class heterosexuality."[6] I am interested in doing the same. Specifically, I am interested in situating asexuality and asexual people within this queer political identity and praxis.

I believe that an asexual consciousness is necessary in the exploration and analysis of compulsory sexuality. Here, I affirm asexuality beyond an orientation label or umbrella term. It also provides a lens through which we can view, take in, analyze, and understand the world and how we exist within it. In my understanding, asexuality exists as a refusal of compulsory sexuality, in defiance of cisheteropatriarchal mandates, and as an opportunity to deeply interrogate how sexual scripts connect with and inform conceptions of gender and race.

Savage Sexuality

Content note: racial fetishism, sexual and reproductive violence, r*pe culture, Black death

> *Western social thought associates Blackness with an imagined uncivilized, wild sexuality and uses this association as one lynchpin of racial difference. Whether depicted as "freaks" of nature or as being the essence of nature itself, savage, untamed sexuality characterizes Western representations of [people] of African descent.*
>
> —PATRICIA HILL COLLINS, *Black Sexual Politics: African Americans, Gender, and the New Racism*[7]

Sex has utility and can be used for many things, and white supremacy often utilizes sex to both carry out and excuse its racist violence. I do not mean only the act of sex itself, as in the colliding and touching of bodies. I also mean everything surrounding sex—one's sexual desirability or appeal, one's sexual "preferences" or proclivities, one's reproduction as a result of sex acts, stereotypes about one's sexuality. The ways sex becomes gendered and racialized become clearer when we understand sex as a utility, especially when we acknowledge the relationship of gendered and racialized people to the nation-state and to the systems of cisheteropatriarchy and white supremacy. This is how sexual violence becomes a tool of war, terrorism, control, and various other interpersonal and systemic abuses.

Black sexuality, as well as reproduction, become heavily policed on interpersonal, social, and judicial levels, as myths of Black sexual deviance are cited as proof of the superiority, purity, and humanity of whiteness. This is why this book is concerned with how Blackness and (a)sexuality fit together. It's also why one of the things this book will do is demonstrate how sex is utilized as a weapon against Black people in one instance and used to show "solidarity" with us in another. In either scenario, entire sexual lives are imposed on us and written onto our bodies without our consent, and both utilizations of sex are driven by the same anti-Black sexual stereotypes. These stereotypes have always been used as justification for the incremental genocide of Black people—for terrorizing Black people and communities; for trafficking, enslaving, torturing, and exploiting Black people; for creating policy and law that specifically targets Black people and Black families. These things are always at work in our sexual lives and in how others engage us sexually. Blackness negates the need for consent in the social imagination since we are constructed as always consenting—either passively or enthusiastically—to the sexualization imposed onto us.

This ever-present "consent" was integral to sexual and reproductive violence on the plantation, the centerpiece of the industry of slavery and Black genocide. White slaveholders, of course, used their own beliefs about the sexual deviancy and subhumanity of Blackness to justify and rationalize their brutalities. Ianna Hawkins Owen writes, in "On the Racialization of Asexuality," a seminal piece on the subject,

> The image of the Jezebel, a stereotype of the black female as erotically deviant, insatiable, and sexually savage, required the disciplining structures of slavery. The reduction of the black female to her libido

rationalized the use of her body as a breeder for slavery and offered a more palatable explanation for nonconsensual sexual relations between enslaved women and their masters.[8]

Under the (il)logic of white supremacy, the sexual and reproductive violences against enslaved Africans, which stripped them of control over much of their own sexualities and family planning, could never be recognized as a violation of consent; white rationale intentionally disallowed access to true consent for Black people by denying Black people access to the category of human. These ideologies have lingered for centuries after, continuing to manifest in how Black sexuality is perceived in contemporary society. Compulsory sexuality and rape culture both work to help keep alive anti-Black sexual stereotypes, which means they both are and always have been tools of white supremacy.

These ideas, and many more, are formed through racist understandings of how sexually savage Black people must inherently be, how sexually available we should be, and how we allegedly use sex irresponsibly and immorally, and therefore do not deserve to have autonomous sexual desires. Meanwhile, others are free to project their own desires onto us. This is the historical and social narrative that works to eclipse the possibility of the Black asexual. For Black people, our asexuality will never be fully separate from larger endeavors to excavate Black sexuality itself from beneath dehumanizing white colonial interpretations.

So, what does it mean for Black people as a whole, but especially the Black asexual, when Blackness and Black sexuality are always already criminalized, moralized, and fetishized under white supremacist and colonial thought? This is one question this book asks and attempts to answer—or at least engage with significantly. The myth of the uncontrollable and socially menacing Black libido persists and finds its roots strongly affixed to white colonial and supremacist rationale. Its result has been psychosexual and sociosexual racism, fetishism, and terrorism against generations of Black people of all sexualities, orientations, and genders. Here, and always, I affirm all expressions of Black sexuality. We deserve to embrace our (a)sexualities outside of the confines of myths about the hypersexual Black body and outside of a need to respond to the various anti-Black claims and mandates of white supremacy.

These white supremacist ideologies have long been and continue to be notably present within queer communities and discourse. In 1984, James Baldwin told *The Village Voice,*

> I think white gay people feel cheated because they were born, in principle, in a society in which they were supposed to be safe. The anomaly of their sexuality puts them in danger, unexpectedly. Their reaction seems to me in direct proportion to their sense of feeling cheated of the advantages which accrue to white people in a white society. There's an element, it has always seemed to me, of bewilderment and complaint. Now that may sound very harsh, but the gay world as such is no more prepared to accept black people than anywhere else in society.[9]

Though Baldwin spoke specifically of gay men, his assessment applies to and is observable in the whole of queer spaces and in dominant understandings of those spaces. Contemporary society imagines all forms of queerness as being overwhelmingly associated and aligned with whiteness. As such, Black asexuals often find ourselves either left out or pushed out of spaces that should be affirming for all on the asexuality spectrum, usually with the claim that "talking about race will only divide us" or "Black people can't be asexual." Another thing this book will demonstrate is why it is past time for asexual communities at large to acknowledge how social anxieties about sexual difference and "deviance" are deeply connected to and informed by anti-Blackness (and anti-Indigeneity), and to recognize how endemic white supremacist thought is to anti-asexual attitudes. Sexual liberation cannot be achieved for those on the margins without challenging both cisheteropatriarchy and white supremacy—systems that cannot be divorced from one another and that Black folks have been writing against for centuries. As Ianna Hawkins Owen affirms for us, "Discussions of asexuality are inextricably linked to the concept of hypersexuality and the consolidation of its discursive attachment to blackness."[10]

With *Aberrations in Black: Toward a Queer of Color Critique,* Roderick Ferguson demonstrates how Blackness and Black nonheteronormative sexual relations became understood as queer under cisheteropatriarchy. As such, Blackness and Black forms of intimacy and kinship have historically been understood as being outside what is considered "normal" in the white imaginary, and therefore, it has always been demonized and punished. Specifically, the state identified Black queerness as a threat and endeavored to effectively outlaw it as a way to further oppress Black people following chattel slavery:

> Emancipation enacted a demand for sexual regulation and the abolition of nonheteronormative practices. In fact, the issue of African American nonheteronormativity was foremost on the agenda of the American Freedmen's inquiry commission, created in 1863 as part of the Freedmen's Bureau's efforts to determine the state's relationship to newly emancipated slaves. [The] commission's reports to the secretary of war express an anxiety about the nonheteronormative practices of African Americans, coding those practices as proof of the "uncivilized, degraded, undisciplined, and … wholly unchristian ways" of the slaves. As the bureau attempted to rationalize African American sexuality by imposing heterosexual marriage upon the freedman through the rule of law and as a condition for citizenship, the racialization of blacks as pathologically nonheteronormative tightened the link between citizenship and a racialized heteronormativity. Those newly freed African Americans who rejected marriage and monogamy were imprisoned and/or denied pension payments.[11]

Beyond this attempt to wipe out forms of nonheteronormativity (and nonmonogamy) among Black people, white queerness became understood as a deviance in line with "savage" sexuality and gender ambiguity, both apparent relics of primitivity and inferior to "civilized" whiteness. *Queering the Color Line: Race and the Invention of Homosexuality in American Culture* by Siobhan B. Somerville makes clear how "the formation of notions of heterosexuality and homosexuality [and other forms of queerness] emerged in the United States through (and not merely parallel to) a discourse saturated with assumptions about the racialization of bodies."[12] Sexologists, biologists, eugenicists, and more produced works that "constructed both the nonwhite body and the nonheterosexual body as pathological,"[13] with several even comparing the genitalia of white lesbians to Black "female" genitalia in order to prove their deviance. "One of the most consistent medical characterizations of the anatomy of both African American women and [white] lesbians was the myth of an unusually large clitoris"[14] and labia resembling "fleshy sacs,"[15] which invoked imagery of "male" anatomy present on the white lesbian and Black "female" body. This gender nonconformity was considered "uncivilized," unevolved, and primitive, with English eugenicist Havelock Ellis remarking that the lack of difference between genders was typically only found in "savage societies."[16]

As Charles W. Mills writes in *The Racial Contract,* "race is in no way an 'afterthought,' a 'deviation' from ostensibly raceless Western ideals, but rather a central shaping constituent of those ideals."[17] Our world is stratified through anti-Blackness; it often functions as a source of unity among non-Black people. Blackness becomes a benchmark, with all others defining themselves and their sex and gender "normality" in juxtaposition to Blackness and the Black body itself—specifically as antithetical to it. When I say "the Black body," it is not to depersonalize, dehumanize, or objectify Black people. It is to highlight how white supremacy depersonalizes, dehumanizes, and objectifies Black people by conceiving of us as only a body, as only a monolithic form, as only a meal to be consumed, as only a singular, grotesque vessel harboring boundless sexual dangers and curiosities. Mills explains,

> The nonwhite body carries a halo of blackness around it which may actually make some whites physically uncomfortable.... Part of this feeling is sexual: the black body in particular is seen as paradigmatically a body. Lewis Gordon suggests that the black "presence is a form of absence.... Every black person becomes a limb of an enormous black body: THE BLACK BODY."[18]

White supremacy and its agents have historically used anti-Blackness to sculpt and define white cisheterosexuality by aligning forms of queerness with Black "savagery" and the Black body. And now, anti-Blackness becomes used to a different end, in efforts to erase Black queerness and promote white people as the most authentic queer projects. Cisheteropatriarchy is a product of whiteness, its delusions of inherent supremacy, and its violent colonial rule. The narcissistic nature of white supremacy means that white queer people often see the subversion of this system as the domain of whiteness as well, rubbing salt in the wounds left by the colonial violence that has tried to snuff out the queerness of Black and Indigenous cultures.

For this reason, Black queer activists have always had to be invested in dismantling white supremacy as the source of both anti-Blackness and queer antagonism.

Meanwhile, white queer activists have been invested in upholding white supremacy, because they continue to benefit from a system that affords power to whiteness and white people, even when they are also queer. What is true of whiteness in every space, even in "progressive" and "inclusive" spaces, is that it will always work to create some form of exclusivity as a means to reassert white superiority. Therefore, white asexuals often claim asexual queerness as a property, just as whiteness itself is claimed as a property, as a space that others are barred from entering into.

The belief that Black people can never disengage from an easily accessible and consumable sexuality is incredibly damaging to Black people as a whole, and uniquely so to the Black asexual. Black asexuality shatters centuries-old beliefs, upheld by caricatures like the Mandingo, the Jezebel, the Mammy, and more. Accepting the existence of genuine Black asexuality would require those who hold so tightly to these myths to do the work of dismantling them. But many people do not want to let go of racist sexual stereotypes because they are comforted by them, they are comforted by the anti-Blackness that is central to their worldview, as it is precisely what affords them their social value. The Black asexual threatens to upend everything they think they know about Blackness, and everything they think they know about themselves as allegedly superior. Black asexuality threatens their worldview, which means it ultimately threatens their world.

I am the descendant of stolen Africans, on stolen land. I came into being within the illegitimate borders of the colonial entity my ancestors helped to build with forced, unpaid labor. As a displaced African born, raised, and living in the so-called United States, the perspective that I write this from will be specific to and reflective of being born Black in a Western society and culture.

I conceived of this book in North Carolina, which has been home to an array of Indigenous peoples, including the tribes and nations of Bear River / Bay River, Cape Fear, Catawba, Chowanoke, Coree/Coranine, Creek, Croatan, Eno, Hatteras, Keyauwee, Machapunga, Moratoc, Natchez, Neusiok, Pamlico, Shakori, Sara/Cheraw, Sissipahaw, Sugeree, Wateree, Weapemeoc, Woccon, Yadkin, and Yeopim. At present, North Carolina recognizes eight tribes: Coharie, Lumbee, Meherrin, Occaneechi Saponi, Haliwa Saponi, Waccamaw Siouan, Sappony, and the Eastern Band of Cherokee.

1

Acephobia

It is axiomatic that if we do not define ourselves for ourselves, we will be defined by others—for their use and to our detriment.

—AUDRE LORDE

DID YOU KNOW THAT some people don't have internal monologues?[1] When this fun fact gained online traction, the internet exploded with curiosity, wonderment, fascination, and disbelief. Not only were people with internal monologues surprised to learn that there are people who do not have one, but those without internal monologues were aghast to learn that there are people who do.[2] This resulted in an exchange between people familiar with both experiences describing what it's like inside their heads, how thoughts form and how often they do or do not talk to themselves.

As someone who has never been able to silence their internal monologue, the concept of having a quieter brain is an incredibly difficult thing for me to process. I don't know what it's like to have that kind of experience with my brain and, therefore, I cannot understand the relationship that someone with no internal monologue has with theirs. Did you notice how I framed the question "Did you know that some people don't have internal monologues?" as if **having one** is the norm and **not having one** is abnormal, as if every person reading this will also recognize and understand internal monologuing as the norm? For someone who understands not having an internal monologue as the "normal" experience, my question will read very differently.

In psychologist Russell T. Hurlburt's 2011 study, subjects experienced hearing an "inner voice" in only 26 percent of all samples, though the frequency at which they heard that voice varied.[3] Hurlburt notes that Bernard Baars, a leading researcher in consciousness science, claims, "Human beings talk to themselves every moment of the waking day.... Overt speech takes up perhaps a tenth of the waking day, but inner speech goes on all the time."[4] He also presents a relevant quote from linguist John McWhorter about what happens in our mind's eye when we use speech: "When we utter a word, we cannot help but mentally see an image of its written version."[5] Both Baars and McWhorter assert these things as universal truths, and they do so with immense confidence and assumed authority over other people's reality. Hurlburt challenges that, highlighting the ways these men center themselves and their own experiences in these generalizing claims:

> Maybe Baars talks to *himself* all the time, and maybe McWhorter *himself* sees images of written words while he talks ... but I've investigated such things as carefully as I know how and [have] become convinced that most people (let alone all people) do not do such things.[6]

Because not having an internal monologue is something so contradictory to my daily life experience, I can never fully identify with it or even begin to imagine what it's like. And because it is something that I didn't even know existed until I read an article about it, it would be rather easy for me to simply dismiss it as an impossibility. I imagine, based on many of the reactions I witnessed, that is precisely how some people chose to respond to learning about this phenomenon.

New information that forces us to reconsider or completely alter our worldview is sometimes immediately rejected. This remains true even as the topic changes—whether it be internal monologues or sexual attraction and desire. When some people feel confusion and discomfort with a new idea, they allow it to push them fully into denial and refusal because they find the new idea too difficult to fathom. So what happens when the worldview you hold about sexual attraction and desire—one molded by a lifetime of external messaging and internal confirmations or contortions—becomes challenged by new information asserting something that is inherently in conflict with what you think you know and have spent your entire life believing? The safest and easiest course is to simply reject it.

Rejecting new information requires very little work on your part because it allows you to continue to believe what you have already accepted as true. It allows you to continue your life unencumbered by this new information, without needing to do any work to open yourself up to it, process it, and expand your imagination to allow the new idea to find a home in it. When we view our own experiences inside our own bodies as what is "normal" and then have that idea challenged by new information, it presents us with an uncomfortable situation, but it also presents us with the opportunity to learn and grow. It expands our world, and makes us more empathetic, when we listen to others share experiences that are different from our own and respect that difference, regardless of how foreign it is to what we have always known.

What contributes to ignorance about and resistance to asexuality among the general public is a lack of teaching about asexuality in sex education, as well as limited interest among sex researchers. **Candice N. Hargons** (she/her) is an associate professor of counseling psychology and the founding director of the Center for Healing Racial Trauma. She is interested in studying Black people across the entirety of the sexuality spectrum, and is doing so through developing projects focused on pleasure. One of her most recent studies includes Black asexuals and their experiences with pleasure, among other things. This type of study is quite rare. "Because a lot of research is 'me-search,' it reflects that there are few sex scientists who are both Black and asexual," Hargons explains. "There is less investment in studying people who are marginalized—and, with at least two intersecting marginalized identities, there is even less attention to Black asexuals."

As a sex researcher, she understands the consequences—both institutional and interpersonal—of not properly educating people on asexuality along with the rest of the sexuality spectrum. Hargons says,

> Without comprehensive, anti-racist, inclusive sex education, we tend to pathologize anyone outside of heterosexuality. People are not exposed to the myriad ways one can experience their sexual identities, and it leaves around 1–5 percent of our population [the estimated number of asexuals] out of the conversation. Even though this percentage is small, they are not any less deserving of empirical inquiry and attention. Everyone stands to learn a lot by understanding asexuality as a part of the sexualities spectrum, despite their sexual identity, because that awareness helps with empathy, connection, sexual wellness, and better science.

Epistemic Authority

Most allosexuals don't understand asexuality. A 2019 Sky Data poll on asexuality found that 53 percent of respondents expressed initial confidence in their knowledge of and ability to define asexuality, but 75 percent of these respondents went on to demonstrate a lack of knowledge about the definition of asexuality and little understanding of asexual people's experiences with sexual desire.[7] While much of this ignorance can indeed be attributed to lack of education and awareness, the other contributing factor is that many allosexuals impede their own education when given opportunities to learn, closing themselves off from their capacity for imagination and critical thought when asexuality is the topic of discussion, even to the point of refusing to acknowledge *allosexual* as a term that describes them.

This response to *allosexual* mirrors the way others have responded to *cis* in conversations about trans and nonbinary identities. or even how some white people respond to being reminded of their whiteness in conversations about race and racism, and this is exactly why the word *allosexual* is necessary. Naming non-asexual people as allosexual encourages them to think more deeply about this aspect of their identity, consider its many implications, and reflect on how they move through this world because of it and how that truth impacts others— even, and especially, if it makes them uncomfortable to do this work. It's a reminder that asexuality exists, and that allosexual is just one identity on the spectrum of sexuality—not the default, neutral, blank-slate, "normal" identity that some have always assumed it to be. So much so that they feel it doesn't even need to be named.

I know from personal experience, witnessing, and testimonials that allosexual responses to asexuals and asexuality are typically rife with misunderstanding, bad faith arguments, brick walls, circular logic, denial, and cognitive dissonance. If you've never had sex, then you **can't** know that you are asexual. If you **have** had sex, then you just haven't had enough sex to know what you like yet. But you also can't possibly be asexual if you've had "too much" sex, especially if you enjoyed any part of it. If you come out as ace before a certain age, then it's too early to know that about yourself. After a certain age, you're a fraud because otherwise you would have come out sooner.

In these interactions, asexuality is always painted as an impossibility according to whatever realm of logic the deniers decide to argue within at any given moment. The parameters are also subject to change at any time, and only **they** get to determine what those parameters are and when they are allowed to change, **never** asexuals. A significant and integral part of acephobia is the stubborn refusal to recognize asexual people as authorities on our own lives, as knowers of our own sexuality. This is what British philosopher Miranda Fricker calls epistemic injustice, "a wrong done to someone specifically in their capacity as a knower."[8] More pointedly, it is what Fricker has termed as testimonial injustice, a type of epistemic injustice that "occurs when prejudice causes a hearer to give a deflated level of credibility to a speaker's word."[9] Ultimately, it means that allosexuals feel entitled to attempt rebuttals against any claims we make regarding both our asexuality and the impact of acephobia on our well-being. Their self-imagined, self-appointed position as unchallenged epistemic authorities and our perceived lack of credibility as knowers gives them undue confidence in their ability to make determinations about our reality, even when they have nothing to couch their counterarguments in aside from personal bias, pseudoscience, and false superiority.

Fortunately, allosexuals are not the authority on asexuality. Allosexual opinions on asexuality will never be the barometer against which I measure myself and other asexuals. Their denial does not negate our existence and their lack of understanding does not taint our authenticity. They can never refute us as epistemic authorities on our own lives, as knowers of ourselves. The very unfortunate reason that we must concern ourselves with the fact that allosexuals overwhelmingly misunderstand asexuality or deny its existence is because of what that misunderstanding and denial leads to: violence and discrimination.

The Scope of Asexual Discrimination

Content note: sexual abuse, coercion, r*pe, r*pe culture

Acephobia is the hatred of and discrimination against asexuals, whether through active targeting, casual gestures and rhetoric, or otherwise. It's rooted in the fundamental belief that asexuality is a wrong or impossible way to exist in the world and that asexual-identified people deserve to be punished, or need to be corrected, or both. Acephobic violence is often entangled with other forms of bigotry, especially misogyny and racism—like the misogynistic idea that women owe men sex for being "nice guys" or the racist myth that Black people are inherently hypersexual. In this way, misogyny and racism, together with compulsory sexuality and rape culture, help to fuel acephobia.

Oppressive ideas are never singular; they are always informed by other interlocking notions of power. We understand oppressions and how they operate much better when we recognize them as being rooted in belief systems that are continually overlapping and converging. Their malleability allows them to take various shapes and manifest in a whole host of ways. The "friend zone" concept—in which men lament being relegated to platonic friendships with women they feel entitled to have sex or a romance with—is a product of both misogyny and male supremacy. Meanwhile, the hypersexualization and adultification of Black children assigned girl, which allows for society to blame them for their own sexual abuse rather than those who perpetuate it, is a product of misogynoir, patriarchy, and white supremacy. Wrapped up with all of this is compulsory sexuality.

The nexus where each of these meet is the ideology that sex is not only obligatory, but that it is a property and a "right" owed, especially for those in power to use as they please. This is the same ideology that forms the bedrock for acephobia. It's also what allows many allosexuals not only to believe that asexuals need to be "fixed" or "realigned" to conform with dominant social expectations, but also to appoint and empower themselves as the duty-bound authorities who must enact this repair and realignment—a delusion driven by their own entitlement and ego. It's a dangerous and perverse savior complex that results in sexual violence against asexual people, and this fact highlights how much acephobia is deeply rooted in rape culture.

Asexual people's "failure" to correctly perform and align with heterosexuality means that a heartbreaking number of us have endured corrective rape and coercive sex because someone thought they could "fix" us, or because they felt we owed it to them, or made us feel like we were somehow hurting them if we did not agree to sex, because their desires were more important to them than our comfort, autonomy, or safety. The term *corrective rape* refers to the rape of any individual who does not conform to gender or sexual norms, committed with the intent to "correct" or punish their transgression. While the term was initially created to describe particular acts of violence against lesbians, it has now been expanded to include gender-expansive identities and other non-heterosexual identities, including asexuals.[10] For asexual people, corrective rape—including sexual assault and coercion—occurs as a means to "help" usher us into socially prescribed allosexuality.

This makes asexual vulnerability to sexual violence distinct from non-asexual vulnerability. Asexuals are susceptible to harm from allosexuals of all sexualities in a unique way precisely because the intent of that harm is often to eradicate our asexuality—it's meant to kill the very thing that sets us apart from all allosexual identities in the first place, that marks our departure from societal sexual norms, and that threatens to expose society's devotion to compulsory sexuality. In the 2015 Asexual Community Census, 43.5 percent of the aces surveyed reported past sexual violence—including rape, assault, and coercion[11]—and 50.6 percent of those respondents had experienced sexual violence with their romantic partners.[12] The 2018 Asexual Census saw that number increase to 79.5 percent of aces surveyed having experienced sexual violence. In each report, racially marginalized asexuals were more likely to have experienced sexual violence.[13]

While these censes did not ask respondents to specify whether or not they believed or knew the rape, assault, or coercion to have been necessarily corrective, it is fair to conclude that a portion of these instances were intended to be corrective and to proceed with that understanding, especially because half of these incidents happened with romantic partners. I believe that the sexual pressure and coercion of asexuals is always corrective in part, as the people who pressure us into sex after we initially, and sometimes repeatedly, decline are always seeking to override our **no** and "correct" our course toward a **yes.**

I also believe that challenges made against the existence and validity of asexuality are inherently challenges to sexual boundaries and consent as a whole. It's a deep, shared denial among acephobes that creates the insistence that asexuality cannot or should not exist, and that it must therefore be "fixed" by them. The fundamental belief at the root of this denial of asexuality is the lie that **none of us** truly have the freedom to set boundaries that honor our own bodies and sexual autonomy because we live in a society in which sex is expected of us.

The boundaries around sex that asexuals set are often indefinite ones. Asexuality is not celibacy, or abstinence until marriage, or waiting for the third date, or anticipating the ninety-day mark because that is apparently the point at which a committed, trusted romantic relationship has officially been formed. Those are all boundaries that allosexuals can understand because they are temporary, because they name an endpoint or acknowledge that there will eventually be an expiration of the no-sex boundary. Allosexuals find it easy to regard asexuals as liars because our no-sex boundary is often an eternal one, and acephobes—having been socialized in a world where sex is upheld as an unavoidable inevitability—do not understand full sexual autonomy as a reality for us because they have never seen it as a possibility for themselves. In order to maintain the world they have accepted as the only possible one, they must regard the sexual boundaries set by asexuals as ones that can and should be challenged, even if through violative means.

I have often wondered how much of asexual discrimination and hatred from acephobes is rooted in projection. How much of their denial and disdain is a manifestation of their frustrations about their own perceived inability to say no to sex, frustrations that become transmuted into anger and resentment toward a subset of people who hold consent as fundamental and central to our (a)sexual being? Acephobes tend to cringe at the very term *acephobia* (like most -phobes), and insist that the animosity they harbor toward us is "not a phobia." They are decidedly "not afraid" of asexuals. But a phobia is something that is also characterized as an irrational disgust for something, and at the root of this is fear. So, I must wonder, what exactly is it that acephobes fear? What is it about the concept of asexuality and the implications of its existence that causes so much inner turmoil and discomfort that acephobes feel compelled to deny and challenge someone else's lived experience, and even visit violence upon them because of it?

What are the things that would have to be unearthed and attended to if more allosexuals took inventory of their sexual lives and realized that some of the sexual experiences they always told themselves were consensual were actually not wanted? What becomes unavoidable if they acknowledge that they may have been sexually violated because compulsory sexuality convinced them they weren't "allowed" to say no? What things might have to be said out loud instead of whispered softly or swallowed whole if they begin to excavate their sexual histories and find that they may have committed violations themselves by disregarding someone else's boundaries because compulsory sexuality assured them that their actions were acceptable and even expected? What if it means that, perhaps, they are more complicit in rape culture than they once thought they were, or more so than they are ready to admit? There are massive implications for acknowledging that compulsory sexuality exists, how acephobia is deeply connected with rape culture, and the many ways that it harms us, and those implications are so terrifying to a lot of people that they simply choose to ignore them. But in an effort to protect themselves and their own psyche, they end up participating in a cycle of sexual harm, against asexuals and allosexuals alike.

But acephobia extends beyond these sexual violations and occurs in nearly every arena of our lives. Asexual testimonies include stories of gaslighting, mockery, and abuse by friends, partners, family, coworkers, clergy, medical professionals, and more because of our relationship to sexual attraction and desire. Many of us have been infantilized and belittled because sex is seen as one of the principal markers of maturity and adulthood. Our nonnormative experiences with sexual attraction and desire have been medicalized and pathologized, subjecting us to ableist and even eugenic thought and rhetoric because something must be physiologically or psychologically "wrong" with us for not experiencing sexual attraction or desire the way allosexuals do.

We are often dehumanized—seen as "failures" of humanity, as inhuman, alien, robotic—because sex is accepted as an essential part of being human, and not wanting sex must mean that we are something else entirely. A 2012 study, led by prejudice researchers Cara C. MacInnis and Gordon Hodson, measured bias against asexuals compared with other marginalized sexual orientations and found that asexuals were "evaluated most negatively of all groups" in a survey of heterosexual attitudes in university and community samples.[14] Of the four sexualities the respondents were asked about—the other three being heterosexual, homosexual, and bisexual+ individuals—asexuals were perceived to be the least "human" and to have the least emotional capacity.[15] Within this dehumanization, asexuals were characterized as more "machine-like" and simultaneously more "animal-like" than people of other sexualities. "Asexuals were seen as relatively cold and emotionless *and* unrestrained, impulsive, and less sophisticated."[16] Along with dehumanizing asexuals more than others, respondents also demonstrated future intent to discriminate against all sexual minorities, including asexuals, in terms of social inclusion, hiring decisions, and housing access.[17]

The more dehumanized a group of people are, the more prejudice and discrimination they face, the more susceptible they are to violence—especially sexual violence—and the more likely it is for that violence to become invisibilized. Dehumanization breathes life into a cycle that makes the dehumanized more vulnerable to and less protected from harm, while others become more emboldened to both enact and deny the existence of that harm. This is the reality for asexuals, and all of this becomes compounded for asexual people who are also marginalized by race, gender, disability, body size, class, and so on because we are even farther removed from the privileged identity categories of white, cis, male, able-bodied, neurotypical, wealthy, and thin.

The MacInnis-Hodson findings are already supported by the stories asexuals have to offer about our lives, but they are even further supported by the Attitudes Towards Asexuals (ATA).[18] This study also found strong bias against asexual people, alongside gay, lesbian, and bisexual+ individuals. Respondents reported feeling greater discomfort renting to or hiring asexual people than other sexualities. They also expressed the least interest in future contact with asexuals, unwilling to pursue or consider friendships with people on the asexuality spectrum.[19]

Both the MacInnis-Hodson study and the ATA scale did two additional things to better contextualize acephobia. The studies simultaneously measured for social dominance orientation and accounted for singlism, meaning they (1) gauged the strength of alignment with dominant social ideologies, and (2) controlled for prejudice against single people—in which singles are discriminated against by both partnered people and social institutions, including the workplace, housing, and health care—to determine whether it could explain respondent acephobia. Overall, bias against asexuals remained strong even after allotting for social prejudice against single people, confirming that acephobia is distinct from singlism.[20] It's important to note, however, that even though singlism and acephobia are distinct from one another (and singlism also significantly impacts aromantic people), singlism and acephobia often overlap, especially because asexuals are more likely to be single than allosexuals. This discrimination can look like unpartnered people being stereotyped as immature, nonfunctional, or unproductive members of society, which are stigmas that are also frequently attached to asexuals.

Meanwhile, respondents to these studies with the most negative attitudes toward asexual people were also more strongly aligned with and entrenched in "right-wing authoritarianism, social dominance orientation, sexism, [and] traditional gender-role endorsement." On average, asexuals were targeted with bias for our "lack of sexual attraction and interest" more than gay, lesbian, and bisexual+ people were for their same-gender or multiple-gender attractions and interests.[21] In other words: acephobia exists and persists, at least in part, because acephobes are uncomfortable with the fact that asexuals do not comply with dominant sexual norms and compulsory sexuality.

In the United Kingdom's 2018 National LGBT Survey, asexuals (on par with pansexuals) reported the lowest level of life satisfaction as a sexual or gender minority in the UK. Asexual people were also found to feel the least comfortable overall and among the most likely to conceal their orientation from friends, family, and coworkers for fear of negative reactions to their sexuality.[22] A major reason for asexual people's unease and sense of insecurity is the amount of microaggressions we experience, which are often not recognized as microaggressions at all by the people around us. Microaggressions are "brief and commonplace daily verbal, behavioral, or environmental indignities, whether intentional or unintentional, that communicate hostile, derogatory, or negative slights and insults" toward members of marginalized groups.[23]

In a 2018 study on asexual experiences with microaggressions, asexual participants reported experiencing invalidation, expectations of sexual or relational normativity, pathologization, generalized prejudice against anyone who is not cis or heterosexual, dehumanization, infantilization, tokenization, sexual threats and pressure, sexual assault or corrective rape, and more. The sources of these microaggressions were family, friends and acquaintances, school systems, religious institutions, non-asexual LGBTQ+ counterparts alongside cisheterosexual people, media, medical professionals, and past or prospective romantic partners. Participants also reported that these microaggressions caused increased anxiety, stress within their interpersonal relationships, general to extreme discomfort, and symptoms of depression.[24]

As a form of discrimination, microaggressions are also associated with negative mental health outcomes, having been shown to have negative effects on the mental health of lesbian, gay, and bisexual+ (LGB) individuals. A 2011 study on the mental health outcomes of LGB individuals identified eight categories of microaggressions that sexual minorities might encounter. Four of those categories are: **exoticization,** in which the targets are dehumanized or treated as objects; **discomfort/disapproval,** in which the targets are treated with disrespect and criticism; **assumption of sexual pathology or abnormality,** in which the targets are considered sexual deviants; and **threatening behavior,** in which the targets experience verbal or physical assault or harassment.[25] As the aforementioned study and many asexual testimonies demonstrate, asexuals experience these microaggressions as well—with even less awareness, understanding, and social acceptance.

Acephobia should be taken as seriously as all other discriminations on the basis of sexuality. There is evidence enough that acephobia exists in multiple life spheres and is an abiding force that has a significant impact on the lives of asexual people. The fact that those who demonstrated the most bias against and aversion to asexuals in the MacInnis-Hodson study were also the most faithful to right-wing authoritarianism, social dominance orientation, sexism, and traditional gender roles highlights how the hatred of asexuals is commonly spurred by a desire for strict adherence to cisheteronormativity and white supremacist settler-colonial ideals. The transgressive nature of asexuality disrupts dominant societal sexual norms, and those who are committed to these norms—to one extent or another—believe we should be punished for it, and many of them attempt to enact that punishment by their own hand. Asexual discrimination cannot continue to go unaddressed, diminished, or denied by anyone who claims to be invested in combating sexual violence and working toward the liberation of all queer identities from the confines of white supremacist cisheteropatriarchy.

2

Gatekeeping

*All of our lives we have experienced ourselves as queer, as not belonging, as the essence
of queer ... queer not as being about who you're having sex with—that can be a dimension of it—but queer as being about the self that is at odds with everything around it
and has to invent and create and find a place to speak and to thrive and to live.*

—BELL HOOKS

Content note: queerphobic violence, including sexual violence
QUEER USED TO FEEL like a lie on my tongue. When I first realized I was on
the asexuality spectrum, I tried mingling in virtual queer spaces. Sometimes,
it was okay. Other times, I felt invisible. Other times, I was pushed out. Someone once told me that the A in LGBTQIA+ did not count, nor did it matter,
and others echoed their sentiment. Someone else once told me that they would
recognize the A in LGBTQIA+ only when asexual people began to experience
discrimination and sexual violence like the people the rest of the acronym represents, and they were unwilling to hear evidence of the fact that we do. I had
my queerness invalidated and witnessed others have theirs invalidated by self-
proclaimed queer experts citing the dangers allosexual queer identities face for
being out or not "passing" as straight or cis. All the while, their arguments rested
on their own view of asexuality through a monolithic lens while making broad
assumptions about what traumas asexual people may or may not have and how
they may or may not be wrapped up with our asexuality. I tried to "come out"
of the proverbial closet, but every time I took a step, there was always someone
there to shove me back in.

I knew I was not straight. I had always failed to perform heterosexuality
correctly, but I was not evidencing my deviation from heterosexuality in a way

that some could recognize as queer enough. And so, what I learned from queer exclusionists is that asexuality will never be loud enough or legitimate enough to be called queer, because queerness is apparently about sex and that fact disqualifies asexuals. I learned that the more pointed terms asexuals use to describe our specific experiences with sex and attraction—like demisexual or aceflux— are just frivolous five-dollar words that mean nothing, excuses wrapped up in a pretty little bow. They taught me that asexuals are liars, just making shit up, vying for special snowflake recognition. Some even informed me, without further explanation, that asexual just means "a sexual predator." Among straight people, I was too queer. But to queer exclusionists, I was not queer enough. So there I was. Floating on a lonely island between two worlds, an illegitimate unwelcome child in both.

I had always understood queer to mean existing outside of traditional, rigid ideals of what normative sexuality and gender look like. But what I learned from trying to engage in queer spaces while ace was that, next to trauma and discrimination, many queer people center sex in their queerness and conceive of sex acts as the catalysts for queerness itself. And if that's where queerness was located, and could only be located according to some, then where did that leave me? I wasn't fucking back against heteropatriarchy, and what's so radical about not fucking back? What's so queer about not fucking, not dating, not loving in the way that society pedestals as the most significant?

In order for asexuality to be understood and recognized as the queer identity that it is, sex acts and sexualization would first have to be removed from the center of dominant conceptions of queer identity. It follows that asexuals would never fit seamlessly into a mainstream queer discourse that largely focuses on sex and how queer folks (are thought to) engage in it, especially as terms like *top, bottom,* and *verse* go more and more mainstream. Hyperfocus on queer sex and sex roles is a direct result of the oversexualization of queerness as a means to construct it as nothing more than sexual deviance and also to reassert heteronormative gender roles within queer relations—i.e., the myth that mascs cannot be bottoms and fems cannot be tops due to the misogynistic idea that masculine sex partners must always penetrate feminine sex partners because both penetration and masculinity are conflated with dominance and control while femininity and being penetrated are each associated with being passive and submissive under someone else's rule. This, too, is a symptom of compulsory (hetero)sexuality and it creates limitations and harms for all queer folks.

Compulsory sexuality and the oversexualization of queerness not only show up in acephobic erasure and exclusion, but also in biphobic, lesbophobic, transphobic, and homophobic beliefs. Many assumptions made about and discriminations against various queer groups are rooted in how they have sex or how other people **think** they have sex. Queer people are often asked invasive questions about our sex lives and our role in sexual situations in the course of benign conversation. These voyeuristic inquiries about the intimate details of queer people's sexual habits, and even about the mechanics of the sex acts we might engage in (for instance, which body parts go where and in what fashion), are about reaffirming queer people and queer sex as exotic curiosities—deviant and other.

This oversexualization is the same avenue by which bisexual+ individuals become thought of as more promiscuous, less trustworthy people.[1] There is a pervasive myth that bisexual+ partners are more likely to be unfaithful and more likely to spread sexually transmitted infections (STIs) among their partners. These beliefs lead to bisexual+ people being vulnerable to sexual violence at higher rates than lesbians and heterosexuals.[2] They are also more likely to experience victim-blaming following an assault[3] because those who are perceived as more promiscuous than what is socially acceptable are more likely to be blamed for the sexual violence they experience.[4] Meanwhile, lesbians being treated as hypersexual in media is a prevailing issue and it directly contributes to the rates of violence against lesbians and people merely suspected of being lesbians. Two queer women were physically assaulted by a group of teenage boys on a London bus in 2019 because the couple were assumed lesbians and refused to kiss for the entertainment of their attackers.[5] Depictions of lesbians in the media often reduce their relationships and interactions with others to sex, and societal misconceptions about lesbian sex and relationships are worsened by lesbian porn that is made largely by heterosexual men for the gratification of other heterosexual men. So, lesbian sex becomes viewed as something to be freely fetishized and consumed by everyone, but especially by heterosexual men.

Invasive inquiries and demands about trans people's genitalia are often born out of curiosity and confusion about how trans people participate in sex, especially whether or not it is penetrative and phallocentric. This intense focus on the genitalia of trans individuals is specifically used to paint trans women as deceptive sexual predators. It manifests in the disproportionate murder of Black trans women[6] (and transmisogynoir cannot be separated from the fear of the Black phallus). And proposed policy like the infamous now repealed North Carolina HB2 Bathroom Bill of 2016, which prohibited trans people from using bathrooms and locker rooms that align with their gender identity in schools and government buildings.[7] And the legalization of homeless shelters' ability to deny trans women care and resources.[8] Beyond that, it helps fuel the mission to further marginalize trans and nonbinary youth through bills that prevent them from accessing gender-affirming health care and even criminalize them by levying legal penalties at trans girls participating in girls' sports. These penalties could send them to juvenile detention facilities—where abuse against trans and nonbinary youth is prevalent[9]—and has the potential to result in a ninety-day sentence and a $1,000 fine for their parents.[10]

Sex and gender roles, and the dynamics thereof, are used as one of the primary tools of understanding human relationships, interactions, and connections in general. And this way of understanding, and of writing meaning onto certain bodies, becomes heightened for queer people—a manifestation of compulsory sexuality and the oversexualization of queerness that imagines queer people as inherently aberrant, perverse, and sinful spectacles meant to be fetishized, feared, and punished.

None of this is to say that the erotic experiences of queer people and the erotic possibilities of queerness are insignificant to me. Quite the opposite. I will always honor how all queer folks use sex as a means to rebel against cisheteropatriarchal systems. I will always revere queer sex as manifesto, as concert, as affirmation. As cherished and sacred, celebratory and subversive. As an avenue to gender euphoria and healing, as both political and apolitical, as simply a matter-of-fact part of many people's queer existence. Because I know the gifts these things hold.

I will always advocate for every queer person's right to be a fully autonomous sexual being—and that always must and always will include asexuals. Recognizing the significance of queer sex should not mean that every queer person should be mandated to meet an arbitrary sexual prerequisite in order for their queerness to be affirmed. Centering queerness around sex leaves very little room for queer folks for whom sex is insignificant, or for whom sex is never or rarely possible, or for queer folks who have never had sex before, or for queer folks whose only sexual experiences have been violent. It also leaves a lot of queer people, especially young ones, feeling pressured to have a certain amount or a certain type of sex in order to legitimate or prove their queerness to themselves or to someone else.

Because of the demonization of queer sex and anxieties about queer sex being used as the basis for many antiqueer discriminations and policies, I understand the train of logic that leads many to conclude that queer sex itself is the sole impetus for queerphobia and that, therefore, queer sex should be the primary marker of queerness itself. But queer sex is not the sole impetus for queerphobia; it is the divergence from cisheteropatriarchal mandates. A 1999 study found that its participants held deep and sustained bias against gay people even when they abstained from sex.[11] These findings, coupled with the proven bias against and dehumanization of asexuals more than other nonheterosexual identities in both the MacInnis-Hodson study and the ATA scale, indicate that prejudice against marginalized sexual orientations is about far more than the sex we may or may not engage in.

If queerphobia is expressed even when queer sex is not present, then queer sex cannot be such a significant factor by which we define queerness that we end up excluding those for whom sex is not central to their queerness. It's evident that queerphobia is about cisheterosexual society's need to assert dominance, maintain social order, and attempt to bring under colonial control anyone who is not cis and heterosexual, regardless of whether we have sex or not. We are made queer by virtue of our departure from cisheteropatriarchal gender and sexual norms, even as our departures lead us toward different paths.

A Hierarchy of Trauma

Content note: death threats, suicide, r*pe culture
It's time for queer communities to abandon the hierarchy of trauma that supports acephobia with the myth that asexuals do not have "enough" trauma related to our sexual identity to be considered queer. Trauma is not a factor by

which queerness should be measured. In fact, I argue that queerness should not be measured at all. If our goal is to arrive at a reality in which none of us have to endure or die from queerphobic abuses—whether institutional, individual, interpersonal, structural, public, or private—then these abuses should not be such a significant part of how we regard queer identities. If we largely define queerness by whether or not we experience these abuses "enough" to be considered authentic, what room does this leave us to embrace our queer identities outside these abuses, especially when our collective goal is to dismantle them altogether? Is a queer child who grows up loved and affirmed in their queerness any less our comrade than the queer child who grows up hated and suppressed for theirs? Would we not welcome them both with open arms?

Excluding asexuals from queerness under the belief that we do not experience discrimination and trauma "enough" only serves to reproduce the same harms as cisheteropatriarchy. Being subjected to and harmed by compulsory sexuality, rape culture, and acephobia is traumatic, and the denial of this works to obscure the very ways in which asexuals have been harmed by people within queer communities. Allosexual queer folks have absolutely been spectators to asexual queering; they have even been participants in moments where we have been queered because of our relationship to sex, attraction, and desire. Acephobic exclusionists must hold two opposing ideas at once in order to maintain their dissonant belief system that if asexuals are not discriminated against in the same ways and to the same degree that they are, then that discrimination either cannot count or must not exist at all. They hold this belief even as they themselves actively participate in that discrimination, and even as they acknowledge that the discrimination faced by other queer folks can and does differ across gender, sexuality, race, class, disability, and more.

So I ask: What exactly is the connective tissue between the experiences of those who call ourselves queer? What is the distinct criteria that supposedly disqualifies asexuals from being able to claim queerness or even exist in "LGBTQIA+" spaces, despite the presence of the *A* in the acronym? Is it discrimination, invalidation, and violence based on their sexual or gender/sex variant identities? Is it failing to perform heterosexual or cisnormative social scripts and being ostracized for it? Is it institutional mandates and unwritten rules that don't take their sexuality or gender/sex into consideration, or are specifically designed to other people like them? Is it having their very existence and the validity of that existence up for constant debate? Is it feeling invisibilized in mainstream media and cultural artifacts because the relationships or gender/sexes depicted therein rarely, if ever, reflect their own experience with these things? Is it feeling largely isolated and distinctly barred from being able to relate in social settings where the conversations operate on the assumption that everyone involved has a universal experience with sexuality or gender/sex, and that experience is typically a cisheteronormative one?

The asexuality spectrum is filled with people who experience these things, as I have enumerated in the previous chapter. Though it does not and should not define us, it is unfortunately true that so many queer people know the feeling of a crushed, dying spirit that comes from feeling forced, coerced, and threatened into performing a sexuality or gender that is simply not a part of our natural way of existing. We know, intimately, the wreckage that it leaves behind, and what it's like to spend a lifetime trying to heal our accumulated wounds. Asexuals know this torment well, and the insistence that asexual folks do not experience any forms of discrimination or violence because of our identities—or not enough for it to count—adds another layer to the cognitive dissonance because perpetuating this myth is itself a form of acephobic harm.

Nevertheless, "asexuals are straight-passing" is an accusation that often gets lobbed at us, along with pointed objections of "asexuals are just straight people who don't have sex." Acephobic exclusionists assert that asexuals cannot be queer because asexual people allegedly never receive the kind of ire and harassment that is informed by someone expressing attraction to the "wrong" person within a cisheteronormative society—someone of the same gender or to people of multiple genders—and, from their perspective, this means that what asexuals experience is "the heterosexual experience." This assumption ignores the fact that many aces pursue and happily commit to relationships and lifelong partnerships with people of the same gender or multiple genders. It also disregards the existence of gender expansive and gender divergent asexuals and how gender identity informs our lived experience. Most significantly, and disingenuously, it omits how heterosexuality demands compulsory (hetero)sexuality and the normative participation in heterosexual attraction, desire, and sex as an essential part of performing the heterosexual script.

Alongside the notion that being cis and heterosexual is the only acceptable way to exist, cisheteronormativity operates on a foundation of understandings, assumptions, mandates, expectations, and permissions for heterosexual people. What it demands, above all, is compliance with and allegiance to heterosexuality. Asexuals do not meet these demands, and this places us squarely outside of the scripted heterosexual experience. Asexuality is always a site of subversion and resistance to cisheteronormativity itself, and is that not what queerness is? What queer exclusionists claim is the "straight-passing" of asexuals is nothing more than others projecting their own heteronormative assumptions onto us based on their own narrow notions of how queerness should be performed. It's rooted in a fundamental belief—although likely a subconscious one—that everyone is categorically heterosexual until the moment they begin to experience, express, and act on sexual attraction to the same gender or multiple genders. This is just one of the ways that cisheteronormativity becomes reproduced in queer communities and queer modes of thinking. It constructs heterosexuality not simply as a default orientation, but also as the blank slate that queerness must be written onto. An insult to us all.

Asexuals being **assumed** as heterosexual by others, based on heteronormative beliefs, does not amount to asexuals "passing for straight." We are assumed to be heterosexual because heterosexuality is compulsorily seen as the default orientation, because people continually fail to learn about asexuality and asexual people when presented with opportunities to do so, and because they often refuse to accept our asexuality as a valid orientation to begin with. What other people choose to see—and what they choose not to believe—from their own biased perspective is not the responsibility or fault of asexuals. Being invisibilized, constantly wading through the expectations and projections of compulsory (hetero)sexuality, and having others consistently assert themselves as the authorities on our lives, experiences, and identities while refusing us the right to have this authority ourselves is not and never will be "passing for straight."

Acephobic exclusionists also argue that any discrimination asexuals experience is only because we can be and sometimes are mistaken for gay or lesbian. With this argument, they veer incredibly close to a vital point, but ultimately fail to grasp it. If and when asexuals are mistakenly read as gay or lesbian, it is because our asexuality—our failure to perform a "normal" heterosexuality—has

36

signaled that there is something nonheteronormative about us; it has signaled our queerness. The fact that those recognizing our queerness can only read it as gay or lesbian, rather than as asexual, is because asexuality is constantly invalidated while gay and lesbian are largely seen as the only valid queer identities. Asexuality, along with other nonmonosexual identities, would be more recognizable if it were not so strongly regarded as an impossible or wrong way to exist.

The many acephobic microaggressions and discriminations discussed in the previous chapter are evidence enough of how often asexuals fail to "pass for straight" and how much it takes a toll on our well-being. Even more, the internet allows for acephobes to run rampant on any given social media platform, and these platforms offer us little to no protection. I've witnessed asexuals navigate vicious bullying and death threats, with some acephobes advocating for asexuals to receive the death penalty, simply because some people think that us having rare or absent sexual attraction or desire means that we shouldn't be allowed to exist at all. Asexual Twitter users have been added to group chats and lists without warning and sent hateful messages, including ones telling us to kill ourselves or that we should have been aborted. People do these things to us because they enjoy it, because they think we deserve it, because they actively want to see us dead, and they do it because we are asexual. None of this is "straight-passing privilege." It's cisheteronormativity and compulsory sexuality being violently projected onto us. It's rape culture. It's a lifetime of people feeling sexually entitled and taking their anger out on us when we don't perform what they consider to be "normal" sexual behavior. It's people hating us because they know we are not like them. It's acephobia.

I have observed queer allosexuals openly admit to their active discrimination against asexuals, only to assert mere moments later that acephobia does not exist and that aces cannot be queer. Meanwhile, others will acknowledge the existence of acephobia and its impact on asexual people's lives, only to then attempt to gatekeep asexuals from claiming any kind of queerness whatsoever. Contradiction after contradiction continually arise in these conversations and efforts to bar us from queerness.

Gatekeeping is always about power—in the same way that borders are always about power, in the same way that policing is always about power, in the same way that categorization is often about determining who should have power over whom. If you can place yourself or your representatives at a border and police who can and cannot traverse its threshold based on how they have been categorized, by you or by someone else, that is about power. The people policing the border may change, the intention behind the policing of the border may change, the criteria by which people are categorized may change, but the refusal or permittance of bodies at the border will always be about power.

What I have come to learn after many years of studying, thinking, and writing about power and oppression is that there will always be factions of marginalized people who do not want collective liberation from the oppressive systems we live and die under. Liberation is simply too big, too daunting, too difficult to fathom. What these people resort to instead is the creation and maintenance of systems in which they have the opportunity to act as oppressors and wield what little power they do have over others. If the world must be structured through hierarchies, then marginalized people who are not fully committed to liberation or the dismantling of these hierarchies must find a way to never be at the bottom. For those marginalized by sexuality or gender within a cisheteronormative system, having this outlook on power and oppression—whether or not they are conscious of it—means that groups who are even more obscure and hieroglyphic to dominant society must be under their boot. In their eyes, asexual people can never be welcomed into queerness.

This is the sort of ugly compromise that makes way for transphobia and transmisogyny within queer spaces. It creates opportunities for biphobia to thrive, for people of nonbinary genders to be further marginalized, for intersex people and their experiences with gender/sex to be erased. It's lateral aggression, and though it may often be trauma-informed, it must still be highlighted and addressed. The same cisheteronormative structures and belief systems that impact asexuals will always impact others in queer spaces, because cisheteronormative modes of thinking will always be violent toward all queer identities.

At the same time, queerphobia will never affect all queer people in the same ways. But regardless of how it manifests, we should always be vigilant of it. That means acknowledging the differences in the forms of oppression we face and being honest about how queer folks can and do sometimes participate in them too, and we can do this while naming that these oppressions and their manifestations all stem from the same place. The previously discussed MacInnis-Hodson study found that, while the amount of bias differed, participants discriminated against gay and lesbian people, bisexual+ individuals, and asexuals alike. Hodson confirms that these biases are intertwined, and heterosexual respondents "who dislike one sexual minority, therefore, also dislike other sexual minorities, even though some of these groups are characterized by their sexual interest and activity and others by their lack of sexual interest and activity."[12]

In her seminal speech "The Master's Tools Will Never Dismantle the Master's House," Audre Lorde offered,

> Without community there is no liberation, only the most vulnerable and temporary armistice between an individual and [their] oppression. But community must not mean a shedding of our differences, nor the pathetic pretense that these differences do not exist.[13]

All queer communities are facing the same enemy: white supremacist cisheteropatriarchy and sexual, relational, and gender normativity. Exclusionary politics keeps us focused on fighting each other for space, connection, and resources rather than using our collective power to combat the beliefs and systems that oppress us all.

Asexual Is Queer

We are the queer groups, the people that don't belong anywhere, not in the dominant world nor completely within our own cultures. Combined we cover so many oppressions. But the overwhelming oppression is the fact that we do not fit, and because we do not fit we are a threat.

—GLORIA ANZALDÚA, "El Mundo Zurdo," *The Gloria Anzaldúa Reader*[14]

Acephobia remains illegible to many allosexual queer folks because asexuality itself is not fully legible to them. But the issue is not a matter of us making ourselves easier for them to read; it's a matter of others doing the work to expand their own imagination. Asexuality will not be legible to them until they interrogate their own allegiance to cisheteronormativity, binary thinking, and compulsory sexuality, because that allegiance is what persuades them to see asexuality as a mode of heterosexuality rather than its own distinct queer identity.

I am queer. I was queer long before I knew I was queer. I was punished for my queerness long before I knew there was even a word for it. Not only because of my tenuous relationship with the carcerality of gender and the gender binary I know myself to be outside of, but also because my experience with sexual attraction and desire is one that has always been distinct from the prescribed "normal" way to experience these things, and that has tangibly impacted my life.

Let me be exceedingly clear: I have no intention of forcing my way into queer spaces where I am not wanted and where I would be subjected to acephobic violence and rhetoric. I also have no intention of relinquishing my claim to autonomous, supportive, loving spaces within queer communities that I and other asexuals unequivocally deserve, especially the ones that we have had a hand in building and nurturing. I affirm that all aces should feel free enough to identify as queer if they so choose. But, ultimately, it is not so much the label of "queer" that matters to me. It's naming that asexual people's experiences fall outside of the "normativity" of sexuality. Of course, that is precisely what the term *queer* is meant to name, but the term itself need not be our only means of naming our queerness.

Asexuals have always been identified as nonnormative in a sex-focused society of people unwilling to consider perspectives on, attitudes toward, and experiences with sex, attraction, and desire outside their own as possible and valid. As betrayers and failures of our social scripts, asexuals have been pressured to contort, deprive, and sacrifice pieces of ourselves in order to make others more comfortable with our existence—so that they might find some relief from their own uncertainties about which unimaginative box to place us in. It will always be disingenuous to say that asexuals have not been read, understood, and constructed as queer under compulsory sexuality, as uncomfortable subversions of society's sexual and relational norms, even as our right to claim that queerness is continually challenged.

I and many other asexuals will continue to embrace our queerness, regardless of how many gatekeepers try to tell us that we are not allowed to for fear that it will somehow diminish their own queerness. What if instead queer folks accepted the truth that queerness is not a diminishing good, that there is no such thing as being "not queer enough"? What if instead we took refuge in the fact that queerness is multifaceted, multitudinous, multidimensional? There is not one singular, monolithic queer community for which we each must pay dues. There are queer communities, and they are abundant. It is rigid, colonial, binary, cisheteronormative thinking that tells us that queer folks are only allowed one space to fit our entire lives into and that some of us don't deserve any space at all. The imposed limitations of cisheteronormativity need not apply to us.

Recognizing and honoring the multidimensionality of queerness, queer experiences, queer lives, and queer truths is what truly challenges the binaries that are upheld through cisheteropatriarchy. It means the visibility and honoring of all of our stories, dreams, and realities without the need for putting our traumas on display in order to have our queerness recognized by the world. Imagine queer communities where we are free from the obligation to revisit our traumas. Here we can find connection through our departures from and subversions of cisheteropatriarchy without relying on the ways in which it has harmed us as our most significant means of connection. We owe more to our queer selves than rearticulating the cunning violences and mandates of cisheteropatriarchy and imposing them on ourselves.

3

Neverland

DURING MY FRESHMAN YEAR of college, my psychology professor said, "Everything is about sex. You are here, at this university, in this class, because you want to have sex." Snickers came from every corner of the lecture hall. "It's the truth," he continued, excited to enlighten his students. "You came to college so that you can go to parties, meet people, and have sex. And so that you can graduate with a degree that will allow you to get a good job so that you can be an eligible dating and marriage prospect, and have sex." All around me, heads nodded while I sat in confusion, unable to wrap my head around the assertion that **everything** is about sex.

I was already exceedingly aware of the fact that my lack of investment in seeking out sexual encounters alienated me from my college peers, especially because some of the people closest to me made it clear, in one way or another, that there was something "abnormal" about this, about me. They viewed me as immature and undeveloped; some even pitied me. I needed to "grow up" or else I would "end up alone," they'd warn. I referred to myself as a "late bloomer" for many subsequent years, often as a sort of apology or disclaimer. Only after affirming my asexuality did I understand that this "late bloomer" rhetoric was an unhelpful sentiment and a reinforcement of the same ideologies that caused others to treat me like an abnormality in the first place. One does not "bloom"—as in, enter into sexual exploration—too late, because there is no set time frame in which one must "bloom." One is not required to "bloom" in this way at all.

Infantilization is a dehumanizing process by which a self-righteous sense of superiority is wielded over someone seen as inferior—assumed to be less mature, more naive, and less worthy of respect. It's closely akin to and often comes with a heaping side of patronization and condescension, with the infantilized being spoken to and treated as if they are unintelligent, unimportant, deserving of pity, and in need of guidance and education from those who are allegedly more superior and more knowledgeable about the world. This often manifests as the infantilizer regarding themselves as more qualified to make decisions on behalf of and about the infantilized, whom they regard as childlike and incapable of making these determinations on their own. The denial of self-governance and authority that comes along with infantilization is informed by the perceived adult superiority and the dehumanization of children already present, pervasive, and normalized in our society.[1]

According to one study, "Societal Challenge and Depression, Self-Esteem and Self-Concept Clarity in Asexuals," 69.4 percent of the asexual participants report having had their identity challenged, and the vast majority of those challenges came in the form of infantilization, with phrases like "you are a late bloomer" or "you have not met the right person yet" being offered in response to them revealing their asexuality or simply being noticeably disinterested in sex.[2] The association of asexuals with childishness and immaturity reproduces much of the same disregard and dismissive attitudes that are typically directed toward actual children. I understand the infantilization of asexuals as its own brand of gaslighting, in which seeds of doubt are continually planted in our minds and cause many of us to question our experiences, desires, and perception of self.

The median age of "virginity loss" in the United States—with the first time engaging in sex being defined here as penis-in-vagina penetration—is around seventeen years old.[3] Many people make the determination that someone is a "late bloomer" or "too old to still be a virgin" by using this approximate age as a measurement. A 2016 study on virginity stigma toward sexually inexperienced people over the age of seventeen researched the impact of being "developmentally off-time with first coitus (i.e., not yet engaging in coitus when most same-aged peers have done so)" and found bias against "older virgins" from both experienced and inexperienced people alike because of the stigma associated with being sexually inexperienced past a certain age.

While virginity prior to marriage has been historically valued, changing sociosexual scripts in the United States have made premarital sexual activity the norm for young adults.... Studies show that being a sexual "late bloomer" may result in negative interpersonal consequences.[4]

Sex, particularly cisheterosexual sex with the potential for procreation, continues to be regarded as a rite of passage and a marker of maturity. According to dominant cultural beliefs, following this socially established chronology is more than simply a rite of passage but a prerequisite for true adulthood under cisheteropatriarchy. Through this ideology, asexuality becomes understood as liminal—as an intermediate life phase or condition, a state that is merely in between, transitional, on the cusp. Asexuals are expected to always be working toward moving out of this perceived liminality and into what is accepted as maturity and adulthood. This is what it means to "bloom," and we mark ourselves as queer and socially other when we live contently in the "phase" that society regards as one that we are all required to transition out of by a certain time. And so, asexuals who deprioritize or completely divest from sex—who refuse to "bloom" and emerge from the liminal space—will never truly grow up.

The Clock in the Crocodile's Belly

What my psychology professor inadvertently highlighted with his "everything is about sex" lecture are the expectations of chrononormativity and how sex—specifically, heterosexual marital sex for the purpose of reproduction—is understood as a significant aspect of said expectations. Chrononormativity, as asserted by feminist writer Elizabeth Freeman in *Time Binds: Queer Temporalities, Queer Histories,* addresses the notion that our lives and the experiences within them are set to unfold in a particular pattern, and this pattern is one that is determined by the social and cultural mandates of the era in which we live. Freeman defines chrononormativity as "the use of time to organize individual human bodies toward maximum productivity [by which] people are bound to one another, engrouped, made to feel coherently collective, through particular orchestrations of time."[5]

Normative chronology is baked into the minutiae of our everyday lives, down to what time we should go to bed, how long we should sleep, when we clock in and clock out of a "normal" workday—all of which are socially constructed and have myths built around them for the benefit of white supremacist capitalism. Even the directive of having three meals a day at what are considered to be appropriate mealtimes is a relic of colonialism. When European colonizers observed Indigenous Americans eating freely—whenever they were hungry, rather than according to the time of day—they interpreted it as evidence that Indigenous peoples were "uncivilized." Abigail Carroll, historian and author of *Three Squares: The Invention of the American Meal,* says that, in the mind of the European colonizer, "Civilized people ate properly and boundaried their eating, thus differentiating themselves from the animal kingdom, where grazing is the norm."[6] Our very concept of breakfast in the morning, lunch in the afternoon, and dinner in the evening is informed by white supremacy and colonial violence.

The chrononormativity applied to our overall existence means that we are expected to ultimately conform, to be compliant, and to align with a normative lived experience with a universality shared among our peers. If we do not adhere to or achieve the arbitrary markers of adulthood—often also considered markers of health, humanness, and civilization—by a certain point in our lives, successfully moving out of the liminal stage, then we are considered "late bloomers" or, worse, failures. Our life trajectory is supposed to be linear and uncomplicated; we are not meant to stray from the path laid out before us: we are born, we go to grade school, we finish high school, we graduate college, we find a job, we get married, we reproduce, we raise our children, we work, we retire, we die. Sex, marriage, and reproduction are especially significant in this timeline because reproduction, and reproductive control, is integral to the white supremacist capitalist system.

In *The Heart of Whiteness: Normal Sexuality and Race in America, 1880–1940,* Julian B. Carter pinpoints the concept of heterosexual sex and marriage as true adulthood emerging in the late nineteenth and early twentieth centuries. Directly tied with the rise of U.S. industrial capitalism—and historian Eric Williams argues in *Capitalism and Slavery* that the industrial revolution was made possible for colonial powers by the wealth gained through the trafficking and enslaving of displaced Africans—it was a means to further establish whiteness as superior to all other races through white heterosexuality. "In 1930 the leftist novelist and critic Floyd Dell argued that the material constraints on earlier civilizations had hampered both their sexual and political development: only with the coming of the machine age, he held, were people free enough to achieve adult heterosexuality," Carter observes. Dell ultimately "conflates heterosexuality with modern marriage, which he describes in terms of the achieved capacity for independence and self-determination."[7] This true adulthood as an exclusive property of "normal" white heterosexuality was defined against queerness and nonmonogamous forms of marriage, which ultimately became associated with non-whiteness.

> For Dell, sexual development from "infantile" perversity (ancient Greek homosexuality, extramarital courtly love) to normal adult heterosexuality (modern marriage) was unmistakable evidence that modern industrial civilization was better than any other had ever been. Dell's argument turned on the conflation of the modern and the adult with the normal, a conflation that underscores the racial assumptions structuring his [enthusiastic praise] to heterosexuality.... The claim that truly modern lovers were the first to achieve true adulthood resonates with the era's racist and imperialist constructions of nonwhite people as permanent children, incapable of self-rule and therefore requiring guidance from more advanced races.[8]

The chrononormativity we are expected to abide by in Western societies is propped up by white supremacy, cisheteronormativity, patriarchy, and capitalism—more specifically, capitalist exploitation of the worker. All of these systems rely heavily on our adherence to a socially prescribed chrononormativity because the timeline we are meant to follow is an essential part of the oppressive systems we live and die under, and we are indoctrinated into the ideology that we are only "successful" if we follow this predetermined timeline when we are young. Anyone who veers from the chrononormative path is devalued and punished, their "failure" becoming constructed—through rhetoric and policy—as being indicative of poor character, morality, intelligence, and worth.

Queer people often navigate life on a trajectory "behind" cisheterosexual people because, due to queerphobia and repression, queer youth largely do not have the same opportunities to engage in the gender or dating rituals and rites of passage that are considered standard during the adolescent years. To this point, many of us understand a common experience of queerness to be an extended or sustained liminality when evaluated by cisheteropatriarchal social and cultural norms. This accepted cisheteronormative chrononormativity contributes to the perspective that asexuals are "late bloomers" because we often do not align with this predetermined timeline. As long as the dominant belief is that sexual relationships are markers of maturity and adulthood, many asexuals will fail to meet that standard.

Here, again, acephobia and singlism overlap. Bella DePaulo and Wendy Morris shared results from an investigation of attitudes toward singles in their 2005 article "Singles in Society and in Science." The pair set out to define and explain what DePaulo calls "the ideology of marriage and family." However, she later remarked that another, better term for what they were studying is "compulsory coupling"—that is, compulsorily entering into sexual relationships and marriage, valuing these partnerships as inherently superior, and assuming that this is a universally desired experience. DePaulo summarizes that the assumptions seen present among respondents that made up their singlist ideology of marriage and family, or compulsory coupling, were as follows:

- "Just about everyone wants to marry, and just about everyone does."
- "A sexual partnership is the one truly important peer relationship."
- **"Those who have a sexual partnership are better people—more valuable, worthy, and important.** Compared to people who do not have the peer relationship that counts, they are probably happier, less lonely, and more mature, and their lives are probably more meaningful and more complete."[9]

Attitudes about those who are not in sexual partnerships and those who choose to deprioritize, "delay," or not participate in the cisheteronormative rituals of sex, marriage, and reproduction are marked by a continual drawing of connections between sexual activity, maturity, and adulthood—as well as the acceptance and promotion of these connections as inherent. In "Possible Reasons US Adults Are Not Having Sex as Much as They Used To," Jean M. Twenge asserts that the decline in sexual activity among younger generations means that "adolescents and young adults are taking longer to grow [in]to adulthood. This includes the postponement of not just sexual activity but also other activities related to mating and reproduction, including dating, living with a partner, pregnancy, and birth."[10]

Societal conditioning and social attitudes reaffirm for us, repeatedly and in multiple arenas, that not participating in or prioritizing sex and the things surrounding it should only be a temporary and transitional period, not a sustained or permanent one. The widely-held assumption is that we will eventually, inevitably, "bloom" out of this liminal state and into a "normal" state in which we do participate in and prioritize these things, and that is when we will finally grow up. And so, infantilized asexuals are provided endless assurance that the "right person" will come along to pluck us from our lonely, immature existence and plant us firmly in the prosperous, fertile soil of adulthood, of normative allosexuality.

Compulsory (hetero)sexuality works to frame heterosexual sex as a necessary fixture of adulthood, which leaves all queer people in a space of extended liminality, where our partnerships, relationships, and sexualities are devalued and invalidated because they do not fit this mold. Queer narratives will always disrupt a chrononormativity and an "adulthood" that is defined by cisheteropatriarchal values, and asexual queerness distinctly challenges the idea that we need to "grow up" in the way that cisheteronormativity demands of us. This omnipresent clock and all of its parts have been socially constructed, and we are not obligated to abide by the timeline set before us, nor should we fear the sound of it ticking in our ears. We are allowed to map out our lives according to our own queer desires and aspirations, because queer timelines need not align with the chrononormative mandates of cisheteropatriarchal systems.

The Lost Ones

Content note: sexual violence, r*pe

White supremacy is a slippery, dishonest adversary, setting the clock but never allowing the pendulum to swing freely. It bends time to its will to suit whatever ugly need it has. In this temporal distortion, Black children never exist. Guided by the hands of this two-faced clock, adultification takes root so that Black youth can be denied a childhood, instead being perceived and treated as if they are older than they really are—a perception based in anti-Black stereotypes and logics.

They are not treated as older than they are in the way that adults are afforded reverence, authority, and respect in a society that infantilizes the people it devalues, but in a way that punishes them more severely and disproportionately for any given transgression, real or imagined. Adultifying Black children is a form of dehumanization, a means to strip them of the presumed innocence that is readily afforded to white youth, and in fact is often used to paint Black children as a threat to white innocence. The world accepts this skewed, anti-Black timeline and actively promotes the idea of Black children as adults or adult-like figures in order to justify abuses committed against them, lack of care given to them, and their criminalization.

A significant aspect of this adultification is hypersexualization, particularly of Black children assigned girl. "Girlhood Interrupted: The Erasure of Black Girls' Childhood" is a 2017 study on adultification bias from Georgetown Law's Center on Poverty and Inequality. The research shows that Black girls are perceived as needing less nurturing, less protection, less support, and less comfort, and are assumed to know more about adult topics and sex than white children of the same age.[11] A follow-up study, "Listening to Black Women and Girls: Lived Experiences of Adultification Bias," confirmed that Black girls as young as five years old routinely experience this adultification bias and the sexualization that comes along with it.[12] Focus groups were surveyed to examine how findings from the original adultification bias study align with the experiences of Black girls and women. The study affirmed that the negative stereotypes about Black women being angry, aggressive, and hypersexualized are indeed also projected onto Black girls.[13]

Historical precedence for this attitude was set by the institution of slavery and the systematic sexual violence it relied on. The rape of Black women and girls—regardless of the race of the rapist—was legal and socially acceptable during chattel slavery and the post-Civil War era.[14] In 1918, the Florida Supreme Court ruled that, in cases of statutory rape—the rape of a minor—it would only be considered rape if the victim had been a virgin prior to the assault.

> Cloaking itself in the mantle of legal reasoning, the court states that most young white women are virgins, that most young Black women [and girls] are not, and that unchaste women are immoral. The traditional law of statutory rape at issue in the [aforementioned] case provides that women who are not "chaste" cannot be raped. Because of the way the legal system considered chastity, the association of Black women with

unchastity meant not only that Black women could not be victims of statutory rape, but also that they would not be recognized as victims of forcible rape.[15]

When we look at this adultification and sexualization of Black children alongside the chrononormativity our society upholds, it both complicates and further highlights how much of the predetermined timeline is rooted in white values, interests, and understandings of the world. Black people never truly get to be seen as innocent or as children, as separate from sexuality, and yet the same colonial thought processes that adultify Black youth also demand that Black people conform to white cisheteropatriarchal notions of chrononormativity for white society's comfort, and demonize us when we do not. When the "normal" timeline is conceptualized in the image of whiteness and as yet another means to reaffirm whiteness and white heterosexuality as superior, Blackness will always fail to meet the expectations of this chrononormativity. The eternal failure of Black people to meet the white standards set before us— and that failure significantly being marked by our mythologized hypersexuality and lack of innocence—is an integral part of white supremacist logics and the eternal project to define whiteness as "normal."

This is further complicated when we consider the reality that Black adults have also been, and oftentimes continue to be, infantilized. But we are not treated as younger than we are in the way that affords us purity and innocence; rather we are treated as younger in a way that paints us as incompetent, foolish, and subhuman. White people invested in continuing the institution of chattel slavery argued that Black people were and are inherently too simple-minded, wayward, childlike, and ill-equipped to be able to survive without the institution of slavery. Vincent Woodard's *The Delectable Negro: Human Consumption and Homoeroticism within U.S. Slave Culture* demonstrates how this belief was and is encapsulated in white hunger and desire—both figurative and literal—for Black flesh. He writes that the staunchly pro-slavery physician Samuel A. Cartwright saw this childlike nature as due to

so-called African biological and racial inferiority, which in his opinion "has rendered the people of Africa unable to take care of themselves." In reality, of course, enslaved black persons took care of whites, who often acted as sycophantic children in their demands, hungers, and insatiable needs. Under this cloud of delusion, wherein whites depicted the Negro as the helpless adult-infant that they themselves embodied, white hungers for and desires for the Negro could flourish. On the level of acquired taste for the Negro, Cartwright's pseudo-medical science portrays how myths of the Negro child, of the exoticized and animal-like African, stoked white appetites and made the Negro into a delectable, desirous object.[16]

With *The Delectable Negro,* Woodward explores instances of symbolic, erotic, and literal consumption of Black flesh and highlights the antithetical reality of this consumption when juxtaposed with white society's insistence that the Black body was and is inherently undesirable. "Such references to black people as animal-like, infantile, and disfigured proliferate in pro-slavery rhetoric," he writes. "They are so common that we do not naturally think of them as indexes of desire—of white people's fixations upon and obsessions with black bodies and sex."[17]

In the social imagination, Black people are never really children. We are adultified in our youth so that we can be readily criminalized, brutalized, and sexualized throughout the entirety of our lives because white supremacy requires it as a means of racial dominance and control. And, in this same imagination, Black people are eternally children. We are inferior, incapable of self-governance, sexually irresponsible, and always in need of white guidance because white supremacy also requires this as a means of racial dominance and control. We are at once never afforded the right to exist in the space of liminality, the transitory period before adulthood, while also always existing as liminal, as too immature to be capable of self-governance and authority. These contradictions highlight the violent, circular logic of anti-Blackness and the malleability of anti-Black racism. Like water, it acquires the shape of whatever vessel it is in.

I understand this "cloud of delusion" as what Charles W. Mills names in *The Racial Contract* as "an agreement to misinterpret the world."[18] White supremacy relies on this silent agreement in order to uphold the Racial Contract in which the "officially sanctioned reality is divergent from actual reality."[19] It anchors the false reality anti-Blackness requires for its sustenance, and the false temporality in which Black people are at once both and neither, yet always a hypersexual body. It creates paradoxes and impossibilities that it cannot reconcile as long as this silent agreement is held by all who are invested in or who have been unwillingly indoctrinated into a white supremacist misinterpretation of the world. As Mills argues, "white misunderstanding, misrepresentation, evasion, and self-deception on matters related to race are among the most pervasive mental phenomena of the past few hundred years, a cognitive and moral economy physically required for conquest, colonization, and enslavement. And these phenomena are in no way accidental, but prescribed by the terms of the Racial Contract."[20]

The Black asexual must exist as a distinct impossibility according to the Racial Contract, the agreed-on misinterpretation of the world that continually (re)produces Blackness and the Black body as hypersexual, as both delectable and undesirable, as both repellent and consumable. Black asexuals, in our impossible existence, are up against multiple overlapping narratives: the blanket hypersexuality imposed on Black bodies, the simultaneous adultification and sexualization of Black youth, the infantilization of asexuality and Blackness in tandem, and the pressure to conform to white cisheteropatriarchal chrononormative ideals while never being able to meet the standards of whiteness, which is continually defined against Blackness. Each contradictory point highlights the imperative for racial analysis and the contextualization of white supremacy and all it begets—the gender binary, cisheteropatriarchy, racial capitalism, and beyond—in the examination of compulsory sexuality and asexual experience.

4

Productivity

WALL STREET IS A HELLSCAPE. So is Reddit. Albeit for very different reasons. In January 2021, the two collided in an unexpected storm that, nearly a year into a global pandemic, served to further highlight how much capitalist systems are rigged in favor of those who already hold the majority of capital and profit from the subjugation and death of others. Institutional Wall Street investors had been short-selling, or shorting, stock for the struggling video game retailer GameStop. Shorting stock is "a practice where you borrow shares for a fee and sell them for (ideally) a high price, then buy them back at (ideally) a lower price to return them. This can make you a lot of money, especially if the company goes bankrupt and you don't have to return the stock! The thing about short selling, though, is that you lose money if the stock goes up."[1] Reddit users in the community r/WallStreetBets took notice of this short-selling and began purchasing stock in GameStop using Robinhood, a stock trading app that takes its name from the fictional hero who steals from the rich to give to the poor. r/WallStreetBets ultimately pushed up GameStop's share price and caused traditional investors to lose money, nearly bankrupting them. By the end of January, GameStop trading had been halted nine times, preventing Redditors from trading or purchasing more stock and protecting the interests of short-selling Wall Street investors, who reportedly lost nearly $5 billion.[2]

There were a variety of reactions to the unprecedented situation. Notably, many celebrated the monetary losses of Wall Street investors, noting how racial capitalism and labor exploitation allowed capitalists to hoard even more money during the COVID-19 pandemic. The fact that GameStop trading had been halted multiple times to ensure the survival of the obscenely wealthy was especially emblematic of how capitalism operates, forever necessitating an uneven playing field. Of course, there were also those—aspiring capitalists and billionaire sympathizers—who lamented the situation and insisted that the r/WallStreetBets Redditors had somehow ruined "the marketplace" with their unsophisticated trades. And then, there were peculiar responses like that of a professor of marketing at New York University, who tweeted this thread:

> "What happened here (i.e., GMS)?
>
> --It's about sex...
>
> --Specifically, young men not having (enough) sex
>
> --Sex leads to relationships, obligations and guardrails (don't get in fights, we need you. Don't gamble your paycheck, we need to save for a house)

> --A bored/angry young man is the most dangerous person in the world.
>
> --When countries have unemployed young men, who are single, the likelihood that country goes to war escalates
>
> --We have cut the share of wealth of young people in half in last 30 years (19% to 9%)

> Arm young men, in a basement, not at work, not having sex, not forming connection, with an RH account, a phone and stimulus and you have the perfect storm of volatility as they wage war against established players while squeezing the dopa bag [...] harder and harder."[3]

Sex and capital have long been bedfellows. "Sex sells" after all. Sex work is a centuries-old profession. People in power often (unethically and exploitatively) trade sex for access and promotion. Viagra helped to create today's billion-dollar erectile-dysfunction industry and many attempts have been made to cash in on a similar pill for people with vaginas. Sex and capital are seemingly inseparable. Even so, I found it profoundly interesting and incredibly revealing when I read this professor's thread and saw how many people agreed with this assessment of the situation—that if the r/WallStreetBets Redditors had simply been having (enough) sex, they would not have nearly bankrupted Wall Street investors.

What struck me most were the sheer amount of assumptions made, based entirely on one central assumption that these people were not having (enough) sex. The audacity of the thread both intrigued and astounded me. Not only does it contribute to the idea that not having (enough) sex is something that is shameful and deviant, but it also upholds the idea that sex is necessary to fuel men's productivity and that it is women's responsibility to provide this fuel, drawing a direct connection between rate of sexual activity and economic outcomes. But, ultimately, it serves as a reminder that people value, privilege, and center sex in many aspects of life—assigning a meaning to sex that they believe is a universally understood truth, but is actually the influence of white supremacist, heteropatriarchal, and capitalist indoctrination.

Beyond this, the connections between certain language used to talk about sex (and reproduction) and the language typically used to discuss economics also intrigue me. From the way misogynists and incels discuss the "sexual marketplace" when theorizing how women make sexual decisions and how those decisions can be manipulated, to the way some scholars use "erotic/sexual capital" and "libidinal economy" to interrogate desirability politics and its tangible impact on our lives. There are a number of terms about sex and sexual activity that mirror economic jargon, and I believe these terms and how they are deployed demonstrate how compulsory sexuality can become wrapped up with capitalist interests.

In December 2018, *The Atlantic* ran a story about a "sex recession" in the United States. Not only are young people waiting longer to begin having sex, but they are also having less of it than older generations did at the same age. According to the Centers for Disease Control and Prevention's Youth Risk Behavior Survey, the percentage of high school students who reported having had intercourse dropped from 54 percent to 40 percent between 1991 and 2017. This means that "in the space of a generation, sex has gone from something most high-school students have experienced to something most haven't" and this decrease in sexual activity apparently signifies that "the delay in teen sex may [be] the first indication of a broader withdrawal from physical intimacy that extends well into adulthood."[4] Additionally, in the General Social Survey's study of U.S. adults born in the 1980s and 1990s—both millennials and Gen Z—were more likely than Gen X—born in the 1960s and 1970s—to report having no sexual partners after age eighteen.[5] Several experts were consulted for the *Atlantic* sex recession story, and they each offered their own hypotheses about why young people are having less sex than the generations before us. The writer summarizes,

> It might be a consequence of the hookup culture, of crushing economic pressures, of surging anxiety rates, of psychological frailty, of widespread antidepressant use, of streaming television, of environmental estrogens leaked by plastics, of dropping testosterone levels, of digital porn, of the vibrator's golden age, of dating apps, of option paralysis, of helicopter parents, of careerism, of smartphones, of the news cycle, of information overload generally, of sleep deprivation…. Name a modern blight, and someone, somewhere, is ready to blame it for messing with the modern libido.[6]

The piece, thankfully, also acknowledges that "some people today may feel less pressured into sex they don't *want* to have, thanks to changing gender [norms] and growing awareness of diverse sexual orientations, including asexuality."[7] Even so, it paints a picture that is marked by anxiety about the so-called sex recession. *Cosmo* responded to the alarmist claim of a sex recession with "The Millennial Sex Recession Is Bullsh*t" in 2019, collecting their own data and providing context that was glaringly absent from other commentary on young people and sexual activity:

> Despite what the media says, we're not lonely, porn-addicted careerists who are too selfish or busy to get it on. According to top experts, *Cosmo*'s exclusive data, and, um, actual millennials, we're the most experimental, enlightened, and sexually fulfilled generation yet.[8]

According to *Cosmo*, millennials are broadening our definitions of sex and what constitutes it, particularly reaching beyond the penis-in-vagina or anal penetrative sex that centers the phallus. Overall, we are less constrained by the traditional, conservative, and puritanical notions of sex and sexuality, a factor not taken into consideration by studies and surveys about sexual activity that ask questions through a heteronormative lens.[9] This means that the so-called sex recession is, more accurately, more of a sexual expansion.

Almost a year after *The Atlantic* declared us to be in a sex recession, and only a few months before the COVID-19 pandemic hit, CNBC warned that the sex recession could potentially lead us into yet another economic depression:

> Forget the trade wars, automation, and even the skills gap. The real threat to the U.S. economy may be that fewer Americans are in the mood for sex.... Enduring reports of America's sexual recession are a sign of a serious problem for a wide ranging list of sectors from real estate, to apparel, to condoms.[10]

According to several studies, technology and its advances are to blame for the decrease in sex rates among younger people. The ease with which we can access sources of entertainment—from video games to social media to porn—means that we have more distractions than older generations ever had, more opportunities to retreat from the world. We have the distinct ability to rely less on material human interaction for our enjoyment and more on virtual.

> The sex recession seems like an even more menacing sign that technology, especially AI technology, is seriously weakening the primordial human desire to mate with other humans and do the work necessary to make that happen. That "work" has been an essential economic component since civilization began.... We've heard of the threats tech poses to job creation, but **the drop in sex rates may be the clearest sign yet that tech's challenges to modern love might be the biggest economic threat of all.**[11]

This discourse around the sex recession and its potential economic consequences presents an opportunity to examine how compulsory sexuality is often upheld by capitalist interests. Furthermore, the rhetoric that accompanies it continues the work of connecting sex to maturity and true adulthood: "**The drop in sex rates and marriage rates are clearly related. Fewer people making adult connections simply leads to a decline in both,** and you don't need to be an economic genius to know that fewer marriages and children weaken economic demand overall."[12]

Chrononormativity, "the use of time to organize human bodies toward maximum productivity," emerges again here.[13] This concept developed by Elizabeth Freeman provides a framework to better understand why and how sex and marriage "deficits" and "delays" can have so much impact on economic demand, as the economy relies on us participating in these things at the "normal" or "right time" in our lives. CNBC reports:

> For men in their 20s and beyond, the sex recession appears to be a symptom of a delayed entrance into the world of fully responsible adulthood. Beating the "failure to launch" trend isn't just about moving out of your parents' house, but it's also about pursuing adult relationships and starting your own family.... **[The] declining sex rates are a sign of a corresponding decline in the adult relationships that stoke acceptance for the costs of dating to the costs of the trappings of domestic family life.**[14]

Alongside and underlining chrononormativity is chronobiopolitics, which Rutgers queer studies professor Dana Luciano names as "the sexual arrangement of the time of life."[15] As already established, our lives are significantly controlled through the regulation of time. It is through societal expectations and social convention that we come to understand the "normal" or "right time" for certain life events to take place, and these individual life patterns are connected with larger socioeconomic patterns. In a capitalist society, this means that these patterns, and the "maximum productivity" of our bodies—including sex and reproduction—become tied to capitalist interests. In her work on chrononormativity, Freeman discusses chronobiopolitics as a process which,

> extends beyond individual anatomies to encompass the management of entire populations.... In a chronobiological society, the state and other institutions, including representational apparatuses, link properly temporalized bodies to narratives of movement and change. These are teleological schemes of events or strategies for living such as marriage, accumulation of health and wealth for the future, reproduction, childrearing, and death and its attendant rituals.... **This timeline tends to serve a nation's economic interests, too.**[16]

Anxiety about the sex recession among young people is also anxiety about an accompanying decrease in marriage, nuclear family making, and home ownership. All of these things are intimately related and impact our economy, especially because they are so easily capitalized on. Those invested in the capitalist system work to convince us that these things are necessary parts of life and that participation in them makes us mature adults and "productive" members of society. As Freeman writes, "In the eyes of the state, this sequence of socioeconomically 'productive' moments is what it means to have a life at all."[17] Therefore, cisheterosexual sex itself becomes a means of productivity because it is understood to ultimately lead to marriage, procreation, and nuclear families, all of which are integral to patriarchal and white supremacist capitalist systems.

In July 2020, Bloomberg published "Americans Aren't Making Babies, and That's Bad for the Economy." The article tells of "The Coming Baby Deficit" and warns that the United States could have "500,000 fewer births [in 2021], which will have repercussions long after the pandemic is over."[18] Earlier that summer, Brookings referred to the impending half-million fewer births as a "large, lasting baby bust."[19] That term stuck, and eventually *Time, Business Insider, The Guardian,* and more would go on to report on the Coronavirus Baby Bust. Here, both "deficit" and "bust" are economic terms used to talk about sex and reproduction, each referring to a period of time in which economic growth—in this case, the growth of the labor force—rapidly decreases, often characterized by a simultaneous increase in demand.

Even before what has now been named the Coronavirus Baby Bust, the United States was already below the population replacement level, meaning there were and are not enough people being born to be able to replace the aging population, contribute to "safety nets" like Social Security, sustain the workforce, and help maintain the capitalist system as we know it, and the pandemic has only exacerbated this. The so-called baby bust is not only marked by fewer births, according to Philip Cohen, a sociologist and demographer at the University of Maryland. It has also resulted in a drop in Google searches for topics related to sex and pregnancy. He also suggests that the pandemic has reduced the amount of hookups and casual sex people typically engage in, which he suspects has contributed to a decrease in the number of unplanned pregnancies.[20]

The number of children (read: future laborers to be siphoned from) the average person with a viable uterus in the United States is expected to birth (read: produce) has dropped from nearly four in the 1950s to less than two in modern times. Meanwhile, at the time of this writing, the U.S. birth rate has dropped approximately 7 percent since the pandemic hit and 34 percent of people are intentionally foregoing pregnancy due to COVID-19, which is causing panic among experts who identify the decline as a "crisis."[21] Cohen says,

> One of the reasons we have falling birth rates is because women are deciding to spend less a percentage of their total lives raising children. So they have one or two children instead of three or four children. And they do a lot of other things in their lives ... which is great for reducing gender inequality. [But] it comes with some challenges.[22]

In June 2021, the World Health Organization (WHO) released their Global Alcohol Action Plan for 2022–2030, in which they strongly recommend that "women of childbearing age" refrain from drinking alcohol, because alcohol consumption could impact their ability to become pregnant.[23] Essentially, it suggests that people with uteruses spend their adulthood being concerned with and policing themselves for the sake of nonexistent, hypothetical future pregnancies. This brings pronatalism and the ongoing fight for reproductive rights and reproductive justice into a particular context. Pronatalism—which I understand to be a sibling of compulsory sexuality—is the policy or practice, particularly on the government level, of encouraging the birth of children without concern for the quality of life or health of those children and the people who birth them. The nation-state's push for reproductive control over those with the ability to be pregnant and the pronatalist push for people to bear more children—especially more white children, as white people deeply fear becoming a racial minority in the West and often propagate a "white genocide" mythos to justify racist violence and reproductive injustice—cannot be divorced from white supremacist cisheteropatriarchy, paternalism, gender inequality, and economic disparity.

It's not difficult to ascertain why birth rates have declined following the emergence of COVID-19, or why they were already declining pre-pandemic. The living conditions created by capitalist exploitation make it impossible for many people to properly house, feed, and otherwise support themselves, let alone any children. Furthermore, the United States continually fails to address the medical racism that leaves Black people with unprecedented rates of mortality during pregnancy and childbirth.[24] Institutional transphobia leaves trans, nonbinary, and gender nonconforming parents to wade through misgendering, medical neglect, and other forms of trauma while seeking out prenatal or perinatal care. There also continue to be gendered disparities in household management, in which the majority of the burden in heterosexual relationships falls on women—a fact that has been starkly highlighted during the pandemic.[25] The reality is that sex, marriage, domesticity, birth, and childrearing are often gendered forms of productivity and reproductive labor under cisheteropatriarchy and capitalism.

The United States also has no paid parental leave for new parents, the only one of the world's wealthiest nations to offer no national paid leave for its citizens.[26] Meanwhile, barriers to postpartum care and support persist, especially for those without health insurance. Costs for child care, health care, and education all continue to skyrocket while most people live paycheck to paycheck. During the COVID-19 pandemic, over half a million have died in the United States alone so far, and many survivors have become disabled due to the virus. There has been an untold amount of collective grief and trauma, with no real support offered or made accessible, on top of a multitude of lost jobs and evictions—all of which have disproportionately affected Black people.[27] It is no mystery why the prospect of giving birth in the United States—which can cost upward of $20,000[28]—is less than appealing, particularly for those who do the birthing and the majority of the subsequent child care, whether in the midst of an ongoing pandemic or not.

In April 2021, an op-ed in the *Chicago Tribune* theorized that millennials might finally start "adulting" whenever the COVID-19 pandemic finally subsides. The writer's evidence was that a few thirtysomethings they spoke to had vowed to get married, settle down, have babies, and buy houses to renovate in the suburbs post-pandemic—all accepted signifiers of true adulthood, maturity, and productivity.[29] Again and again we see the conflation of sex, marriage, and reproduction with true adulthood, and the criteria for that adulthood is tied to capitalism and the patriarchal nuclear family—which takes its moniker from the belief that this particular family structure is and should be the nucleus, or the center, of society. Anthropologist George Murdock defines this family structure as "a social group characterized by common residence, economic cooperation, and reproduction." He adds that it "contains adults of both sexes"—meaning one cis man and one cis woman—who "maintain a socially approved sexual relationship, and one or more children, own or adopted, of the sexually cohabiting adults."[30]

U.S. capitalism coupled with white cisheteropatriarchy created an essential need for the nuclear family structure, a remnant of white European colonization of the Americas. This family structure was, of course, also forced on stolen Africans and their descendants. As Roderick Ferguson explains in *Aberrations in Black,* the nonheteronormative, nonnuclear family structures and kinship connections of Black families became evidence of their instability, dysfunction, savagery, and primitivity, and it therefore needed to be eradicated. He writes,

> Common law marriage, out-of-wedlock births, lodgers, single-headed families, and unattached individuals [were] all indicators of African American disorganization defined in terms of its distance from heterosexual and nuclear intimate arrangements that are rationalized through American law and cultural norms that valorize heterosexual monogamy and patriarchal domesticity.[31]

Anti-Black sentiments about Black family-making and kinship outside of the patriarchal nuclear family structure continue to paint Black families and individuals as immoral, immature, and unproductive drains on society.

Furthermore, traditional (read: colonial) attitudes about and social mandates for sex, marriage, reproduction, the patriarchal nuclear family, and the "normal" or "right time" for these things to happen directly contribute to the disdain for and infantilization of millennials. Many refuse to acknowledge us as true adults if we don't prioritize getting married, having kids, and buying houses. All the while, they ignore the reality of our financial precarity. Even though we make up the majority of the current workforce, with approximately 72 million millennials represented, our generation controls less than 5 percent of the country's total wealth, making us collectively four times poorer than baby boomers were at our age.[32]

But these numbers do not contextualize the gender wage gap, wherein nonmen are compensated at much lower rates for performing the same labor as men. This gap is a guarantee that millions will never be able to crawl their way out of poverty, and it impacts racially marginalized people most significantly. It also means that many are forced to resort to heterosexual marriage for a chance at having some financial stability. Also not addressed or contextualized is the racial wealth gap—a direct result of chattel slavery and the wealth it allowed white families to pass on to their descendants—and the fact that wealth for Black households has decreased consistently over the decades. Prosperity Now and the Institute for Policy Studies estimate that, at this rate, Black (and Latinx) families will have $0 wealth by 2053.[33] So, what little wealth our generation has is not equally distributed among us. Charles W. Mills writes in *The Racial Contract:* "This huge disparity in white and black wealth is not remotely contingent, accidental, fortuitous; it is the direct outcome of American state policy and the collision with it of white citizenry."[34]

Malcolm Harris, author of *Kids These Days: Human Capital and the Making of Millennials,* said during an interview with *Vox,*

> If we want to understand why millennials are the way they are, then we have to look at the increased competition between workers, the increased isolation of workers from each other, the extreme individualism of modern American society, and the widespread problems of debt and economic security facing this generation.[35]

During the COVID-19 pandemic—in which millennials have been the majority of "essential workers" significantly at risk of contracting the virus—the working class collectively lost $3.7 trillion[36] while the billionaire class gained $3.9 trillion.[37] The cost of living in the United States continues to increase while workers' wages remain stagnant. A depressing number of young adults can barely afford to pay rent, let alone put a down payment on a house and maintain upkeep of the property. Our lives have been marked by imperialist wars and bloated military budgets, multiple economic collapses, and the impending doom of climate change that will impact economically marginalized people far more than the wealthy. We are underinsured, overworked, and drowning in debt from predatory student loans after having college shoved down our throats throughout our formative years. Harris believes that

> Marxists would refer to this [divergence between productivity and compensation] as an increase in the rate of exploitation, meaning workers are working longer, harder, and more efficiently but are receiving less and

less in return.... Conventional American economists don't really have a term for this—it's not something they like to talk about because they don't recognize that capitalism is built on exploitation.... Workers have always been exploited, but that rate of exploitation ... is increasing exponentially for millennials.[38]

The eldest millennials are now in their forties and the youngest are in the second half of their twenties. Despite this, we are still not considered to be true adults until we demonstrate a desire, or at least a willingness, to conform to the chronobiopolitical patterns set by white cisheteropatriarchy—patterns that asexuals are less likely to participate in. And it is the prioritization of sex, marriage, and reproduction of the patriarchal nuclear family to help sustain a deeply unequal capitalist system that remains ever at the center of this true, "productive" adulthood. We are always expected to mold ourselves into "properly temporalized bodies"—as named by Elizabeth Freeman—and we are blamed for harming the economy when we do not mold ourselves accordingly.

Rather than indicting the capitalist system for its labor exploitation and its exacerbation of the racial wealth gap, the gender wage gap, extreme poverty, homelessness, housing instability, food insecurity, health care inequality, environmental racism, climate crisis, and more, many place the onus of sustaining the economy on the exploited workers—on the use of our bodies toward economic growth and population maintenance. It is profitable to ensure that workers are not paid a living wage and have limited socioeconomic mobility while pronatalist governance ensures both the production of a future workforce and the racial majority of white people within white supremacist nations. Sex becomes yet another means of productivity to sustain the exploitative system.

The connection between sex, capital, and the economy inevitably makes way for the constitution of sex as productivity, and our productivity is the bedrock of the capitalist system as the principal driving force behind the wealthy class's ability to hoard capital. Under capitalism, being productive is what makes us valuable to the system itself, and this has long been conflated with our value as human beings. If we are not being productive and using whatever free time we have to work toward ways to become even more productive or "useful," then we are not doing enough to make ourselves valuable. This system, which encourages us to understand ourselves and our value through our productivity and labor, makes it more and more difficult to view ourselves as having any purpose outside of laboring within and for the system.

We become only bodies for the nation-state's use, and our bodies become instruments for amassing capital that marginalized workers will never be able to partake of as long as this system persists. Those who deprioritize or divest from sex—and often marriage and reproduction along with it—regardless of the reasons why, become a threat to the established systems that rely and thrive on the exploitation of and extraction of labor from our bodies, including sexual and reproductive labor. In this system, those who exist outside of normative sexuality, particularly those socialized as women who do not perform adequate sexual and reproductive labor for male partners, are disordered problems to be fixed. Compulsory sexuality contributes to this construction of our bodies as instruments for capital, and the rhetoric around the so-called sex recession and Coronavirus Baby Bust reveals how our value becomes measured through our sexual and reproductive usefulness to the economy and the nation-state.

5

Desire

If you are told over and over that you are a being who has profound sexual needs the
odds are very good that you will discover that you do. Particularly when other outlets
are forbidden or discouraged. Particularly when it is emphasized that those who do not
feel these needs are frigid, neurotic, sexually maladjusted (which for a woman means
essentially maladjusted) dried-up, barren, to be pitied.

—DANA DENSMORE, "Independence from the Sexual Revolution"[1]

"LOW" SEXUAL DESIRE IS still often considered a physiological disorder, which means that asexuality can be and often is regarded as a physiological disorder as well. A 2021 paper, "The Heteronormativity Theory of Low Sexual Desire in Women Partnered with Men," addresses the pervasive belief that "low" desire is both a problem and an individual responsibility. "The idea that low desire rests in the individual reflects an essentialist view of sexuality that has been advanced by the medical field for decades," the authors assert. "In essentialist views of sexuality, sexual desire is considered an innate and universal part of human biology. It is assumed to be built into all people," and this, of course, is what we know as compulsory sexuality. "Guided by these assumptions, medical approaches have framed sexual desire as a result of physiological processes that are essential to 'normal' human functioning and survival. Accordingly, problems like 'low' desire have been framed as a result of physical dysfunctions within individuals."[2]

Framing "low" desire as an inherent problem and individual responsibility not only demonizes those on the asexuality spectrum, but also ignores how systemic and environmental factors impact people's relationship to sex and desire. The mental, physical, and economic strain of living under capitalism[3]—having our labor exploited, our energy drained, our time stolen—lowers sexual desire[4] and impacts our lives in various other ways, something not always properly contextualized by those who lament how the sex recession and Coronavirus Baby Bust will affect our economy. It is the white supremacist capitalist system, cisheteropatriarchy, and other systemic oppressions that need to be examined and properly addressed, even as we push back against the idea that there is a universal "normal" level of sexual desire and that "low" desire is a problem to be fixed. But capitalism is always invested in convincing us that we are flawed in order to sell us remedies.

There have been a number of pharmacological attempts to treat what the *Diagnostic and Statistical Manual of Mental Disorders, 4th Edition, Text Revision (DSM-IV-TR)* termed hypoactive sexual desire disorder (HSDD), defined as "persistently or recurrently deficient (or absent) sexual fantasies and desire for sexual activity" which causes "marked distress or interpersonal difficulty."[5] The *Diagnostic and Statistical Manual of Mental Disorders, 5th Edition (DSM-5)* split HSDD into two gendered categories, male hypoactive sexual desire disorder (MHSDD) and female sexual interest/arousal disorder (FSAD). Thanks to advocacy by asexual activists, there are asexual exceptions included in the definitions. The "Diagnostic Features" section for FSAD state, "If a lifelong lack of sexual desire is better explained by one's self-identification as 'asexual,' then a diagnosis of female sexual interest/arousal disorder would not be made."[6] For MHSDD, it says, "If the man's low desire is explained by self-identification as an asexual, then a diagnosis of male hypoactive sexual desire disorder is not made."[7] Unfortunately, these exceptions are still not enough, especially given the scare quotes around "asexual" in the diagnostic features for FSAD, a subtle invalidation. Furthermore, these exceptions mean that patients need to already know asexuality exists, since they include no mandates for physicians to either educate themselves about asexuality or encourage patients to explore asexuality and determine whether or not it is something that explains their relationship to sexual desire.

Addyi/flibanserin is one of the aforementioned pharmacological attempts to treat HSDD/FSAD. The U.S. Food and Drug Administration (FDA) rejected the drug twice before finally approving it in 2015. Sprout Pharmaceuticals claimed that the psychoactive drug would increase sexual desire for premenopausal patients. According to the *American Family Physician Journal,* "Although flibanserin results in a modest improvement in the number of satisfying sexual events (approximately one more per month versus placebo), it does not improve other measures, is considerably expensive, and has significant adverse effects. In addition, its approval process and the role of its manufacturer in that process have sparked controversy."[8] The pill must be taken daily, a one-month supply of it costs more than $800, and many health insurers refuse to cover it.[9] As for the drug's approval process, its manufacturer, and the controversy it sparked—it's messy:

> Several well-respected health and women's groups rallied around [Addyi/flibanserin] as part of the Even the Score campaign, a supposedly grassroots effort to expose gender bias at the FDA as the root of the disparity in treatment options—men have Viagra and several other sex boosters to choose from, they argued, while women have none.... When Addyi was approved, organizers called it a win for sexual parity, but some suspected they had been manipulated to score one for Big Pharma.[10]

The "grassroots" effort to have Addyi/flibanserin approved turned out to have been funded and pushed behind the scenes by its own manufacturer, Sprout Pharmaceuticals. Meanwhile, the FDA's approval of the drug actually overturned its own internal reviewer recommendations. Steven Woloshin and Lisa M. Schwartz, founders of the pharmaceutical education company Informulary, published "U.S. Food and Drug Administration Approval of Flibanserin: Even the Score Does Not Add Up," in which they offer this:

> Flibanserin (Addyi), the new female libido pill, is about desire, arousal, and satisfaction. The manufacturer, Sprout Pharmaceuticals (a division of Valeant Pharmaceuticals North America LLC), clearly had desire. They purchased the rights to the drug even after its initial rejection by the U.S. Food and Drug Administration (FDA) and persisted through 2 contentious review cycles. Sprout worked hard to arouse support for the drug, helping create and fund "Even the Score," an advocacy campaign pushing the message that sexism—not legitimate scientific questions—motivated the drug's rejection. And within 48 hours of FDA approval, flibanserin was sold to Valeant Pharmaceuticals for about $1 billion in cash. Very satisfying.[11]

Schwartz also told The Cut, "When we looked at the new data for Addyi, it was hard to understand why the drug was approved the third time around because there was a new alarming drug interaction study—so alarming that it was stopped early because so many people had low blood pressure or fainted."[12] According to the FDA, "Major safety concerns regarding flibanserin include risks of hypotension [low blood pressure], syncope [loss of consciousness], and central nervous system (CNS) depression [slowing of the body's normal neurological functions]."[13] Despite these serious health risks, the drug was pushed through and was met with low sales. While taking Addyi/flibanserin, "[cis] women in monogamous, heterosexual relationships with no known cause of HSDD reported an average increase of 1.6 to 2.5" sexual events per month, according to the *American Family Physician Journal*. However, these women "typically did not notice an increase in the intensity or frequency of sexual desire. In two of the three studies, distress associated with low sexual desire was not significantly improved with treatment compared with placebo."[14]

Addyi/flibanserin was supposed to be "the pink Viagra," but it did not provide the revolution pharmaceutical giants had hoped to cash in on. The authors of "The Heteronormativity Theory of Low Sexual Desire in Women Partnered with Men" observe,

> Locating the problem of low desire in individuals' bodies has high financial stakes.... Naming low desire as an individualized biological dysfunction creates a demand for biological (i.e., medical) solutions; thus, pharmaceutical companies stand to gain by selling a "treatment." It is therefore perhaps no surprise that those with a vested interest in the *DSM-5* criteria for sexual dysfunctions sometimes have strong ties to the pharmaceutical industry or that this industry has invested millions of dollars into making sure that [we] see "the female Viagra" as the most logical (and purchasable) solution to their sexual problems.[15]

Asexual activists were concerned that, with the approval of Addyi/flibanserin on the pharmaceutical market, many asexual people could be coerced into taking the drug by either selfish partners or physicians ignorant of or discriminatory against asexuality. Sprout Pharmaceuticals addressed these concerns in 2015, telling *Newsweek* that, **"Asexual individuals are not distressed,** and therefore would not be a candidate for treatment with Addyi. Sprout is committed to educating health care providers about Addyi to help facilitate informed, educational conversations with their patients."[16] But Sprout's statement actually demonstrates their lack of knowledge about asexuality and asexual experience. Many asexual people do feel distress about their relationship to sexual desire prior to learning about the asexuality spectrum, identifying with it, and finally feeling comfortable in their identity. And this distress comes from the experience of navigating compulsory sexuality and acephobia—societal, medical, and inter-personal pressure to have "normal" sexual desires, shame of not conforming to social or cultural norms, fear of losing important connections, and especially cisheterosexual expectations of dutiful sex for people socialized as women.

According to a 2019 study by the Williams Institute at the University of California, an estimated 1.7 percent of sexual minority adults identify as asex-ual, with about 27 percent of asexuals identifying as women and 72 percent being nonbinary or genderqueer. Overall, 86 percent of asexuals were assigned female at birth.[17] The fact that the vast majority of asexuals are assigned female means that we must take gender into account when examining asexuality's disruption of cisheteropatriarchy and the medical industry's response to it. From the decades of debate about whether or not the "female orgasm" really exists, to the fact that people assigned female frequently receive inadequate health care because we are regarded as hysterical and untrustworthy when presenting concerns to medical professionals, misogyny in medicine has been well documented. The general resistance to asexuality, an orientation which mostly people assigned female and socialized as women identify with, cannot be divorced from this misogyny.

Disorder and Dysfunction

Content note: r*pe, conversion therapy

Humans are more variant creatures than many of us know or care to admit. The capacity for difference among us is truly incredible and endlessly fascinating. Yet, despite the plethora of ways for us to take shape—in terms of sexuality, gender identity and expression, body type, and more—dominant society and institutions continually strive to limit what is a "normal" way for us to exist. This "normal" way of being—which we are all expected to strive toward, regardless of whether or not it is possible for us to achieve on an individual level—is defined by white supremacist, patriarchal, and capitalist influences. These same systems also define what is order and disorder, function and dysfunction.

In medicine, something is classified as a disorder when it causes a disturbance of "normal" functioning of the mind or body. Order and disorder, function and dysfunction, normal and abnormal, healthy and unhealthy are largely socially constructed and socially determined. This remains important as I consider sexual disorder and dysfunction according to medicine—and according to common folk who believe themselves qualified to diagnose others. Compulsory sexuality and the idea that "low" sexual desire is disordered, dysfunctional, abnormal, and unhealthy have a tangible impact on people's lives, whether they engage with the medical system or not, and can be barriers to understanding one's own sexuality.

Ev'Yan Whitney (they/she) had been a sex educator for nearly ten years before they began to truly understand their own sexuality and finally affirmed their place on the asexuality spectrum. "This idea of compulsory sexuality has really been a blanket across my entire sexual experience, and it's something that I've been waking up to. It's definitely informed the way I see myself.... And to have that epiphany about what compulsory sexuality is, it's beautiful," they tell me. "It's relieved a lot of pressure that I put on myself about how I'm supposed to be sexual, and particularly this pressure I put on myself as a sex educator that I should be sexual in a particular way."

Many years ago, Ev'Yan thought they needed medical help for their perceived low sexual desire, so they sought out a physician. "I talked to a psychiatrist, trying to figure out what my 'sexual issues' were, why I had this block, why I didn't have much desire. Sex was giving me a lot of anxiety as well.... I even played around with the idea of getting on Viagra.... I tried so many things. I tried warming lubes, I tried breathing techniques.... There were so many things I tried to change in the way I interacted sexually, to change the way I was attracted to sex and attracted to other people."

Like many blossoming or questioning aces, Ev'Yan also sought answers online, and found compulsory sexuality rhetoric. "When I was on the internet trying to figure out what was going on with me, a lot of what I heard was, 'Just have sex anyway. Create this muscle memory where your body will associate sex with desire, attraction, fun, and pleasure!' So, essentially, override your body. If your body is like, 'I'm not interested in sex; I'm not attracted to sex' or whatever, just do it anyway. Then that 'natural urge' and 'natural instinct' will kick in, and then you'll be the sexual person you want to be. And, believe it or not, there are still people—sexuality professionals, educators, and therapists—who are prescribing that for their clients." Ev'Yan tells me about a potentially asexual client of theirs whose sexual psychotherapist once told her, *"Have sex. It's what you're supposed to do. That's your duty as a wife, to have sex with your husband. The more you do it, the more these instincts will come up in you."*

The medical and scientific communities continue to remain split on whether asexuality should be considered a sexual orientation or a physiological-psychological disorder. One barrier seems to be that the official medical definitions for several sexual desire disorders can also describe the experiences of many people who are on the asexuality spectrum. Sexual aversion disorder (SAD), for instance, is defined as "persistent or recurrent extreme aversion to, and avoidance of, all (or almost all) genital sexual contact with a sexual partner."[18] And while the *DSM-IV-TR* lists six different subtypes—lifelong, acquired, generalized, situational, due to psychological factors, and due to combined factors—it would be all too easy for a practitioner who is either ignorant of asexuality, denies its existence, or thinks asexuals are fundamentally in need of "fixing" to diagnose an asexual patient with such a disorder and try to convert them to allosexuality.

The authors of "Asexuality: Dysfunction or Sexual Orientation?" offer a brief reflection on the challenges that asexuality presents for the study of human sexuality, as well as the relationship of asexuality to medical and social practices. They highlight the school of thought that has shaped the academic and scientific imaginations that help to produce the social conditions and determine the standards and parameters for "normal" sexuality.

> By the end of the twentieth century, the lack of libido or sexual desire had been defined by science as an irrefutable condition of a psychological and physiological disorder related to sex. [It was] assumed that sexual involvement is a natural and immutable force, prior to social life, and is expressed as an innate instinct that represents a biological and essential need to humans.[19]

As such, the absence or rarity of sexual desire becomes medically framed and socially understood as disordered or dysfunctional. The logic produced from this accepted model of "normal" sexuality is one that is necessary to maintain said normality as superior, and one that must proclaim that perceived low sexual desire is either an indicator of poor health or that it will inevitably result in poor health outcomes, and it must therefore be medicalized and pathologized in order to be "fixed," i.e., capitalized on. This ideology not only impacts those on the asexuality spectrum, but also allosexuals who experience desire in ways not considered "normal," especially those socialized as women. And a lack of teaching about asexuality and the natural variety of desire in sex education further contributes to this. "I think that sex educators are doing the folks we are educating a massive disservice by not talking about the different ways that folks experience desire," Ev'Yan says.

In *Come as You Are: The Surprising New Science That Will Transform Your Sex Life,* Emily Nagoski identifies three types of desire: spontaneous, responsive, and context-dependent. She writes, "Where spontaneous desire appears in anticipation of pleasure, responsive desire emerges in response to pleasure," and meanwhile, context dependent desire fluctuates between spontaneous and responsive, based on the situation.[20] In our male-centric culture, spontaneous desire is what is regarded as "normal" and expected because this is how the majority of cis heterosexual men experience sexual desire, and they are considered the default.[21] Nagoski estimates that "about a third of women experience primarily or exclusively responsive desire,"[22] and says there is an "existing narrative" that a lack of spontaneous desire is disordered or dysfunctional.[23] The dismissal of responsive desire as a valid way to experience sexual desire is, of course, rooted in cisheteropatriarchy, misogyny, and phallocentric understandings of normative sexuality and desire.

This "existing narrative" is upheld, in part, by the sexual response cycle as proposed by William H. Masters and Virginia E. Johnson in the 1960s, and later modified by Helen Singer Kaplan in the 1970s.[24] The sexual response cycle is a model of the physiological and emotional changes expected to occur linearly leading up to, during, and after sex. It has four phases: (1) desire (excitement), (2) arousal (plateau), (3) orgasm, and (4) resolution.[25] This model places desire first—i.e., spontaneous desire—and fails to account for those who arrive at desire differently. Most sexual dysfunctions are defined and diagnosed based on this sexual response cycle, determined as occurring when one of the stages of this cycle is interrupted, and they are most often identified in people socialized as women.[26]

"The Heteronormativity Theory of Low Sexual Desire in Women Partnered with Men" presents four hypotheses for the prevalence of "low" sexual desire perceived and diagnosed in cis heterosexual women. They are: "inequitable gendered divisions of household labor, having to be a partner's mother, the objectification of women, and gender norms surrounding sexual initiation."[27] Therefore, what contributes to lowered levels of sexual desire are the social and cultural expectations that women partnered with men—and women are always expected to be partnered with men under cisheteropatriarchy—exist as eternal and tireless household laborers, while being caregivers and nurturers who mother their male partners (who often deploy weaponized incompetence) as well as any children they might have and their aging parents. Cisheteropatriarchal expectations also dictate that women must strive to live up to the constant pressures of fitting into racist, ableist, anti-fat, capitalist beauty standards and follow established gender roles by never showing "too much" sexual enthusiasm, but always being congenial when their male partners initiate sex, as "turning him down" is perceived as selfish and insubordinate.

These things remain unaddressed in dominant discourse surrounding sexual desire because it is more profitable and more in alignment with cisheteropatriarchal mandates to identify "low" sexual desire in cis heterosexual women—relative to cis heterosexual men—as an individual problem that they must take responsibility for fixing in order to satiate their male partners. Heteronormativity, misogyny, and male-centrism are all deeply embedded in medical understandings and diagnoses of sexual desire disorders:

> When a woman experiences lower desire than a man partner, her desire is often labeled low. In the converse situation, however, men are still the referent: in the case of a man reporting lower desire than a woman partner, the woman's desire is labeled too high (e.g., they are labeled insatiable or "sluts" in negative ways), rather than the man's desire being labeled too low.... **This highlights the gendered subjectivity inherent to conceptualization of low desire, where low desire is most often seen as residing not just in bodies, but in women's bodies relative to men's desires.**[28]

All things considered, it is important to question how much of HSDD/FSAD diagnosis and treatment is merely an attempt to coerce people assigned female toward performing sexuality in alignment with people assigned male, as that is what is considered "normal" sexuality. What an asexual lens offers us in the face of this questioning is the opportunity to unburden ourselves by affirming the validity of all forms of desire, banishing phallocentric, heteronormative, and misogynistic thought from conversations about and understandings of sexual desire, and divesting completely from a singular view of "normal" sexuality.

The attempt to orient a person with a nonnormative sexuality or gender toward "normal" cisheterosexuality through medical or psychiatric "treatment" is known as conversion therapy, and this can take many forms, ranging from pseudo-psychological treatments and spiritual counseling to surgical or hormonal interventions to corrective rape.[29] Many know that these tactics have long been used against people with nonheterosexual attractions and gender expansive identities, but the mainstream understanding of conversion therapy needs to be expanded in order to account for the ways it is also used in the attempt to orient those with "low" sexual desire toward "normal" sexuality and asexuals toward allosexuality. The 2018 National LGBT Survey "Research Report" had approximately 91,000 respondents. It found that **asexuals were the most likely to have undergone or been offered conversion therapy,** and racially marginalized people were more likely to have undergone or been offered conversion therapy than white respondents.[30]

The medical industry has a distinct history of medicalizing, pathologizing, and punishing things that fall outside "normal" and that do not align with white cisheteropatriarchal and gendered expectations. Ultimately, the medical community must reconcile its reliance on antiquated ideas about "normal" sexual desire, interest, and activity. Holding onto these ideas produces detrimental outcomes, especially for asexuals who are continually understood as sexually disordered or dysfunctional because of a nonnormative relationship with desire.

Help Not Wanted

The fact that sexual disorders and dysfunctions are mostly diagnosed in people socialized as women, coupled with the fact that people assigned female are more likely to be asexual, is not insignificant. In her 1977 essay "Asexual and Autoerotic Women: Two Invisible Groups," Myra T. Johnson describes asexuals as people who prefer not to engage in sexual activity, while those who do experience sexual desire but have no wish to satisfy it with others are called autoerotic.

Asexuals socialized as women, as well as those of other nonheterosexual orientations, experience oppression through societal expectations and mandates that we subscribe to, and perform the roles that have been determined as "natural" and "normal" for "women" under cisheteropatriarchy. Otherwise, we are "unfit" for society. These misogynistic ideologies become present in psychiatry and, therefore, "psychiatric consensus oppresses not only asexual women but also all the women who avoid, or are dissatisfied with, their 'naturally assigned functions.'"[31] Johnson notes that, therefore, lesbians, bisexual+ individuals, sex workers, and the nonmonogamous could all be "construed as violating 'reproductive family-oriented morality'" but asserts that "of all these violators, however, asexual women seem to be the most invisible."[32]

Johnson proceeds with an analysis of how asexuality and autoeroticism were treated by psychiatry at the time, which is, frankly, not significantly different from how they continue to be treated in psychiatry and beyond today: "Rarely conceded a unique identity by a therapist, professional agreement seems to hold that really asexual women simply do not exist.[33] ... New oppression seems to lie [in the] excess psychiatric consensus that **women who deny their 'natural' female functions are just repressed heterosexuals in need of 'a good fuck.'"**[34] She reasons that asexuality and autoeroticism easily met the criteria for sexualities understood as "dysfunctional" by psychiatry and its practitioners of the time, as researchers, practicing psychiatrists, and psychoanalysts had produced "a trend to term any sexual behavior which violates traditional [heterosexual] reproductive morality or which seems dysfunctional to the family as abnormal, disorganized, or immature."[35] A trend that continued for decades after and directly contributed to the oppression of queer people through the pathologizing and moralizing of nonheterosexual and non-cis gender identities.

Johnson goes on to analyze letters to the editors of various women's magazines in order to spotlight readers who found themselves failed by the "sexual revolution" of the 1960s and 1970s, which emphasized sex as freedom. One person lamented the fact that those who spoke up about how the "sexual revolution" did not serve them, and in fact could even be harmful for them, were often pathologized and dismissed, saying, "We mustn't breathe a word of opposition though. We must be all salivating at the sight of the fourposter [bed] and if not, seek therapy."[36] Another offered an astute observation about how many people conceive of "sexual freedom" through a narrow, individualistic lens: **"Individuals 'discuss' sexual freedom all too often in terms that will serve only to reinforce the choices *they* have made."**[37]

For Johnson, the "help" offered to asexual and autoerotic women wasn't help at all, but merely a means to "correct" or convert them toward heterosexuality. Among autoerotic women, masturbation was seen as an "immature" expression of sexual desire, and so they were often sent to therapy to "help" orient themselves toward more "mature" heterosexual behaviors. She writes, "'Helping,' therefore, takes on the discriminatory tone that robs women of the truth of individual experience when it makes them victims of excess consensus, with the underlying assumption being that *all* or *most* asexual or autoerotic women, because of their orientation, *need* help."[38]

Asexuals often experience concern-trolling, criticism presented with the false air of concern from people who only seek to invalidate asexuality, usually insisting that we all need immediate "help." We encounter aggressive assertions that we are sick and we should see a doctor because asexuality isn't real—all the while being reassured that they only have our best interests at heart; they just want us to be "healthy." This sometimes results in overbearing parents forcing their asexual children into (conversion) therapy or in abusers violating their asexual partner's boundaries. Our society upholds "regular" sex and desire as facets of health, especially within marriage, but our understandings of health are so often determined by white supremacist cisheteropatriarchal factors, and "sexual fitness" is no different. Ev'Yan repeats the familiar refrain:

> If you are a "healthy" human, then you are meant to be sexual, and if you're not, then there's something wrong with you. That idea was always a part of my experience.... It was one of the foundations that brought me to doing [sex education] work. I was attracted to this work because I wanted to "fix" myself. I wanted to figure out, "Why is it that everyone else seems to be having sexual experiences and pleasure and attraction and desire that I just don't have?" I got into this work trying to diagnose and trying to figure out: What are the blockages? Do I have health issues?

I was really coming at it from a place of [understanding it] as a medical issue that was preventing me from being this sexual being.

Because having a "normal" sexuality and "normal" sexual desire are conflated with sexual health, a significant amount of acephobia is rooted in healthism and ableism, and we live in a culture significantly marked by these things. While ableism is the discrimination against people with disabilities—actual or perceived—or who fall short of societal understandings of health and "normal" bodily or neurological function, healthism is the belief that health is a moral imperative and an individual responsibility. This so-called responsibility extends beyond the personal and also becomes an unyielding pressure for us to signify our health to others according to their perception of what health is. Healthism positions this personal pursuit of health—or at least appearing to be healthy— as a reflection of morality and as one of the most important aspects of life, encouraging us to judge our worth and moral standing according to our health status, both our actual health status and our perceived health status. Moreover, it emboldens people to criticize those who do not pursue health with the enthusiasm and commitment we are expected to, and also to scold those who do not appear to be ashamed of any perceived poor health status.

The healthism and ableism that asexuals are subject to becomes yet another aspect of acephobia we must wade through. People's feigned concern for our perceived sexual health, and insistence that we are immoral failures if we are not constantly working toward that sexual health, is a smokescreen for their anti-asexual attitudes, a manifestation of their inability to imagine sexual lives outside of normative allosexuality. Of course, their concern is a lie; in projecting and forcing their own ideas of sexual health onto asexuals, they demonstrate that they have no consideration for how emotionally distressing it is to be repeatedly told that you are a failure, you are sick, you should be "fixed," you need "help" because your relationship with sex and desire makes other people uncomfortable and challenges their narrow worldview. Ev'Yan reflects:

The thing about my ace experience is that it's combined with so much— it's combined with sexual trauma, it's combined with social conditioning, it's combined with my mental health issues. My task right now is learning to see it as the whole thing that it is, as opposed to fragmenting it. Within the last year, I'd say, it's been a very new experience of seeing myself through this lens, the asexual lens, and [accepting] the notion that there's nothing wrong with me. It's just that I relate to sexuality in a different way.

What must always be affirmed and reaffirmed is the truth that having rare, absent, or "low" sexual desire is not shameful. It is not an inherent aberration that needs to be urgently fixed—regardless of what the reasons behind it may or may not be, regardless of what other things it might be tangled up with—especially if the methods for "fixing" it come with side effects that negatively impact our actual health, and if the reasons for why we feel the need to "fix" it are due to societal, medical, or interpersonal pressures.

"I wish there were more conversations when I was growing up, and when I was coming into this field in particular, about the different ways people experience sexuality, sexual attraction, sexual desire. I think it would help a lot of people feel more seen, because I think we are excluding a lot of people," Ev'Yan explains. "We are not allowing people to know what is possible." An untold number of people would be significantly helped if there were more awareness of asexuality and the different ways sexual desire can show up. "I know for a fact that if I had seen more representation, or had more conversations or just more education about it, I would not have been as troubled, would not have struggled as much as I did in the beginning," Ev'Yan says.

Asexuals, as well as allosexuals with perceived low sexual desire, do not owe the narrow ideal of sexual health to anyone, particularly when we know that the "healthy sex life" others demand of us, and that we often feel pressured to seek out, would be detrimental to our actual health and well-being. The history of how people socialized as women have been medicalized, pathologized, and "helped" through their rare, absent, or "low" sexual desire is especially revealing of how the urgency to align divergent sexualities with sexual normativity has been and continues to be a product of white cisheteropatriarchy.

6

Frigidity

A great many women are what we call frigid, cold. That is, they either have no sexual desire or experience no sensation during the act. Some even have an aversion to the act. This condition of frigidity is sometimes also referred to as sexual anesthesia....

Now, if you are one of those frigid or sexually anesthetic women, don't be in a hurry to inform your husband about it. To the man, it makes no difference in the pleasurableness of the act whether you are frigid or not unless he knows that you are frigid. And he won't know unless you tell him, and what he doesn't know won't hurt him. Heed this advice. It has saved thousands of women from trouble.

—DR. WILLIAM JOSEPHUS ROBINSON, *Married Life and Happiness or, Love and Comfort in Marriage*[1]

HISTORICALLY, PATHOLOGIZING AND MEDICALIZING "low" sexual desire or sexual aversion has not only been about "correcting" people's sexual behavior toward a socially acceptable heterosexual performance. It has also largely been about the ongoing need to bring those socialized as women under cisheteropatriarchal sociosexual control, to ensure that we remain "fit" for society. For me, the pathologization and medicalization of asexuality—hypoactive sexual desire disorder (HSDD) and female sexual interest/arousal disorder (FSAD) specifically—cannot be separated from the history of "frigidity." Many people on the asexuality spectrum today would have been diagnosed as frigid when it was still considered a legitimate diagnosis, and I understand frigidity— generally defined as the absence of sexual desire, arousal, or pleasure—to be a type of asexual identity in many cases; other instances were likely cases of responsive or context dependent desire or other forms of nonheterosexuality.

Frigidity has been present in discourse about sex and desire since at least the thirteenth century. *Frigiditas* was understood specifically as an obstacle to fulfillment of marital and procreative duties, and the concept was also connected with men's impotence and sterility for a time before it became distinctly associated with (presumably cisheterosexual) women's "inability" to properly perform sexually in their marriages. In *Frigidity: An Intellectual History*, Peter Cryle and Alison Moore provide a thorough investigation, tracing the history of frigidity to more contemporary understandings of "female sexual dysfunction."

> It remains the case [that] **many psychiatrists and sexologists of our time continue to elaborate a complex network of ways in which women can be considered abnormally lacking in desire, pleasure, or orgasm....** We have found an increasing refinement and complexification of female sexual coldness over time. At various points, a "moral" interest in the health and welfare of women led to increasingly detailed knowledge of female desire and pleasure—always within the framework of heterosexual coitus. The knowledge developed was both enabling and constraining, both supportive and invasive. "Frigidity" actually made women's sexuality important where it had not always been so. But the recognition it gave was achieved at enormous cost. Talk about frigidity, anaphrodisia, vaginismus and the like put women's desire and pleasure into a space of anxious fragility, a domain of knowledge surrounded by diagnostic scrutiny and coercive therapeutic attention.[2]

Cryle and Moore begin by looking at the place of frigidity within the canon law of the Catholic Church. Pope Gregory IX (lived 1145–1227) identified the two principal causes of impotence as *frigiditas* (coldness) and *maleficium* (sorcery) in the thirteenth century, and was quoted as an authority on the subject for centuries after.[3] Tomás Sánchez, a Spanish Jesuit, referenced him when he published *De sancto matrimonii sacramento dis putationum* (Disputations about the holy sacrament of matrimony) in 1605. According to Sánchez, frigidity was what rendered a spouse impotent (unable to perform sexually) or sterile (unable to reproduce). While Sánchez did not believe frigidity, or "coldness of passion," was absent in women, he did not consider it to be of sufficient enough consequence to warrant a marriage annulment, as he believed it did with men.[4]

Later, Italian physician Paolo Zacchia's *Quaestiones medico legales* was post-humously published in 1661, in which he asserts, "Those who can properly be called frigid [are] those who because of listlessness of the genital parts or **lack of native heat** are impotent to engage in coitus." In his work, he responds to the *Cum frequenter* of 1587, which stated that "[perfect coupling] should include erection, intromission [penetration], and ejaculation of *verum semen* [true seed]."[5] His writing attempted to redirect the purpose of marital sex toward not simply reproduction but "copulation that satisfied desire."[6] Zacchia also responds to Italian physician Girolamo Mercuriale's 1587 "study of illnesses in women" in which Mercuriale theorized that "in women there is no sickness [*morbum*] which takes the form of a **lack of desire for coitus.**"[7] Zacchia, however, maintained that such a "sickness" did exist in women, declaring that "women, like men, can be frigid by nature, not only by **feeling no venereal irritation [sexual arousal]**, but also by not producing any seed within themselves whose stimulus would move them to coitus."[8]

By the eighteenth century, the understanding of frigidity had begun to evolve. Whereas it had been considered solely a physiological issue in prior centuries, it now became understood as being also a psychological impairment. Throughout the 1700s and 1800s, the questions surrounding frigidity were still significantly focused on whether or not it should constitute an annulment of marriage, as it was a failure of conjugal duty, and sexual coldness in men was again seen as more significant. *Dictionnaire des sciences médicales* from 1816 includes a lengthy entry called "Frigidité" that is attributed to French encyclopedist Julien-Joseph Virey, who believed that there were likely more frigid women than men. However, like Sánchez, he maintained that frigidity in men mattered more. His reasoning was that "the effect is not equal in society and marriage, for **the woman can always receive**, unless her sexual organs are misshapen."[9] As long as wives were still physically capable of sex with their husbands—able to "receive" a penis as fulfillment of their conjugal duties—whether or not wives **desired** this sex was of little concern.

In the 1880s, French physician Pierre Garnier made sure to separate impotence, a physiological issue, from frigidity, or anaphrodisia, the causes of which he identified as entirely psychological.[10] His work acknowledged that sex could occur "in complete anaphrodisia, especially where the woman is concerned."[11] Because of this, Garnier reasoned that frigidity was not a physical sickness, but a "neurosis."[12] Furthermore, Garnier was of the belief that "**the primary func-tion of the female genital organs [are] to increase pleasure in the male during coitus, and thereby maintain his erection.**"[13] Therefore, addressing frigidity for Garnier and his ilk was never about improving a woman's experiences with sex, but about ensuring that she would continue to perform coitus for her hus-band's pleasure. A woman was only a receptacle, a masturbatory aid.

French physician and researcher Jean-Baptiste Fonssagrives published *Dic-tionnaire encyclopédique des sciences médicales* in 1864, which sought to clarify the definition of frigidity:

> We consider the word frigidity to be a synonym of anaphrodisia, and we define the latter as follows: the absence, whether congenital or acquired, of the genital arousal necessary for the regular accomplishment of the sexual functions. Normal arousal is manifested in fact in three differ-ent ways: (1) by venereal appetite; (2) by tumescence [orgasme] which brings the apparatus to the point where it is able to function physio-logically; (3) by the sensation which satisfies desire and constitutes the cerebral or voluntary spur to its later recurrence. Anaphrodisia exists whenever one of these conditions of the normal sex act is missing.[14]

According to Fonssagrives, "femmelettes" or "excessively soft and feminine women" were not as prone to frigidity as "viragos" or women who were more "masculine," dominant, and assertive.[15] There has long been a practice of con-necting gender performance and the gender binary with sexuality. That is: there are only two genders and marked differentiation between the two genders is an important feature of whiteness and white supremacy, which requires women to be appropriately "feminine" and men to be appropriately "masculine." Following this, exclusive heterosexual attraction, desire for, and sexual activity with the "opposite sex" are specifically scripted as part of both gender performances, and women fulfilling their obligation to dutiful sex is essential to white cisheteropatriarchy.

An 1882 text by French physician Jules Guyot, *Bréviaire de l'amour expéri-mental* (A manual of experimental love), includes a preface by Georges Barral and Charles Dufaure de la Prade that declares that it is not possible for women to opt out of sex. All women needed to participate in the "physiology of love," for failure to do so would result in "the worst kinds of pathology," such as hys-teria.[16] They assert that "**there are no women without needs. There are no**

women deprived of their senses. There are no women who are impotent for the genesic spasm."[17] For Barral and de la Prade, women who seemed to be frigid were merely victims of unfortunate conjugal circumstances in which their partners did not properly or adequately pleasure them. This position had been articulated perhaps even more succinctly in 1859 when French physician Félix Roubaud wrote that frigidity was, simply put, "a condition particular to woman in which she participates only passively in the act of copulation."[18]

While the idea that wives are duty-bound to have sex with their husbands and the myth that not having sex would generate psychological consequences are transparently rooted in misogyny and cisheteropatriarchy, the accompanying logic regarding the passivity with which many cisheterosexual women participate in sex with partners who care very little or not at all about their pleasure or comfort is not completely without validity. The orgasm gap—wherein cisheterosexual women orgasm significantly less than cisheterosexual men and queer women—reveals how unfortunately common it is for cisheterosexual women to have subpar sexual experiences.[19] There is also a pastime of disregarding or even demonizing engagement with the clitoris, with the likes of Sigmund Freud declaring clitoral orgasms to be "immature" and pathologizing those never able to reach orgasm through penis-in-vagina sex alone,[20] which nearly 75 percent of people with vaginas are unable to do.[21] Cultural scripts for cisheterosexuality continually fail people socialized as women, whether asexual or not. But I digress—this is not a discussion about cisheterosexual men's long history of sexual ineptitude fueled by both societal and individual phallocentric and misogynistic scripts for cisheterosexuality.

The aforementioned Roubaud and others initially regarded frigidity as a complex disorder, as "for some, frigidity was the absence of venereal desires, while for others the word referred to the absence of pleasure" during the act.[22] During his career, Roubaud's work helped to further entrench ideas of "normal" desire and sexuality in the medical field, ultimately expanding the diagnosis of frigidity to include more than absence of sexual desire or pleasure:

> A form of medicine predicated on the concept of normal desire and pleasure was now able to make a triple set of moves: **every departure from the norm was a perversion, every perversion a lack, and every lack part of the same general pathology.** As a consequence, the theoretical

and clinical scope of "frigidity" was much extended: it became a generic diagnosis for masturbation and same-sex attraction, and later for sadism, masochism, clitoridism [the need for or reliance on clitoral stimulation] and androgyny.[23]

This not only demonized any orientation outside of heterosexuality, or any gender performance or presentation outside the socially acceptable, but regarded any sex act other than "vanilla" penis-in-vagina intercourse, even among heterosexuals, as disordered. All ways of being that were not directed toward the accepted vision of cisheterosexuality became understood as forms of frigidity, and this idea continued to gain popularity in both sexological and psychoanalytic circles during the late nineteenth and early twentieth century. According to Cryle and Moore, "Frigidity was not always named as a perversion in its own right, but took its place within a tableau of anomalous sexual functions. By insisting that frigidity could account for all noncoital desire, Roubaud took a decisive step toward a view of **sexual pathology as lack, and indeed of lack as perversion.**"[24] Asexuality is so commonly understood as being defined by lack, and is therefore viewed as a perversion of "natural" sexuality. Such a perversion—whether by the name asexual or frigid—cannot be tolerated in a society that upholds heterosexuality and specific heterosexual sex acts as normal, superior, and healthy.

To remedy this problem, Roubaud became concerned with how frigidity would be treated by medicine. As he and many others understood it, those diagnosed with frigidity needed to be persuaded to adopt "normal" desire and sexual habits, by whatever means this persuasion required. In Roubaud's advocacy, we can see the seeds of what would eventually develop into what we now know as conversion therapy. By 1899, German psychiatrist Albert von Schrenck-Notzing would claim to have successfully converted a patient toward heterosexuality using hypnosis and suggestion theory.[25] Many doctors would go on to practice conversion therapy throughout the twentieth century. Even now, it continues to leave queer people scarred and traumatized.

By the twentieth century, the work of Pierre Garnier had helped to make the term *frigidity* associated with a psychological condition or syndrome exclusive to women.[26] In 1909, a Dr. Riolan published the eighth volume of his *Collection exclusive d'hygiène et de médecine* (Exclusive collection of hygiene and medicine) in which he offers this definition: "Sexual frigidity, or anaphrodisia, is **indifference to the pleasures of love, absence of venereal desires.**"[27] This aligned somewhat with what French physician Auguste Ambroise Tardieu called an overall atony (lack of tone; muscular weakness) of the genitals and "**a more or less complete absence of need for and pleasure in physical love.**"[28] However, a Dr. Eynon asserted that frigidity or anaphrodisia was largely artificial.

> Eynon simply declared that a frigid woman was one whose senses had not been properly awoken. He supposed that **a capacity for natural sexual response lay dormant beneath the symptoms of anaphrodisia,** and that it was subject in principle to transformation by some agency. In Eynon's view—and all of his views were widely shared—"true" anaphrodisia of an enduring kind was to be understood not as a pathological condition in its own right, but as the consequence of some other illness.... This is a decisive articulation at the heart of the theme of frigidity: **frigid women can and should be awoken from their state through the sexual agency of men.**[29]

Reflecting Eynon's understanding of frigidity, early-twentieth-century romantic and erotic fiction painted frigidity as a temporary state for its characters. The "frigid woman" needed only to be seduced by a "virile man" in order to be cured of her sexual apathy or aversion, and this trope can still be found to some degree in modern erotic narratives. "It has become one of the clichéd verities of female sexuality: natural desire is the truth that underlies apparent frigidity, and it is just waiting to be revealed by potent males," observe Cryle and Moore. "The frigid woman's narrative destiny was to undergo the treatment called for by her disorder: to be subject to the agency of others and be brought, no matter how long that might take, to the fullness of sexual pleasure."[30]

Along with this view that "most apparently frigid women were thought to be simply alienated from their own true desire and pleasure and might well come to be reconciled with it"[31] also came the accusation that some women remained "cold" toward men out of resentment, stubbornness, or ill will. *Le Mensonge du féminisme* (The lie of feminism), by Théodore Joran, a story published in 1905, follows a character who does just this. "As if on purpose, she remained the passive, inert being," Joran describes. "[She is] **the living corpse who puts up with embraces but does not return them, who carries out the divine act with the**

indifference one brings to a chore. She remained the one who paralyses the flesh and chills the heart."[32] Cryle and Moore highlight that her male suitor identifies "the inhuman temperament that lies at the heart of feminism: **frigidity is diagnosed as a stubborn refusal of normal, male-centered sexuality.**"[33] Stories like this would help to fuel the social attitudes that would allow terms like "frigid bitch" to become commonly used as insults against people socialized as women who were noncompliant with cisheteropatriarchal sexual demands.

For Cryle and Moore, it is in these fictional writings that we can perhaps most clearly see the reproduced mythology that "(a) all women are filled with [sexual] desire deep down, even if they often seem cold on the surface; (b) frigid women need men to awaken them; and (c) women who criticize or resist domination by men have perversely chosen to be frigid."[34] Fictional writing and medical writing informed one another, and together they worked to broaden the general public's exposure to the term and concept of frigidity as a distinct and pathologized failure of womanhood. Indeed, "through repeated affirmation and narrative representation, they established a number of functional 'truths'" about frigidity and those who allegedly or apparently suffered from it.[35]

From the late nineteenth century through the twentieth century, frigidity or "sexual coldness" became regarded less as an absence of pleasure during sexual engagement and was more associated with an absence of sexual desire. "**Frigidity or anaphrodisia was now primarily a terrible malfunction of desire.** Frigidity had become interesting and seductive because it was understood to be quite other than the natural absence of sexuality."[36] An indifference for or aversion to sex and low sexual desire were framed as anything but naturally occurring, especially because it was a phenomenon associated significantly with people socialized as women, much like the modern understanding of asexuality. The stronger this association became, the more frigidity became conceived of as blasphemy. Women's low sexual desire was an affront to cisheteropatriarchy, and specifically to men's ability to dominate sexually.

Wilhelm Stekel, an Austrian physician and psychologist who became one of Sigmund Freud's earliest followers and a loyal protégé, published *Frigidity in Women in Relation to Her Love Life* in 1926. In this work, Stekel declares, "To be roused by a man means acknowledging oneself as conquered," then, at the conclusion of sex when she can take no more, she should acknowledge herself "defeated, subdued, in the game of love" by the man who has dominated her.[37] Moreover, he declares that **"sexual frigidity enables woman to domineer, to triumph over man. [Frigidity], therefore, is to be interpreted as a phase in woman's struggle for equal rights; it is distinctly a social manifestation."**[38] For Stekel and his followers, it was feminism and women's desire to play "men's roles" and be in "men's positions" that was actually producing so many cases of frigidity. Therefore, according to Stekel, the "only hope for relief from an epidemic of frigidity lay in a return to traditional roles: A woman can never become a man."[39] All that was needed was a "return to the calling of motherhood under equal political, social and sexual rights."[40] This abandonment of feminism alone would "furnish woman the opportunity for love without humiliation."[41] The conflation of appropriate "femininity" with proper gender performance for women as it relates to sexual, social, and reproductive obligation appears repeatedly in these conversations among men. There is a strong connection between anti-feminist attitudes and anxieties about frigid or asexual women causing the decline of white supremacist civilization by eschewing traditional cisheteropatriarchal roles.

While white patients were not the only ones who were diagnosed with frigidity, it was believed that it occurred far less among "uncivilized races." Frigidity was understood by people like English physician and eugenicist Havelock Ellis as a threat to "civilized" white society and imagined white superiority. In fact, Ellis considered frigidity to be merely a cultural phenomenon, remarking that "among most uncivilized races there appear to be few or no 'sexually frigid' women,"[42] a convenient position aligning with racist stereotypes of an insatiable "savage" sexuality. In the minds of whites who thought like Ellis, it was near impossible for "uncivilized" nonwhite races to experience any absence of sexual desire. This cannot be separated from the enduring racial fetishism, sociosexual terror, and mythologized hypersexualization of the "savage." Also inseparable from this are white anxieties about "race suicide." If the white race does not reproduce at rapid and consistent enough rates, then surely they will be overtaken by the "uncivilized races" and inevitably forfeit their institutional and political power to oppress all others. Not only was frigidity a threat to "civilized" white society, but also to the promise of continued racial dominance, and it therefore warranted pathologization. Sexologist William Robinson was one among multiple white physicians to affirm that "every sexual deviation or disorder which has for its result an inability to perpetuate the race is ipso facto pathologic, ipso facto an abnormality."[43]

In concluding their trek through the history of frigidity, Cryle and Moore offer:

> Among the continuing mass of treatments and concerns about the lack of orgasms and erections, only the tiniest of minority voices dares to suggest a more radical alternative: not only that the perceived need for sexual desire and satisfaction and the types of pleasures sought or experienced might vary enormously from one individual to another, but that some people may not be suited to sexual intimacy at all. The psychiatric understanding of sex is still being put to the test in this regard, and it will be a significant event indeed if the notion of a nonpathological asexuality finds acknowledgment in future editions of the *Diagnostic and Statistical Manual*.[44]

Indeed it will be. In this history of frigidity—of which I have provided only a glimpse—misogyny, phallocentrism, cisheteropatriarchy, compulsory (hetero) sexuality, the gender binary, and anxieties about the preservation of whiteness are all present and integral to the very concept and diagnosis of frigidity, which I understand to be asexuality by another name. While frigidity, or anaphrodisia, came to be defined and redefined throughout the centuries, absence and rarity of sexual desire were consistent factors, and this is what I believe directly connects frigidity to the modern understanding of asexuality. Regardless of how it was defined, frigidity has always been produced by the standardization of sex and desire according to patriarchal and phallocentric parameters, and it brings starkly into question gendered sexual disorders and dysfunctions like HSDD/FSAD. The same field that regularly dismisses asexuality as a valid orientation and has a documented history of diagnosing women as sexually dysfunctional according to men's standards cannot be trusted to determine whether anyone has a genuine sexual obstacle or if they are on the asexuality spectrum.

"Perhaps the strongest force now helping to maintain female sexual failure as a pathologically defined condition is the uptake of disorders such as FSAD by multinational drug corporations intent on profiting from the sale of chemical treatments for stimulating sexual arousal," write Cryle and Moore. "[And] drug companies appear intent on developing and selling arousal-stimulating drugs to women."[45] I see HSDD/FSAD as clearly descended from and closely akin to frigidity—they are arguably even mirror images. These heteropatriarchal endeavors work together to fuel the medicalization and pathologization of asexuality, which affords the medical industry and pharmaceutical companies opportunity to capitalize on the socialized shame of rare or absent sexual desire. And this prescribed heterosexual desire and compulsory sexuality are essential to cisheteropatriarchy, the gender binary, and the sociosexual control of those socialized as women.

7

Unfit

THE GENDER BINARY HAS borders. It is a structure that requires the policing of those borders in order to remain intact. Not only are we relegated to existing on one particular side of the binary, but we are also not allowed to traverse or transverse the binary's borders. And not only must these two binary extremes be explicitly different from one another, but one must be subjugated by the other. This Western gender binary has long been a racial project. In the nineteenth century and early twentieth century, policing gender became necessary for the "advancement" of the white race and the maintenance of white supremacist cisheteropatriarchy. In order to further entrench myths about the natural superiority of white men, gender policing became a means to help establish whiteness as "civilized" and all other races as inferior savages. In *Manliness and Civilization: A Cultural History of Gender and Race in the United States, 1880–1917*, Gail Bederman details how "'civilization,' as turn-of-the century Americans understood it, simultaneously denoted attributes of race and gender. By invoking the discourse of civilization in a variety of contradictory ways, many Americans found a powerfully effective way to link male dominance to white supremacy."[1] In white civilized society, "women were womanly—delicate, spiritual, dedicated to the home [and] civilized white men were the most manly ever evolved," and these differences were an "intrinsic and necessary aspect of higher civilization."[2]

Men's institutional power within cisheteropatriarchy is dependent on strict gender differences, the gender binary, and specifically on defining "woman" as inferior to "man," identifying sexual roles as intrinsic to both gender categories. In our modern society, performing womanhood means to eternally strive toward appealing to male attention, approval, and comforts, which are expected to be valued above all others. Dutiful sex and sexual submission to men—meant to be reflective and reproductive of social submission to men—are integral to this script. People understood to be women who defy these expectations by not seeking out, not resigning to, and not prioritizing or pedestaling monogamous heterosexual relationships are an affront to cisheteropatriarchy and rigid ideals of womanhood. As such, those who fail at this womanhood—by virtue of nonnormative sexualities that do not center or cater to men—sometimes may recognize and name their gender as something else entirely.

Monique Wittig examines heteronormativity in her essay "The Straight Mind," indicting heterosexuality as a system that requires the submission of women and the preservation of the gender binary, observing that "straight society is based on the necessity of the different/other at every level. It cannot work economically, symbolically, linguistically, or politically without this concept.... 'Man' and 'woman' are political concepts of opposition."[3] She also presents an analysis of the compulsory nature of heterosexuality and how it is upheld through a shared consciousness:

> The consequence of this tendency towards universality is that the straight mind cannot conceive of a culture, a society where heterosexuality would not order not only all human relationships but also its very production of concepts and all the processes which escape consciousness, as well.[4]

For Wittig, "lesbian" exists as a category distinct from but not dichotomous to woman, as "woman" was, and continues to be, defined by men on the basis of the relationship of women to men, a relationship in which women are intended to be eternally subjugated under male dominance. She writes, "'woman' has meaning only in heterosexual systems of thought and heterosexual economic systems. Lesbians are not women."[5] To be lesbian—to exist outside of heterosexuality and the cisheteropatriarchal norm of "woman" as defined by men—is to be something other than woman. Because society continually structures gender itself through compulsory adherence to heterosexuality, gender and sexuality are always informing one another. Therefore, the liberation of the lesbian and other nonheterosexual identities would require the abolition of gender categories altogether, and along with it, gendered understandings of both the sexual and the social.

But while it is true that some people's determinations about their gender identity are deeply informed by their sexuality, it is also true that some assess and affirm their gender based entirely on other factors that do not bring sexuality into account at all. What Wittig's "lesbians are not women" claim gives us is not a gospel, but a framework for interrogating the relationship between sex-(uality) and gender within a cisheteropatriarchal system and white supremacist civilization. People who do not perform heterosexuality are a threat, especially women—affirmed or assumed—because the social and sexual control of women is essential to cisheteropatriarchy. Because the gender categories of "man" and "woman" require heterosexual expression as an authentication of each respective gender, it is useful to question, as Wittig does, whether deviation from this expected heterosexuality ultimately means not fitting into these gender categories at all.

Indeed, it would be entirely valid for a person to conclude that if they do not, or cannot, perform prescribed womanhood accordingly and have no inclination to orient themselves toward a "correct" performance of womanhood, then they are evidently not a woman. But it is necessary to understand "womanhood" and the criteria for membership to it beyond Wittig's analysis. The gender binary, with "man" and "woman" as the only gender categories, is an invention of whiteness, defined against the "savagery" of other races. "Man" and "woman" are, therefore, categories that only white people have full access to. Bederman details how it came to be "true" that gender among the more "advanced" and "civilized" white race was characterized by pronounced and evident differences between manly men and womanly women, whereas nonwhite "savage" races displayed little to no gender differentiation:

> Civilized white men were the most manly ever evolved—firm of character; self-controlled; protectors of women and children. In contrast, gender differences among savages seem to be blurred. Savage women were aggressive, carried heavy burdens, and did all sorts of "masculine"

hard labor. Savage men were emotional and lacked a man's ability to restrain their passions [and] Savage men even dressed like women, in skirts and jewelry. In short, the pronounced sexual differences celebrated in the middle class's doctrine of separate spheres were assumed to be absent in savagery, but to be an intrinsic and necessary aspect of higher civilization.[6]

Black people socialized as women—lesbian, asexual, and otherwise—ultimately fail at womanhood because "uncivilized" Black people on the whole already fail at white supremacist interpretations of gender altogether. Sarah Haley's *No Mercy Here: Gender, Punishment, and the Making of Jim Crow Modernity* demonstrates how "gender is constructed by and through race and that the production of woman and other stable gender categories required violence."[7] The way Black women were regarded by white society reflected "an uneasy antagonistic relationship between Blackness and femininity in the white popular imagination"[8] and its understandings of gender:

> In the white imaginary "black woman" was an oxymoronic formulation because the modifier "black" rejected everything associated with the universal "woman." The black female subject occupied a paradoxical, embattled, and fraught position, a productive negation that produced normativity. She was an invention of a white supremacist imaginary defined in part by subjection to extreme violence and terror.[9]

The Black "female subject" may be called woman but is never truly understood as woman. Instead, we exist somewhere in the space between or outside of "man" and "woman." Zakiyyah Iman Jackson names, in *Becoming Human: Matter and Meaning in an Antiblack World*, "Female, rather than woman, African femaleness is paradoxically placed under the sign of absence, lack, and pathology in order to present an idealized western European bourgeois femininity as the normative embodiment of womanhood."[10] This means that those of us assigned, assumed, or affirmed as Black women are continually barred from a coherent gender identity. This, among many other things, is why the gender binary, and the sexual expectations aligned with it, will never serve us. But even as Black people are barred from full entry into white colonial conceptions of gender and sexuality, we are still expected to abide by the social contracts associated with these categories. We are punished for our failure to properly align ourselves with them, even as such an alignment would be impossible because these categories have been defined against Blackness itself. Anxieties about those who do not follow the strict gender "rules" of the binary are also racial anxieties about the preservation of white ascendant ideologies of gender and sexuality.

The authors of *The Gender Accelerationist Manifesto*—in which gender accelerationism is defined as "using gender's own process of decay to destroy the gender class system"[11]—name that, in any given culture, "Gender is produced primarily by the division of reproductive labor. Reproductive labor is any labor that helps to produce the next generation, including sex, birth, child care, and homemaking, and gender is defined by how this labor is divided up, with the different genders being distinct classes which are expected to perform specific sorts of tasks regarding reproductive labor."[12] The gender binary of the cisheteropatriarchal Western world means that the definition of gender also becomes (re)produced through socially prescribed sexual roles and who must be in sociosexual submission to whom. Men are to penetrate and dominate women, and women are to offer themselves as submissive receptacles for men's lust and venom. Those socialized as women are "expected to engage in sexual relations, but have the relations controlled by the man. They have their labor controlled and confined by men and have the fruits of that labor commanded by men. This is reflected in the superstructure around them. They're expected to be subservient and passive, to accept that which comes for them."[13]

With all of this in mind, my intentions here are to acknowledge connections between experiences of asexual and lesbian existence within the gender binary and cisheteropatriarchy. Asexuals and lesbians have resisted within the same system, and this system would rather we submit to misogynistic, male supremacist sociosexual rule and strict gender roles. When Wittig writes that "lesbians are not women," she also affirms that "no more is any woman who is not in a relation of personal dependency with a man."[14] Asexuals, too, can identify with what Wittig describes as the audacity to "reject the obligation of coitus and the institutions that this obligation has produced."[15]

Gender Traitors

Earlier in the century ... expert observers often associated lesbians and "mannish women" with unmarried career women, social reformers, and feminists. By the 1920s, all these women were vilified for their gender transgression. In this earlier version of the "lesbian threat," white middle-class lesbians, and unmarried women generally, threatened "race suicide" by rejecting or otherwise compromising their proper and "natural" social role to bear and rear children. These prewar New Women were castigated primarily as asexual gender traitors.

—DONNA PENN, "The Sexualized Woman: The Lesbian, the Prostitute, and the Containment of Female Sexuality in Postwar America"[16]

In 1917, Correa Moylan Walsh wrote *Feminism,* a lament on and castigation of the women's suffrage movement and what he saw as "the anti-child-bearing mania" that feminism produced.

> Women's concern with the concerns of men is contrary to the nature of things, and the nature of things will prevail. The principle of the survival of the fit women, in the order of nature, means also the passing away of the unfit women.... The women who act the parts of men will not perform the function of women: they will not leave offspring. Their progeny will die out. Only the progeny of the women who remain women will abound. Thus feminism, in all its elements, is doomed.[17]

To Walsh, those who did not remain in their intended place would also not "remain women," which indeed echoes Wittig's claim that "lesbians are not women." He would go on to call these feminists who would not "perform the function of women"—as a comment on their refusal to be sexually subservient to men—asexual. "It would seem to be a law of progress that advancing civilisation tends to produce asexual women,"[18] he opines, recognizing heterosexuality and gender binary differentiation as integral to the established male-dominated social system. The maintenance of the status quo would necessitate men's continued sexual and social oppression of others. What "asexual women" signified for Walsh, and other men who shared his perspective, was a looming danger that threatened to upend the social structure that served white men above all others.

As such, he feared that the asexual's dreaded feminism would become appealing to more and more "normal" heterosexuals.

> The asexual women behave like sexless men, enter men's professions, support themselves, do not marry, or at all events produce next to no children and—both they and their male similars, who likewise refrain from marriage—die out.... Feminism, begun among the asexual, is spreading to those with normal sexual instincts.[19]

It is not insignificant that Walsh uses "asexual" to besmirch and rail against those who refused to enter into monogamous heterosexual relationships, marriage, and servitude to men. Revealing his anxiety about child-free "asexual women" to also be a racial anxiety, he writes, "[It is] the primary difference of reproductive function that constitutes the sex differentiation [whereas] in backward barbarous and savage races of mankind there is somewhat less differentiation between men and women than in the more highly civilized."[20] Walsh, and those who thought like him, recognized "asexual women" as a threat to the social order, as heretics who would surely bring about the destruction of society and the decline of white civilization as a whole. Regardless of whether or not the feminists Walsh wrote about would be considered asexuals or lesbians (or both, or neither) by modern standards, they posed the same threat. In Walsh's time and in ours, these anxieties apply to both asexuals and lesbians, as any refusal of the role of traditional womanhood spells doom for the white cisheteropatriarchal gender binary system.

This separation of "women who remain women" from asexuals and lesbians can be found elsewhere. The political magazine *The Westminster Review* published an essay titled "An Interrogatory Note on the Franchise of Women" by Unitarian minister John Lionel Tayler in 1907. While he does not seem to oppose feminism and women's suffrage, Tayler is quite concerned with the preservation of white society's vision of traditional sexual and gender roles.

> Men may be on this basis divided into three groups. (1) The type that is characteristic of its sex, the manly or masculine man. (2) The type that is womanly, or feminine. (3) The type that is very little sexed, and looks on sexual things either with distaste or an unhealthy curiosity. There are three corresponding types of women.

In each case, it is the first type, the manly man, or the womanly woman, that is characteristic of its sex, and is socially of value. This is so not only for reproductive reasons, but because **the fullest sexualised types lead a healthier life, and *mentally are more original, healthy, and sane.*** [21]

Tayler draws a definitive line between the "womanly woman"—the only type that is "socially of value"—and the masculine, presumably lesbian, and the asexual. In Tayler's view, both "masculine" and "asexual women" were dangerous to the "womanly woman" who would undoubtedly find herself silenced by the colluding, overbearing, less "womanly" types.

> The masculine woman is self-assertive, **the asexual woman wishes to banish all sex-beauty which she does not feel and understand from life,** and both are demonstrative, and tend to dominate the woman who is womanly.

> The womanly woman represents womanhood, but she is not self-assertive, is inclined to prefer a private home life to a public one [while] the masculine woman, who likes publicity, who is either unmarried or if married often neglectful of her home, will tend to predominate, and she will in most cases be supported by the asexual woman. The control of the committee-room and the platform means also largely the control of propaganda and ideas generally. [22]

By Tayler's understanding, the masculine and asexual feminists would not only dominate the appropriately feminine and timid "womanly woman," but they would ultimately betray the cause with their lack of femininity and ruin the feminist movement altogether.

> A masculine ideal modified by non-sexual tendencies will, therefore, tend to be voiced and represented, and the womanly woman, by the passing of an unmodified woman's franchise bill, will be increasingly controlled by the masculine woman to the nation's permanent loss.

> Further, the whole object of the woman's movement, which is to emancipate woman as woman, will be defeated. The predominance of masculine and asexual women will strengthen unhealthily the man's influence and woman's ideals will be lost. [23]

What both Walsh and Tayler reveal in these works is how asexual existence—whether in concept or in name—has long been recognized as queerness, as non-normativity, as outside of binary understandings of sex and gender. Asexuals have long been associated with those of other nonheterosexual sexualities and nonconforming gender expression because all nonnormative expression has been stigmatized as deviant, abnormal, and dangerous to cisheteropatriarchy and white civilization.

Compulsory (Hetero)Sexuality

Adrienne Rich's "Compulsory Heterosexuality and Lesbian Existence" is considered a seminal feminist text, especially among lesbians. It calls for heterosexuality to be understood and studied as a "political institution" that constantly works to "disempower women" sexually and socially.[24] Within said institution, lesbianism is "perceived on a scale ranging from deviant to abhorrent or simply rendered invisible" in a society invested in compulsory heterosexuality.[25] In this work, Rich identifies compulsory heterosexuality as the assumption that all women are heterosexual. She also details the institutional agenda to convince women that their attraction to and heterosexual involvement with men is inevitable and obligatory, creating barriers to seeing lesbianism as a valid existence:

> Messages to women have been, precisely, that we are the emotional and sexual property of men, and that the autonomy and equality of women threaten the family, religion, and state. The institutions by which women have traditionally been controlled—patriarchal motherhood, economic exploitation, the nuclear family, compulsory heterosexuality—are being strengthened by legislation, religious fiat, media imagery, and efforts at censorship.[26]

Here, I would be remiss not to acknowledge Rich's transphobia. She was an ardent supporter of Janice Raymond, who conceived of the deeply anti-trans book *The Transsexual Empire: The Making of the She-Male,* which accuses trans people of "coloniz[ing] feminist identification, culture, politics, and sexuality."[27] According to Raymond, "Transsexuals merely cut off the most obvious means of invading women, so that they seem noninvasive."[28] After its publishing in 1979, it

103

would directly contribute to the oppression of and violence against trans people for decades.

That being said, Rich's essay and the development of "compulsory heterosexuality" have been invaluable for an untold amount of queer people who are expected to perform heterosexuality and womanhood. She gave us much-needed language to talk about what we experience as people who do not fit easily into heterosexuality or the gender binary but are instead coerced into it. Moreover, various scholars—asexual and otherwise—have built on Rich's concept of compulsory heterosexuality in order to identify and analyze the phenomenon of compulsory sexuality. Though Rich does not explicitly name asexuals, she includes *"femmes seules"* (lone women), "marriage resisters," and "spinsters"[29] in her discussion. Asexuals exist in each of these categories, all likewise experiencing the "violent strictures [that are] necessary to enforce women's total emotional, erotic loyalty and subservience to men."[30]

Rich also notes that people socialized as women often "endure sexual harassment to keep [our] jobs and learn to behave in a complacently and ingratiatingly heterosexual manner ... the woman who too decisively resists sexual overtures in the workplace is accused of being 'dried-up' and sexless, or lesbian."[31] Both "dried-up" and "sexless" echo the language around "female sexual dysfunction" or "frigidity" and are understood as undesirable, shameful ways to exist in a society that demands our sexual availability to men and that socializes us "to feel that male sexual 'drive' amounts to a right."[32] Asexuals and lesbians are often similarly put in the position of having to appeal to men, abide by certain expectations of traditional womanhood, and comport ourselves in an "ingratiatingly heterosexual manner" for our livelihood and survival. There are, in fact, social ramifications for not making oneself desirable to men in a system where men carry institutional power over women and other marginalized genders. And this reality, and the compulsory nature of (hetero)sexuality, can skew our understanding of our own sexualities and attractions.

Socialization

Am I really straight, or have I just been socialized toward heterosexual attraction? Have I just been conditioned to unquestioningly value and participate in

heterosexuality? Have I spent my life mistaking a desire for attention and vali-
dation from certain people as attraction to them? How much of the way I (think
I) experience attraction has been determined by social norms and compulsory
heterosexuality?

At the time of my writing this, the internet seems to be practically bursting with people asking these questions, or variations thereof. The Lesbian Masterdoc is making its rounds and finding its way into the hands of questioning lesbians and other queer folks who can identify with it. Originally published as a Tumblr post by the blogger @cyberlesbian in 2018, the Lesbian Masterdoc exists now as an organized, sharable document that illustrates how attraction is often coerced and informed by gendered societal conditioning through the upholding of cishetero-patriarchal gender ideals, especially the myth that we are required to make our-selves appealing to and engage in sexual/romantic relationships with men.

In reviewing the document myself and witnessing others sift through it on TikTok and YouTube to arrive at their own epiphanies about their sexuality, it's not difficult to see where the experiences of asexuals and lesbians align and over-lap in regard to socialized attraction to men under cisheteropatriarchy, gender binarism, and compulsory (hetero)sexuality. Some of the scenarios described that could resonate with (questioning) asexuals, lesbians, and other queer folks coming to understand their socialized attraction to men are as follows:

- being repulsed, frustrated, or deeply confused by certain dynamics of heterosexuality that are considered to be the norm or standard behav-iors, often regarded as universal and inevitable
- being able to identify things that are merely tolerable about performing heterosexuality, but not necessarily things that are enjoyable or actively desired
- reading nervousness, being flustered, or having "butterflies" as attrac-tion, but later coming to understand these things as manifestations of anxiety or panic
- choosing "crushes" rather than genuinely developing them
- mistaking a desire for male validation for heterosexual attraction to men

As Adrienne Rich writes, "women have been convinced that marriage and sexual orientation toward men are inevitable—even if unsatisfying or oppressive—components of their lives."[33] Compulsory heterosexuality and male supremacy teach us that we should accept the bare minimum—ill treatment, poor communication, emotional immaturity, and even hurt, discomfort, and sometimes feeling emotionally or physically unsafe—from heterosexual relations with men. Moreover, those of us who are expected to be attracted to men are sent an array of messages throughout our entire lives, in pornography and otherwise, that work to convince us that "enforced submission and the use of cruelty, if played out in heterosexual pairing, is sexually 'normal.'"[34] The idea that penis-in-vagina sex is "supposed to be painful or uncomfortable" for people with vaginas continues to be especially pervasive. These messages, and more, result in many asexuals and lesbians spending years mistakenly believing that unsatisfying, miserable, and traumatic experiences with heterosexuality are "normal," unavoidable, and as to be expected. Therefore, we may never even consider, until many years later, that we are incompatible, misaligned, or at odds with heterosexuality itself.

What the Lesbian Masterdoc and responses to it make clear for me is that asexuals and lesbians often embark on a similar journey when beginning to question whether or not our heterosexual attractions and desires are genuine or influenced by compulsory (hetero)sexuality and gender binarism. We may come out on the other end with different conclusions about our sexualities— which may sometimes even overlap—but both of these conclusions mean that we have arrived at an existence that, as Rich says of the lesbian existence, is "the rejection of a compulsory way of life [and] also a direct or indirect attack on male right of access to women."[35]

The dehumanizing hypersexualization of Black "female" bodies compounds many of the things explored in the Lesbian Masterdoc and the work of Adrienne Rich—particularly because, as Zakiyyah Iman Jackson puts it, "racialized formations of gender and sexuality are actually central rather than subsidiary to the very human-animal binarism."[36] Sexual accessibility is constantly demanded of us via both white supremacy and Black patriarchy. When we fail to meet the expectations created by centuries-old myths built around Black sexuality, we can find ourselves on the receiving end of angry resistance, aggressive sexualization, and even physical violence from those who have written that narrative onto us—even as we are also shamed for any sexuality we might choose to express.

When misogynoir is ever-present, and when there is a long history of racist, fetishistic, and patriarchal sociosexual terrorism against Black people assigned "womanhood"—albeit not the same class of womanhood as whiteness affords itself—this undoubtedly has an influence, not only on how we understand our sexuality, but also how we are expected to perform "womanhood" within the Western gender binary.

Ultimately, the very same expectations of womanhood that lesbians resist have also been placed on asexuals. Like lesbophobia, much of anti-asexual bias is rooted in misogyny and the white cisheteropatriarchal system's need for "women" to "remain women"—to remain subservient, in both the social and sexual realms—as the "binary opposite" of men in order to uphold an intentionally inequitable civilization. In reading the work of lesbian theorists through an asexual lens, and witnessing people awaken to their lesbian identity by publicly examining compulsory heterosexuality and socialized attraction, I believe resemblance in how these two queer identities maneuver the expectations of cisheteropatriarchy and gender roles is evident. I therefore see potential for more intentional queer kinship and coalition building between asexuals and lesbians based on this overlap. Asexuals and lesbians will always be unfit for a society that only understands "women" as fit when we are sexually and socially submissive to men.

8

Unhuman

And, reflected Kronsteen, much of her success was due to the peculiar nature of her next most important instinct, the sex instinct. For Rosa Klebb undoubtedly belonged to the rarest of all sexual types. She was a Neuter. Kronsteen was certain of it. The stories of men and, yes, of women, were too circumstantial to be doubted. She might enjoy the act physically, but the instrument was of no importance. For her, sex was nothing more than an itch. And this psychological and physiological neutrality of hers at once relieved her of so many human emotions and sentiments and desires. Sexual neutrality was the essence of coldness in an individual. It was a great and wonderful thing to be born with.... Her urge for power demanded that she should be a wolf and not a sheep. She was a lone operator, but never a lonely one, because the warmth of company was unnecessary to her.

—IAN FLEMING, *From Russia with Love*[1]

ROSA KLEBB IS ONE of the villains of Ian Fleming's fifth James Bond novel, *From Russia with Love,* published in 1957. She is the head of Otdyel II, the execution department of the Russian counterintelligence agency, SMERSH. Sadistic, cruel, and predatory, one of her favorite things to do is oversee the interrogation and torture of enemy agents, after which she manipulates them into divulging information by feigning warmth and empathy she is incapable of truly possessing. Though she has sexual encounters with men and women alike, it is only to satisfy an "itch" and use them to her advantage. She cares not for genuine human connection, only for amassing power and using that power to control and harm others. I, and many others, read Rosa Klebb as an asexual antagonist.

From Russia with Love also features a character named Grant, who is explicitly described as "a narcissist and asexual [whose] tolerance of pain [is] high."[2]
This asexual serial killer begins his foray into his macabre obsessions in the way
that many real-life serial killers are known to—by harming animals. At sixteen,
"[when] he first got 'The Feelings' as he called them to himself, he went out and
strangled a cat. This made him 'feel better' for a whole month."[3] He goes on to
kill a sheepdog and a cow, then some geese and chickens, until his urges ultimately direct him toward human prey: "When he killed the occasional girl he
did not 'interfere' with her in any way. That side of things, which he had heard
talked about, was quite incomprehensible to him. It was only the wonderful act
of killing that made him 'feel better.' Nothing else."[4]

Goldfinger is the seventh novel in the Bond series, published in 1958. Its
main antagonist is Auric Goldfinger, a gold smuggler who has an obsession
with the precious metal. He, too, is presented as being asexual, having no
sexual interest in other people, and his obsession with gold flows deeper than
a surface-level hunger for astronomical wealth. Upon their first meeting, Jill
Masterson tells Bond that Goldfinger "loves gold, really loves it like people
love jewels or stamps or—well ... women."[5] In 1961's *Thunderball,* the ninth
James Bond installment, the criminal mastermind Ernst Stavro Blofeld has
"never been known to sleep with a member of either sex."[6] Blofeld's equally
evil right hand, Irma Bunt, introduced in *On Her Majesty's Secret Service,* can
also be read asexually—her only apparent interests being her loyal service to
Blofeld and her ruthless death work. Additionally, in the 1965 *Thunderball*
film adaptation, a character called Vargas is raised from a relatively minor
role to one of the supporting antagonists, a trusted henchman of the main
villain, Emilio Largo. At one point, Bond is told by Largo, "Vargas does not
drink. Does not smoke. Does not make love." Then, he asks, "What *do* you do,
Vargas? Every man has his passion."[7]

Indeed, the Bond series seems to have a peculiar interest in asexual and aromantic antagonism and villainy. And each of the aforementioned characters are
contrasted with the heroic Bond's aggressive, virile heterosexuality—which he
even uses to "cure" femme fatale Pussy Galore of her lesbianism. This trope is
a more common one than some may realize. A number of antagonists, villains,
criminals, killers, and otherwise amoral or unpleasant characters are coded

as asexual or aromantic, and their abnormal nature is framed as being directly linked with their asexuality or aromanticism.

Among the most recognizable of these is Dexter Morgan, the main character of Showtime's *Dexter* television series. He is a serial killer who targets other serial killers and criminals as a convenient outlet for his psychopathic urge to kill, which he very much enjoys doing. When we first meet Dexter, he lacks understanding of human emotion, connection, and intimacy. The closest person to him is his adoptive sister, whom he says that he is merely "fond" of. Dexter also feels indifference toward sex and romance, entering into a relationship only to maintain a public image of appearing to be "normal." As the show progresses and he becomes more "human," he enters into sexual and romantic relationships because he feels drawn to the women, not to simply use them as beards for his secret life as a serial killer. Ace- and aro-coded characters like Dexter and the Bond antagonists are removed from humanness in some fashion—more aligned with blood-thirsty beasts or cold, unfeeling machines—embodying the Villainous Aromantic Asexual trope:

> Media that features characters with psychopathic [or antisocial] traits often try to play up their inhuman nature as much as possible. Many decide a good way to hammer the point home is to have the character reject all forms of sexuality. It's the norm for humans to feel sexual attraction (or at least romantic attraction), so something must be fundamentally wrong when someone rejects such basic instincts. This trope also enforces the idea of heteronormativity, alongside similar tropes like Depraved Bisexual, Depraved Homosexual, and Psycho Lesbian.

> Villainous Asexual and/or Aromantic characters often also dismiss friendships, familial relationships, and other human relationships [and] tend to have a Lack of Empathy as well. Characters might be interested in nothing but their work or might have a near-sexual interest in sadism. If they ever have sex, it's only to further some agenda.[8]

This sort of characterization is not reserved only for asexual and aromantic criminality. Beloved protagonist Sherlock Holmes is coded as asexual and aromantic (and neurodivergent) in Arthur Conan Doyle's adventure crime stories. Though Sherlock is a popular hero who continues to be portrayed in endless adaptations and reimaginings, he is unlikable, selfish, arrogant, and obnoxious in most iterations and describes himself in the BBC *Sherlock* series as a "high-functioning sociopath."[9] Being deeply devoted to his detective work, he views sex and romance as unnecessary distractions. In one of his earliest stories, "A Scandal in Bohemia," narrator Dr. John Watson reflects on Sherlock's aversion to and disdain for emotionality, likening him to automata:

> It was not that he felt any emotion akin to love for Irene Adler. All emotions, and that one particularly, were abhorrent to his cold, precise but admirably balanced mind. He was, I take it, the most perfect reasoning and observing machine that the world has seen, but as a lover he would have placed himself in a false position. He never spoke of the softer passions, save with a gibe and a sneer.[10]

Here, I return to the MacInnis-Hodson study discussed in chapter 1 on anti-asexual attitudes and how they impact asexual lives. The study recognizes two types of dehumanization categorized by psychological researcher Nick Haslam: animalistic and mechanistic. Haslam's work, which seeks to better understand and analyze the meaning of "humanness" itself, identifies two types of dehumanization, each involving the denial of different aspects of humanness: (1) uniquely human (UH) characteristics that differentiate humans from nonhuman animals, and (2) human nature (HN) characteristics that are considered fundamental or central to the human species. When dehumanized based on the perceived absence of "uniquely human" characteristics, people are considered animalistic. When dehumanized based on the perceived absence of "human nature" terms, people are seen as mechanistic.[11] Haslam argues that "uniquely human" and "human nature" are "distinct senses of humanness."[12]

MacInnis and Hodson examine two bases through which people become dehumanized: (1) trait-based, as in the denial of human traits, and (2) emotion-based, as in the denial of human emotions.[13] Before presenting their data, they offer some context and share their predictions:

> Sexuality has become inextricably linked with "humanness." [Many] scholars have discussed the extent to which sexuality has become intimately connected with nearly all aspects of human social life. Human sexuality is thus a socially constructed phenomenon with strong prominence and importance in our lives. Given the strong overlap between

sexuality and "humanness," asexuals were expected to be dehumanized generally, as an atypical, deviant, and low-status outgroup. Given their defining lack of sexual desire, we predicted particularly strong human nature dehumanization, with heterosexuals representing asexuals as cold and machine-like, relatively devoid of fundamental aspects characterizing humanity.[14]

Their predictions were right. Asexuals were seen as the least human, as both animalistic and mechanistic, and were believed to have the fewest "uniquely human" and "human nature" traits among all sexualities included in the study. Asexual people are accustomed to hearing dehumanizing rationalizations for why asexuality either cannot possibly exist or for why asexuals are deviant, with variations on the claims that asexuality "goes against (human) nature" or that "sex is what makes us human." But many asexuals have taken this in stride, (half-jokingly) concluding that, if we are not human, then surely we must be displaced gods. Regardless of what the category of "human" denotes or symbolizes, humanness and sexuality need not be in conversation in a way that posits one as a prerequisite for the other. Tethering humanness to sexuality has only ever provided opportunities to further marginalize people without legible sexualities or with sexualities understood as nonnormative in a white cisheteropatriarchal system.

The authors of "Asexuality: Dysfunction or Sexual Orientation?" offer some insight as to why sex and "humanness" are so strongly linked in the social imagination, using Abraham Maslow's theory of hierarchy of basic human needs (which he misappropriated from Native Americans). This motivational theory is a five-tier hierarchical model of human needs, often depicted as a pyramid, which places our most basic physiological needs on the bottom tier and our other needs on the tiers above it in order of importance. Created in 1943, this model of human needs is still used in modern psychology.

Importantly, this theory categorizes human needs in a descending order. According to its concept of relative necessity, a need can only be met from the satisfaction of other needs considered most important, which are located at the base of the hierarchical pyramid. **Maslow places the sexual act at the base of this pyramid, as a basic, natural, and physiological need, disregarding the complexity of the human being,** refusing to analyze the individual from a holistic, historical, social, and cultural perspective and reducing them solely to the biological dimension.[15]

According to Haslam, "UH characteristics primarily reflect socialization and culture, whereas HN characteristics would be expected to **link humans to the natural world, and their inborn biological dispositions.**"[16] Furthermore, "HN characteristics should be seen as deeply rooted aspects of persons: parts of their unchanging and inherent nature. HN should be seen as that which is essential to humanness, the core properties that people share 'deep down' despite their superficial variations. In sum, HN should be **essentialized, viewed as fundamental, inherent, and natural.**"[17]

While both forms of dehumanization impact asexuals, it is "human nature" that many acephobes reach for when drawing an inherent connection between sex and humanness, and thus invalidating asexuals based on this imagined connection or barring us from humanness. Popular media makes use of both forms of dehumanization, creating asexual characters who are detached from both "uniquely human" and "human nature" traits, and framing them as animalistic, mechanistic, or a combination of both. And though onscreen asexual and aromantic representation is gradually improving, in both quality and quantity, the dehumanized asexual or aromantic character trope continues to occasionally show its unpleasant face.

Ace of Spades

Content note: Spoilers for *Selah and the Spades* (2020)

There is something ever so slightly off about Selah Summers. It's like she is more an observer of human interactions than a participant in them, like she isn't actually connecting with the people around her so much as she is interested in studying them. She could very well be described as having an antisocial personality. At the very least, she is extremely toxic—deceptive, calculating, and dangerous, with a pattern of causing direct harm or injury to others and attempting to evade accountability. The movie *Selah and the Spades* (2020) is an unflinching teen melodrama that takes the common social hierarchy of high school and amplifies it in a beautiful and quiet, contemplative tragedy. Selah (Lovie Simone) is at the center of the story as leader of the Spades. Alongside her closest friend and right hand, Maxxie (Jharrel Jerome), Selah oversees and facilitates the distribution of an array of drugs and alcohol to the student body, ruthlessly imposing her will.

It's the spring semester of Selah's senior year and she must find someone to whom she can pass on her power and leadership position. Enter newcomer Paloma (Celeste O'Connor). They meet when Paloma is tasked with photographing the spirit squad, of which the high-achieving Selah is the captain. Soon after, Selah begins to groom Paloma, both as her protégé and as another person to have under her boot, to use for her own interests. During Paloma's first visit to her dorm room, Selah talks about her lack of interest in sex and romance. She tells Paloma, "I don't do that ... dating and sex and, like, making out. I don't—I don't do it.... I never wanted to.... I don't think I'm waiting for some 'right person.' I just don't think I'm interested in the thing itself."[18] This is essentially the only time we get any real insight into Selah's inner world, and this emphasis on an absence of sexual and romantic interest stands out. It seems to ultimately serve as a means to paint Selah as starkly different from her peers, to point to her inability to develop significant emotional connections, to further demonstrate that she is devoid of certain "uniquely human" and "human nature" qualities.

Before she realizes the magnitude of her situation, Paloma has been sucked into the power-hungry Selah's vortex of secrets, lies, and cruelty that swallows up anyone who dares to get in her way, undermine her authority, or defy her command. Even longtime friend Maxxie eventually becomes a pawn in Selah's political game. Though the film provides some context for Selah's complicated life, showing her cowering under the immense pressure of her highly critical perfectionist mother, it ultimately leaves her as both the star and the antagonist. Like the various Bond villains, Selah's aromantic asexuality is wrapped up in her antagonism. Her disinterest in sex and romance becomes a function of story—another way to demonstrate her apathy, narcissism, detachment, and disregard for others; to drive home the fact that there is something ever so slightly off about Selah Summers.

Melanie Ojwang (she/they) is a Black ace writer and creator of the YouTube channel "Voice Memos for the Void." This is where I encountered their video analysis of *Selah and the Spades* and its handling of Selah's aromantic asexuality. I reached out to Melanie, who shared her thoughts on how Selah fits in with established tropes of asexual and aromantic characters in media. "Selah is popular, but always alone, seemingly unable or unwilling to have even small connections outside of Maxxie and Paloma for most of the film. Despite being the leader of the spirit squad, for example, we don't see her interact with the other members at practice or in the hallways or in class," Melanie observes. "There is the suggestion that she struggles to build emotional intimacy with others. Selah treats her friends terribly, but unlike other popular girls who are shown as **strategically** emotionally manipulative (think: Regina George [from *Mean Girls*]), Selah operates in a way that suggests she isn't invested in emotions or her friends' well-being at all."

Selah spikes Paloma's drink as retaliation for an imagined slight, and Paloma eventually becomes unresponsive. Selah panics and runs to Maxxie. She explains to him that Paloma's head was "just getting so big," rationalizing what she's done, but he sees through her bullshit. "You can't keep doing this, Selah!" he explodes, confirming that she has done this before and got away with it. Once it is made clear to a now-conscious Paloma that Selah drugged her to keep her "humble," she is rightfully furious. But Selah is dismissive and gaslights her, saying, "You're making a big deal out of this for nothing."[19] Paloma slaps Selah and runs off into the woods in a stupor, nearly falling over a cliff, which might have killed her. After having caused this perilous situation to unfold, Selah offers no apology.

"It isn't until after drugging Paloma that Selah has any emotional response to someone else's well-being. But the last scene of the film has Selah standing at the edge of a cliff, away from her struggling friends in the background, for a long and tense moment." Then, Melanie asks, "Why is the decision to **still** show this strong detachment instead of finally having Selah be emotionally invested?" To me, Selah's "emotional response" seems to be more about a fear of possibly having to face serious consequences for her illegal, unethical, impulsive, and dangerous actions than it is about Paloma's well-being. Selah's self-centeredness and emotional detachment is central and constant, and she seems to have no remorse for what she has done.

"It's harmful to suggest that asexual and aromantic people are incapable of forming any kind of emotional intimacy or care for others, especially when this is attached to antagonists. There's a message of 'Be careful around these people because there's something about them that might make them behave without care for others' melding with the idea that being ace or aro means you're broken somehow," Melanie says. "Ace or aro coding as a stand-in for a disinterest in **all** intimate connections often trickles down to a lack of character development. A lot of our media depicts intimacy as only a sexual or romantic experience, so removing the interest for romance or sex from a character [often] means removing the potential for showing them forming deeper relationships with **anyone**." Among asexual and aromantic characters, there is a clear pattern of dehumanization through constructing them as people without empathy and without any real concept of the emotional complexities of humans. With *Selah and the Spades*, Selah's Blackness will always complicate and magnify this dehumanization.

NHI

Content note: police brutality, serial murder, whorephobia

Following the acquittals of the Los Angeles Police Department (LAPD) officers who assaulted Rodney King in 1991, the 1992 Los Angeles Riots erupted. Rage and bewilderment fueled the rioters, who witnessed the brutal beating of the unarmed King on video. Amid the aftermath of the trial and subsequent chaos, new information about the LAPD's protocols emerged. Cultural theorist Sylvia Wynter wrote an open letter to her colleagues that named the anti-Blackness in the Los Angeles justice system. Reports had revealed that "public officials of the judicial system of Los Angeles routinely used the acronym NHI to refer to any case involving a breach of the rights of young Black males who belong to the jobless category of the inner-city ghettoes. NHI means 'no humans involved.'"[20]

Six years before Rodney King's violent arrest, a serial killer began targeting victims in South Central, Los Angeles. Much later, this killer would come to be known as the Grim Sleeper, a name derived from a supposed fourteen-year hiatus in his reign of terror, from 1988 to 2002. His real name was Lonnie Franklin. It would eventually be discovered that the killing never stopped, and Franklin likely ripped at least eleven women from the world during those fourteen years. In all, investigators suspect that he killed at least twenty-five women, but it is likely that he took the lives of far more. There were over 1,000 photos of at least 180 unconscious women found in his home. Many still have not been identified.[21]

Like many serial killers, the Grim Sleeper targeted drug users and sex workers, the unhoused and housing insecure—people he knew could disappear and would not be missed by society. He discarded their remains in alleyways, dumpsters, and industrial yards, amid the city's filth and garbage and unwanted things. The LAPD was aware that a serial killer was active as early as 1985, but they failed to alert the community of this danger until 2007. HBO's *Tales of the Grim Sleeper* (2014) documentary reveals that the LAPD used "NHI" to refer to many of Franklin's victims because they were Black drug users and sex workers. One woman who managed to survive an attack in 1988 was assumed to be a crack user by responding officers. As such, they did not follow up on the account she gave about her attack. Lonnie Franklin was not apprehended until 2010, nearly twenty-five years after the killings began. Many, including me, believe he would have been stopped sooner if the world had cared more about his victims.[22]

The use of NHI by law enforcement is the logical end of anti-Blackness and white supremacy. Humanness and who is allowed access to it, as understood through white ascendant ideals and white knowledge production, is limited—from the once fracturing of Black people into three-fifths a person[23] to Dred and Harriet Scott's 1846 lawsuit to have their personhood recognized[24] to our ancestors being treated as cargo, chattel, and commodity. Black people have not had access to the category of "human" since the jaws of colonialism took hold of Africa. As Zakiyyah Iman Jackson writes in *Becoming Human: Matter and Meaning in an Antiblack World*, "Gendered and sexual discourses on 'the African' are inextricable from those pertaining to reason, historicity, and civilization, as purported observations of gender and sexuality were frequently used to provide 'evidence' of the inherent abject quality of black people's human animality from the earliest days of the invention of 'the human.'"[25]

Impossibility

Content note: lynching, r*pe

"Human" so often becomes one of the uses of sex. Many people use sex, and the things surrounding it, to codify and define humanness for themselves and others, and therefore to exclude asexuals from the category of "human." At the same time, sexuality has historically been used to beastialize Black folks, that is, to make our alleged animalistic engagement with sex into the evidence of our monstrosity. **Tea Troutman** (they/them), a geographer, urbanist, and cultural commentator, sees the utilization of sex to authenticate humanness as inseparable from anti-Black authentications of humanness:

> I think people use sex to authenticate humanness for a number of reasons, chiefly among those are to establish and maintain hegemonic, patriarchal power dynamics and to enforce codes of desirability. I also think sex(uality) and humanness, or the sexual as constitutive of "proper" humanness, cannot be separated from the establishment of anti-Black, white supremacist, colonial notions of morality.

The way sex is used and has been used to reify white ascendant ideals of personhood is revealed in how entire Black communities and lives have been destroyed under the guise of protecting white women from Black sexual appetites. Consider Emmett Till, the Scottsboro Boys, the Central Park Five, and many more unnamed and unknown to us. Tea explains:

> As an urban studies scholar, I've found that phenomena like racial segregation, "progressive reform," and outright slum clearance and communal displacement are all rooted in the logics of negrophobia that constitutes Black folks (as well as other nonwhite colonial subjects) and our communities as sites of hypersexuality, sexual impurity, and inherent immorality and uncleanliness. This is especially prominent in the reconstruction South, where even the emergence of white terrorist organizations like the KKK and the culture of lynch law emerged in response to the necessity to police the Black in the name of protecting white women, white femininity, and the white family order. White masculinity, white femininity, and the adherence to the patriarchal structure mandates that "proper, moral" humanity be stabilized through sexual coherence and the policing of deviant sexualities.

So what does it mean for Black people—asexual or not—when our sex is always already criminalized, moralized, and fetishized, to the point where Black asexuality is seen as a distinct impossibility, even among other asexuals? What does it mean for Black asexuals when we are told that sex is a prerequisite to be considered human under compulsory sexuality, even as Black people always already fail at being human under white supremacy, and that dehumanization is achieved through the myth of Black animalistic hypersexuality? Moreover, what limitations does this place on our understanding of sex, humanness, Blackness, and asexuality altogether? Is it possible to sever the connections imagined as inherent between them? And what possibilities might arise if we did?

"[Our world] constitutes Blackness as always inherently sexual," Tea offers. "Or as Frantz Fanon notes in *Black Skin, White Masks* when attempting to make sense of the origins of negrophobia and its anti-Black violence: 'The Negro symbolizes the biological danger.... To suffer from a phobia of Negroes is to be afraid of the biological'[26] and 'one is no longer aware of the Negro, but only of a penis; the negro is eclipsed. He is turned into a penis. He *is* a penis.'"[27] This fear of "the biological" explored by Fanon is paralleled by Jackson's *Becoming Human,* which asserts that "the African's 'failure' to achieve humanity has historically been thought to be rooted in 'the body,' in an insatiable appetite that made it impossible for the African to rise above 'the body,' 'the organ,' in order to come back to itself in self-reflection, never achieving the distance required in order to contemplate the self."[28] As Tea affirms, "Fanon, like other scholars of anti-Blackness and sexuality-desire, understands that the logics of an anti-Black world—and the notion of humanity it constitutes—cannot understand the Black as separate from an insatiable sexual appetite that makes the notion of a Black (moral, non-perverse) humanity impossible."

As scholars of various disciplines continue to interrogate humanness to understand the ways certain groups become dehumanized, I also want us to interrogate how sexuality has become regarded in the social imagination, so that asexuals are understood as abnormally lacking sexuality to the point of dehumanization while Blackness is hypersexualized to the point of dehumanization. We must think more deeply and ask more questions about what it means when these two phenomena happen simultaneously. Black asexuals have the anti-Black dehumanization we experience compounded by asexual dehumanization. If Blackness and asexuality are both abjections that cannot live up to humanness, where does this leave the Black asexual—both in terms of narrative explorations like *Selah and the Spades* and navigating real-world acephobic dehumanization alongside anti-Black dehumanization? Blackness always already fails to be everything that white supremacy names as "normal," and asexuality makes us into failures in the same right.

"To me, an understanding and recognition of a Black asexuality quite literally threatens the white supremacist social order," Tea argues, echoing my own conclusions. "Taking Fanon's understanding of the negro as biological danger that animates the classical white fears and anxieties that structure 'amalgamation'—whether through the constitution of Black male sexuality as always a threat of rape or Black female sexuality as that of an always consenting temptress/Jezebel—threatens the racial-biological purity that makes whiteness and white humanity coherent and dominant. [With] the overrepresentation of the Black as sexual, Black asexuality is not simply erased.... The idea of a 'Black asexual' is impossible given the logics of anti-Black humanity."

I hope to see scholars of critical race studies, sexuality studies, and more interrogate how humanness has become defined through and attached to allosexuality—or, at the very least, the performance of allosexuality—alongside race, as I believe it will produce new insights and create new interventions in multiple fields of study. It is imperative that we critically engage with what it means for there to be such a connection between humanness and sexual engagement, and to have this connection regarded as eternal, innate, and inseverable. This entanglement of humanness with allosexuality is foundational to compulsory sexuality, and this entanglement necessitates the dehumanization of the asexual.

If asexuality and Blackness both make one unhuman for diametrically opposing reasons, then "human" as a category is movable and arbitrary, yet always unattainable for the Black asexual, left to exist in a state of impossibility. The position this places Black asexuals in only further demonstrates the malleability of humanness, a tool to reify white supremacy. As Zakiyyah Iman Jackson attests, "Eurocentric humanism needs blackness as a prop in order to erect whiteness: to define its own limits and to designate humanity as an achievement as well as to give form to the category of 'the animal.'"[29] Tethering sex to humanness is simply one more avenue by which white supremacy seeks to enact sexual control, cultivate sexual shame, and reinscribe white cisheteropatriarchal ideals as "normal" in every arena. The Black asexual is rendered impossible through the (il)logics of anti-Black sexual racism, white supremacy, and compulsory sexuality. A world that allows for Black asexuals to be seen as possible, to live more freely in our asexuality, would also be a revolution for all others racialized, gendered, and queered. Such a world requires us to combat white supremacist ideologies and the very idea of "human."

9

Utility

Sex as Racial Containment

Content note: racial fetishism, pornography, racist violence, r*pe

WHITE SUPREMACY ITSELF IS a sexual fantasy—preoccupied with power, violence, and domination. Therefore, sexual fantasy is an opportune space for sex to become utilized toward white supremacist ends. Anti-Black and white supremacist uses of sex seem to now stand at the threshold between taboo and socially acceptable. People of all races are encouraged toward demonstrating their anti-Blackness through sexual expression or finding sexual gratification in racist spectacles, especially through pornography. The cultural and political climate allows for racist porn to thrive, in part because racism is woven into the very fabric of some of it. Porn is the perfect medium for the eroticization of white supremacy to be explored, through the likes of videos featuring neo-Nazis inked with swastikas performing in front of Confederate flag backdrops or scenarios with white cops brutalizing and hurling racial slurs at Black performers before dominating them sexually.

Running alongside these overtly white supremacist sexual fantasies brimming with racial hatred is the more mainstream porn that centers racial fetishization. According to Pornhub's 2019 insight report, "Eight out of the top twenty-five most popular search terms were nonwhite racial or ethnicity descriptors.... Not one of those top-ranking terms referred to whiteness or Caucasian ethnicity. In fact, the terms 'Caucasian' or 'white' have never once appeared on Pornhub's top search lists throughout the years."[1]

Stereotypes about the dangerous Black phallus and immediate sexual accessibility of "Black pussy" are abundant and evident in porn titles and action. The same is true of myths about the purity of whiteness, the exoticism and fire of Latinx performers, the supposed natural tightness of the tiny Asian's vagina, and so on. Each of these racist mythologies function as truisms in pornography because, as a form of media made for sexual consumption and geared mostly toward white men's sexual indulgences, it "offers a generative site to explore the representation and potential enactments of racial fantasy. It is a genre of the body, and economy of visible flesh, designed for the specific purpose of titillation and arousal."[2]

While racism in porn is not a direct response to current times, what we see produced by the porn industry is indeed a reflection of our society. With the rise and cult worship of Trump within the last decade, the naming of the alt-right, the neo-Nazi resurgence, the battle over Confederate flags and monuments, the fear of "white genocide," and ongoing KKK rallies and marches, overt racism and bigotry are very much a part of current popular culture because white people react violently to calls for Black liberation. Reactionary white supremacist violence and racial anxiety show up in sexual spaces as well as social ones, sometimes simultaneously.

"Cuck" reared its head during the Trump presidency as one of the favorite insults among white conservatives deployed against other white people who they felt were not conservative enough. As a shorthand for "cuckold"—taken from an Old French term referring to the cuckoo's habit of laying its eggs in another bird's nest—this term comes with racist and pornographic undertones that white men use to transmute their fears about loss of institutional and racial power into a weapon. Derived from a popular pornographic scenario in which a white man is cuckolded by, and obliged to watch, a Black "bull" fuck a white woman who is understood to belong to the white man in some way, this insult—and sexual fantasy—has layers. One porn producer told *Slate* that

> his most popular movies are those where "the purity of the sacred white women is compromised." Another pornographer told Adult Video News, "My customers seem to enjoy black men 'taking advantage' of white women: seducing their white daughters and wives. The more 'wrong' a title is, the more appealing it is." This explains why interracial porn geared toward white men is more dominated by Black male porn performers than any other ethnic group.[3]

The Black phallus holds a distinctive place in the social imagination in regard to Black sexuality and masculinity. It conjures up images of the Black Brute, the Black Buck, the Black Breeder, and the Mandingo—all differing versions of the same lie about the aggressive, animalistic, sex-crazed Black man who preys on innocent white women and breeds countless Black children.

> Most commentary on the Mandingo as an archetypal character tend to center on white male heteropatriarchal fantasies. It is, of course, from the viewpoint of the white male—in the realms of both political economy and psychoanalysis—that the dangerous black buck stereotype emerges. According to this commentary, the Mandingo stereotype emerges through the interplay of desire as discussed both as an expression of the real fear and envy that white men have toward black male sexuality.[4]

This renders the Black phallus desired and fetishized on the one hand, but feared and demonized on the other. In "The Negro as a Distinct Ethnic Factor in Civilization," Dr. William Lee Howard asserts, "Every unphysiological and antisocial act that tends to breed degenerate human beings, sinful, vicious, and lustful, lies inherent in the African to-day," and details the inherent sexual perversion of Blackness, often focusing on the size of the Black phallus as evidence. This work appeared in a medical journal published in 1903:

> When education will reduce the large size of the negro's penis as well as bring about the sensitiveness of the terminal fibers which exist in the Caucasian, then it will also be able to prevent the African's birthright to sexual madness and excess—from the Caucasian's view-point.

> During these periods of sexual madness, the negro has all the symptoms of lycanthropia. There is a loss of controlling power over the higher centers of the brain, or else the rabid impulses due to overdevelopment of sexual energy in certain portions of the brain, which the normal power of inhibition—that which the white man possesses—cannot control.[5]

The social fear of and preoccupation with the Black phallus carries with it a particular history that has left a trail of thousands of Black people lynched for even looking at white women: "The most common justification for lynching was the claim that a Black man had raped a white woman. The thought of this particular crime aroused in many white people an extremely high level of mania and panic.

One white woman, the wife of an ex-Congressman, stated in 1898, 'If it needs lynching to protect woman's dearest possession from human beasts, then I say lynch a thousand times a week if necessary.'[6] Those lynchings often included castration specifically because of the fear of Black sexuality, the Black phallus, and the harm that might be done, or allegedly had been done, to white women. The fascination with this particular sexual trope has played out on the screen since the beginning of cinema, most notably with D. W. Griffith's *The Birth of a Nation* (1915), in which a Black man (a white actor in Blackface) is depicted as violently lusting after a young white woman and stalking her until she willingly leaps from a cliff to escape his unwanted advances.

Over a century after the release of Griffith's white supremacist manifesto on film, which sparked a resurgence of the KKK, the subject of the Black phallus is still explored on screen. With *The Hateful Eight* (2015), Quentin Tarantino imagines the Black phallus as a weapon wielded by Major Marquis Warren (Samuel L. Jackson) in an act of sexual violence against a white man as a perverse form of racial justice, and it is later violently removed from his person, seemingly as another form of justice. Jordan Peele contemplates the Black phallus again with *Get Out* (2017), although less explicitly, via the fetishization of Black male sexuality in Chris Washington (Daniel Kaluuya) and his interactions with a white woman who blatantly sexualizes him, touches and inspects his muscular arm without his consent, and asks his white girlfriend if sex is better with him than with white men. Understanding the anti-Blackness inherent to this violation and fetishization of Chris, the Black phallus, and Black sexuality—especially engaged with white women—is key to understanding the work the film does as a whole.

Porn is "a genre that makes visible the proof of the Mandingo's threat.... The Mandingo archetype has been the overriding frame for representing black men's sexualities and pornography, a powerful mechanism for the eroticism passion of interracial, black-white sex. This pornography demands that black men perform a typically assertive, sometimes brutish, sexuality, because the Mandingo figure defines black masculinity as such."[7] The term "cuck," as discussed earlier, not only calls up white men's historied sexual anxieties about Black men's lust for white flesh and sexual ownership over white women—and the simultaneous fear and fetishization of the Black phallus—but it also speaks to their contemporary social anxieties.

In the scenario in which a white man is cuckolded, "erotic tension is produced in the fantasy of the black man's extreme sexual prowess and the threat that he will displace the white husband.... This fantasy demands a particular kind of labor on the part of black men in that they are called on to perform the role of a Mandingo who uses his sexual prowess to seduce white women and undermine white men."[8] The use of "cuck" by white men as an insult directly challenges the masculinity and virility of any white man who does not take racist, xenophobic, and nationalist enough stances against immigration and efforts toward racial equity. Fear of the corruption of "white purity"—whether by nonwhite immigrants and citizens gaining institutional power over white nationalists, or by the Black phallus gaining sexual power over white cuckolds and miscegenating with white women—is also a fear of sexual and social humiliation.

These fears are tied up with the white fetishization of power and the gendered power dynamics of heterosexual sex and the heteropatriarchal family. The "cuck" insult—and its conflation of the social with the sexual—demonstrates how compulsory sexuality can pull sex into other arenas and specifically utilize it toward white supremacist ends. The white superiority mythos not only manifests, but fully flourishes in porn and pornographic language. White supremacy and its agents—and even white people who believe themselves to be progressive—continually use sex to uphold racist ideology.

Sex as Racial Solidarity

Content note: state violence, Black death, racial fetishism

In the summer of 2020, amid nationwide uprisings following the state's murder of George Floyd, a friend sent me a captured image of Pornhub's website with a banner saying, "We commit to stand in solidarity and take action with the Black community as they rightfully demand justice. That's why from June 6th–12th only ebony videos will be available on our website." I immediately questioned whether or not it was real. Rumor has it that it *was* real, but Pornhub took it down after receiving complaints. I do not know whether those alleged complaints came from angry racists, from users who immediately recognized what an abhorrent gesture it was, or both.

The image—if it was parody—was likely created as a commentary on and an example of the absurdity of certain companies claiming solidarity with Black communities while profiting from anti-Blackness. In May 2020, @Pornhub tweeted, "Pornhub stands in solidarity against racism and social injustice."[9] Like many other porn sites, Pornhub is brimming with racist content and videos with titles that intentionally play into hundreds of years of propaganda about the inherent sexual deviance of Black people. Regardless of whether or not the image my friend shared with me was real, what is remarkable about it is the fact that it is wholly believable and, frankly, unsurprising that Pornhub would implement something like "only ebony videos" as a form of "activism" for and "solidarity" with Black people, especially given some of the content that emerged on their site during that summer.

> Pornhub saw the rise of a new subgenre: Black Lives Matter porn. One such video is called "White Girl Moans Black Lives Matter While Getting Fucked #BLM." Another is "Black Anal Matters." There is also a subcategory called BLM protest that mainly shows Black men penetrating white women during a supposed Black Lives Matter protest. Some of these women have "BLM" written on their backs, while others are in jail cells being penetrated by Black porn performers dressed as police officers. In a classic marriage of racist themes, one video purports to show a "black lives matter thug choking out a white cop daughter." ... The recent subgenre on Pornhub that sexualizes and trivializes Black Lives Matter highlights the hypocrisy of [their] public relations effort: With more than 1,000 such videos already on the site, Pornhub is drawing revenue from the exploitation of the protest movement, with recycled racist themes to boot.[10]

People were photographed with signs that do the same kind of work while attending protests against police brutality in the summer of 2020 and beyond. One white woman carried a sign, embellished with an eggplant emoji, which read, "I only suck Black [dick]" and, at the bottom in much smaller text, "Fuck racism." Another non-Black person offered a novel suggestion: "We just need to keep fucking each other until we're one color." A Black Power fist punctuated their words. Another asked, "So you will open your mouth for Black dick but keep it closed for Black matters?" Another declared, "I love Black dick so you will hear me speak." And yet another read, "Love Black people like you love Black dick." These signs—and the collective, cultural understandings behind each of their creation—were an unintentional display of one of the many ways race gets wrapped up in sexual politics and vice versa, of how so many people utilize sex in ways that uphold racist ideology.

The following January, when Georgia "turned blue" during the 2021 Senate runoff elections, credit was heaped on former gubernatorial candidate Stacey Abrams. Alongside Black Voters Matter founder LaTosha Brown and Black grassroots organizations, Abrams led campaigns to register hundreds of thousands of Georgians to vote, focusing on Black voters to push back against anti-Black voter suppression efforts.[11] What happened next was a display of sexual and political fetishism when white liberals began to overtly project sexual fantasies onto Abrams in the wake of the Democratic victory. A few of the now-deleted tweets read, "I'm gonna go fap to Stacey Abrahms now" and "I want to bear Stacey Abrams's children" and "A Democrat senator needs to personally eat Stacey Abrams ass every day for the rest of her life." These tweets, and more, were posted on the morning of January 6, the same day white supremacist nationalists invaded the U.S. Capitol.

Both the overt sexualizing of Stacey Abrams and the overtly fetishistic signs at protests are demonstrations of a grotesque political performance non-Black people often use to signify their solidarity with Black people, in public and private spaces. Whether propagating anti-Black sexual stereotypes or showing their "support" through our fetishization, sex often becomes a tool of control. Make no mistake, the immediate sexual projection onto Abrams was an attempt at controlling the public image of a Black woman and her body. The ease with which white liberals were able and willing to connect their political support of a Black woman with the sexual use of a Black woman was unnerving, but revealing. Abrams seamlessly became a sexual object, delectable flesh to be shared among and consumed by others, immediately after proving her usefulness as a political object. Her political labor so easily translated to sexual labor in the white liberal imagination because both forms of labor became understood as useful to the performance of white liberalism in that moment.

When we don't acknowledge how the uses of sex can and sometimes do align with white supremacy and anti-Blackness, people can easily convince themselves (and others) that having sex and reproducing with Black people, or at least expressing a desire to do so, absolves them of their anti-Blackness. They feel confident in using their engagement with Black desirability and sex as a shield against any accusations of racist behavior. Moreover, they offer it up as evidence of their anti-racism, or support for Black lives, or political liberalism. The fetishization and hypersexualization of Black people continue to provide a mask for the dehumanization of Blackness itself, but so many have swallowed the lie that white desire is somehow evidence of care for Black life. White supremacy is always invested in segmenting and reducing us into easily consumable pieces for its own pleasure. We become only our Black skin, only a Black phallus, only a Black pussy, only a Black ass, only a Black body. Delectable morsels.

These ideas about white desire and Black sex are deeply ingrained, and compulsory sexuality allows for people to continuously use sex as a lens for understanding racial solidarity and offer up Black people as conduits for sexual pleasure. Even though they may not name it explicitly as such, people recognize that there is utility in sex—sex as an answer to racism, sex as a defense against accusations of racism, sex as a tool of anti-racism, sex as a means of creating a post-racial world—however futile their attempts might be.

Sex (and Asexuality) as Racial Superiority

Content note: racial fetishism, r*pe, sexual violence

Ianna Hawkins Owen argues in "On the Racialization of Asexuality" that it is essential for us to "interrogate how the historical discourse of asexuality became useful to our society and what logic or illogic it abides by [and] the ways representations of sexuality and asexuality have been deployed to support white supremacy."[12] The use of sex toward white supremacist ends in our past is what has given way to how we see it being utilized in our present.

Asexuality—in concept, rather than in name—has been utilized to prop up mythologized white superiority and to serve white interests. In her seminal essay, Owen interrogates "the deployment of asexuality in the dominant discourse as an ideal sexual behavior to justify both the empowerment of whites and the subordination of blacks to uphold a racialized social and political system."[13] Utilizing the asexual Mammy, characterized as middle-aged, fat, and dark-skinned (i.e., undesirable), became yet another tool of racial-sexual terrorism, specifically against Black "female" subjects. The system and the (il)logic of chattel slavery were maintained in large part through the invention of the Jezebel and the Mammy, creating a sexual dichotomy. Together, they embodied "the sexual ideologies of, respectively, hypersexuality, which provided a rationale for racial violence, and asexuality, which assuaged the moral concerns confronting the system."[14]

Mammy was desexualized and constructed as asexual—stripped of any sexual desire or desirability—to paint her as safe in contrast to the typical sexual savagery of the Jezebel, as savage sexuality is largely what makes Blackness so dangerous in the white imagination. "As the tamed and docile black woman bereft of sexual desire, the image of the Mammy not only represented the so-called benefits of slavery for the enslaved as domestication, but also reconciled the problem of the proximity of blackness in the house and among the children."[15] Her alleged sexlessness qualified her for entry into a white space and eased the worries of polite white society that the presence of a Black body might corrupt or endanger the white household. Essentially, her prescribed asexuality made her nonthreatening.

White supremacy is maintained through intentional misinterpretation of truth and a mythology that "recognizes some as more human than others, distributes benefits accordingly, and takes such a system to be 'normal.'"[16] This is the "agreement to misinterpret the world" identified in Charles W. Mills's *The Racial Contract;* it dictates, "One has to learn to see the world wrongly, but with the assurance that this set of mistakes and perceptions will be validated by white epistemic authority."[17] Owen asserts that asexuality "has operated within, and as an extension of, this misinterpretation of the world,"[18] given how it has been utilized to prop up mythologized white superiority by applying it to the Mammy as well as white morality.

Discussions of asexuality are inextricably linked to the concept of hypersexuality and the consolidation of its discursive attachment to blackness. To this end, whiteness marshals the concept of asexuality-as-ideal to substantiate its claims to racial superiority and "fitness" to rule. Asexuality as ideal is the misinterpretation of asexuality as the honorable achievement or performance of sexual restraint; the white practitioner [of asexuality-as-ideal] is considered pure and deserving of reverence, while the black asexual figure is considered less threatening than her hypersexual counterpart.[19]

White people, white women especially, were expected to deny their sexual desires, living a life in a sort of imposed and moralistic nonsexuality, as proof of white superiority, purity, and willpower—and this also served to deny the ways white slaveholders enacted systematic sexual and reproductive abuses against their captives. Meanwhile, the Mammy's apparent asexuality served to rein-scribe the hypersexuality and lasciviousness of the Jezebel, which was utilized to justify the sexual and reproductive violence visited on her body. The plantation was indeed a site of endlessly incongruent narratives and cognitive dissonance.

Owen also makes interventions by reading Mammy's body alongside Sarah Baartman, an enslaved African who was exhibited as part of nineteenth-century European "freak shows" in which white patrons paid to marvel at her "steato-pygia," or large buttocks. Until 1974, her brain, skeleton, and sexual organs remained on display in a Parisian museum, commodifying her body and con-tinuing the grotesque "freak show" for over a century after her death in 1815. Baartman "received unprecedented sexualized racial attention, and the alleged size of her genitalia constituted the draw of her exhibition. This perception led to the production and circulation of commercial images that emphasized 'Blacks' sexual nature' for the first time."[20] Whites used said images to promote their anti-abolitionist messaging, arguing that such sexually primitive peoples could never be fully or properly integrated into "civilized" white society. Infantile and sexually irresponsible Black people needed to be enslaved; they needed to be subjugated; they needed the guidance and policing of superior whites. "The image of Baartman provided a concrete, physical form on which white British [and U.S.] discourses were able to locate the boundaries of so-called respectable sexuality as well as the embodiment of normal citizenship. The protections of whiteness and racial purity are carried out through the crafting of a sexualized racial threat."[21] Baartman and her apparently primitive sexuality were used as tools to reify both white sexual purity and Mammy's safe asexuality as respectable, and to argue for the continued enslavement of stolen Africans and their descendants.

Reading Mammy and Baartman alongside each other makes plain how white people have used—and often continue to use—a mythical sexual superiority to reinforce their imagined racial superiority, and how "the discourses of black sexuality, conflicting reports though they may be, reveal the strategy of the othering of Black sexuality to support the (il)logic of white supremacy."[22] Again and again, we see the violent, circular, contradictory logic of anti-Blackness. In the same way that it bends time, white supremacy thrives on revisionist histories, false narratives, and disingenuous misinterpretations.

Quiet as it's kept, Mammy often also served as "surrogate mistress" in Southern white households.[23] But white Southerners would continue to uphold and propagate the myth of the docile asexual Black woman dwelling in their homes, the perfect domestic worker. The myth conveniently obscured the reality of the Mammy as "mistress," of Mammy's body as a site of sexual violation, because it would break the illusion of the sexlessness inscribed onto her and the impossibility of white flesh desiring such an undesirable form.

In her dissertation, "Misreading Mammy: Towards a Sexual Revolution of Contemporary/Third Wave Black Feminisms," Nicole Carr endeavors to write "white women's history of violence back into the historical record."[24] She does so by examining their relationship to and violence against Mammy in the household and other Black women on the plantation in order to reveal the role of white women in the horrors of chattel slavery and their complicity with white men in the subjugation and abuse of Black women:

> White women not only identified with white men's patriarchal power, but they developed their own unique methods for renegotiating the terms of their own subordination vis-à-vis the black female body. A substantial amount of my research centers on examining white women's primary role in commodifying, erasing, and sexually assaulting black women via the mammy archetype. I plumb the depths of white women's refusal to acknowledge black women's sufferings to consider white women's

utilization of the mammy myth as a tactical method for silencing black women's voices and sanitizing black women's unique subjectivities.[25]

Carr examines the writings of white mistresses who recorded their private thoughts on and reactions to the Mammy, the "fat buxom wench"[26] whom they often viewed and treated as a threat. This reality, of course, contradicts the mythology built around Mammy by Southern whites, which framed her as non-threatening due to her asexuality. Carr's dissertation is ultimately concerned with "explicating white women's imaginings of black women as trespassers tainting the plantation household as it dispels notions of sexless, benevolent black mammies whose noticeably inferior bodies and beauty stood out in stark contrast to their white mistresses."[27] White women's journals and letters make evident how they "assigned a pathological blackness onto black women that essentially erased enslaved black women's rape, subjugation, and economic exploitation."[28] Between the public image of Mammy as sexless and undesirable versus the private reality of Mammy as the receptacle for both white men's desire and white women's ire, Mammy's body became a battleground.

The stereotypical image of her as middle-aged, dark-skinned, fat, "amorphous and enormous"[29] is not the only form that Mammy took. She was a domestic worker, nursemaid, washer, cook, child-rearer, a bottomless source of household labor whose appearance took various forms. But the image of an undesirable Mammy was useful because her "wide smile and hefty body conceals her own rape at the hands of the white men."[30] Naming this truth is essential for Carr, and it is essential to my work as well. It is this archetype of undesirability and asexuality used to conceal sexual violence against Mammy that Carr understands to be central to removing the demure Southern belle archetype from white women. What is instead revealed is their active participation in the industry of chattel slavery and its many forms of violence, particularly their "utilization of the mammy trope as a means of erasing black women's sexuality from view in order to bolster their femininity as the pure ideal."[31] As always, white womanhood becomes reified and pedestaled through its juxtaposition with Blackness.

The nexus between mammy's gender and race produced a useful device by which white women could freely deliberate their own repressed desires without sullying their own purity. Mammy's unchanging image assisted in the tampering down of black women's sexuality, which white women regarded with equal parts fascination, disgust, and desire. This last factor is critical. Although mammy has been stripped of all sexuality in the popular and current imagination—her toothy grin still the standard for pancakes, syrup bottles, and good Southern comforts—white women's anxious interactions with her and the physical connotations lodged within her body suggest that her body signified carnality too visible to ignore. In reality then, mammy existed as a receptacle for forbidden topics too offensive for polite Southern ladies to mention. **Though supposedly benevolent, mammy's presence on the plantation was a decidedly threatening one based on the latent sexuality concealed within her body.**[32]

Mammy had to be made into a threat, otherwise white mistresses would have to contend with "the truth of their sexually predatory husbands."[33] To shield themselves and their psyche from this truth, white mistresses often punished Black women for their husband's sexual violence against them and even "derived a titillating pleasure from whipping black women."[34] White mistresses "utilized the black female body as a textual script for meditating on their own imprisonment" within a white patriarchal society,[35] transposing their frustrations about their own subjugation onto Mammy and other Black women on the plantation. And the violence they enacted also served to help to assert their own status and racial dominance as white women.

Perhaps the image of the asexual Mammy and the way it was utilized in order to subjugate her and other Black women leaves some Black people reluctant to accept the existence of a genuine Black asexuality, especially their own. Mammy's desexualization and asexualization are constructed, in large part, through her perceived undesirability. It is her stereotypical dark-skinned Blackness and fatness that assist in her uglification and dehumanization. The hesitation to identify with a term associated with her is understandable. White supremacy and the narratives it creates seep into every part of our lives and continually influence how we see ourselves, and even what we believe we are or are not allowed to see in ourselves. Mammy's legacy means that Black people, especially those socialized as women, are never allowed to claim asexuality or sexlessness unless such an existence works to reinforce stereotypes about Black bodies and Black undesirability in ways that are rooted in anti-Blackness, misogynoir, and anti-fatness.

It is important to name that Mammy's asexuality was and is imposed on her, just as Jezebel's hypersexuality was and is. These figures are fabricated, not based in reality. We can, and we must, find our way to authentic Black (a) sexual expression, regardless of these caricatures and the stereotypes they hold. We must also name that it is white supremacy that allows society to willingly accept a Black asexuality that is nonconsensually written onto Mammy, yet refuse a Black asexuality that is individually self-determined. Only through white supremacist misinterpretations of the world can the Black asexual Mammy be granted, or cursed, with her existence, even as the Black asexual is otherwise rendered a distinct impossibility.

Compulsory sexuality, cisheteropatriarchy, and white supremacy work to prevent us from having true bodily autonomy, self-discernment, or epistemic authority over our own sexuality. When asexuality is socially prescribed and written onto a particular group of people, it can be used as a tool of control—whether it is to abuse and debase Black people, or to project an image of white sexual purity and superiority. If we are granted the freedom to individually determine our asexuality, then asexuality becomes more difficult to utilize as a tool of white supremacy. Filtered through white supremacist logics, the prospect of Black asexuality that does not resemble the undesirable Mammy—a docile servant to whiteness and an ever-present canvas for its violence—cannot be understood as legitimate or possible.

10

Refusal

People have the right to call themselves whatever they like. That doesn't bother me. It's other people doing the calling that bothers me.

—OCTAVIA E. BUTLER

I OFTEN FIND MYSELF wondering how many of our ancestors may have occupied the realm of asexuality or aromanticism, as sexual and relational misfits, but were unable to fully live in that truth. How many did not get to be their most authentic selves? How many, both living and gone, have been coerced into following strict cisheterosexual, chrononormative, and chronobiopolitical conventions, especially those marginalized by gender? How many have been assigned other, more legible queer identities, because the idea of an asexual or aromantic existence—whether in concept or name—was unfathomable to those around them? How many have found themselves living a life under duress, even as they have known themselves as beings not aligned with societal understandings of intimacy and connection? These lingering questions are what lead me to ruminate on the possibility of unseen and unhonored Black asexuality and aromanticism.

Here, I ruminate on such a possibility for the legendary Octavia E. Butler, not only because of her legacy as one of the most profound and respected wordsmiths of the last century, but even more so and especially because I am fascinated by and enamored with her as an enigmatic gem after my own heart. In the wake of her death, lesbianism has come to be regarded as her true sexual identity, accepted as canon, even though this idea was born as speculation.

Butler is not the only Black icon whose sexuality and queerness have been the subject of speculation. Langston Hughes is another example of someone whose identity has been debated over because of how he refused and eschewed cisheteronormative expectations in his lifetime. There is mystery and friction surrounding the sexuality of the late Hughes. It has been said by some, in more ways than one, that this important figure of the Harlem Renaissance and his sexuality were guarded and obscure—and sometimes said in a way that suggests that his unwillingness to divulge more details about his life translated to a cagey dishonesty. The poet's primary biographer, Arnold Rampersad, describes his sexuality as a murky and imprecise subject. In *The Life of Langston Hughes, Volume II,* he writes:

> Although many people approached for information confirmed that he was thought to be gay, no one could offer the name of a man who had been involved with Hughes, or recall an incident, even at second hand, involving Langston's presumed homosexuality ... yet for some people the idea was fixed: Langston Hughes was a homosexual. For the greater part of his life, Hughes made almost a fetish of the secrecy about his sexual interest, so that from the start of his adulthood even close friends of liberated sexuality, such as Countee Cullen, Wallace Thurman, Carl Van Vechten, and Bruce Nugent, vouched privately **not for the nature or relative strength of his sexuality but for its maddening elusiveness.**[1]

Writer and theater critic Hilton Als offers that "Rampersad's biography, which is as rich a study of a life as one could wish for, was criticized by gay readers.... In Rampersad's work, **Hughes emerges as a constantly striving, almost asexual entity—which is pretty much the image that Hughes himself put forth.**"[2] Still, many insist on unequivocally naming Hughes as gay and even project internalized homophobia and shame onto him as the reason for why he never "came out" as gay. Jim Kepner, founder of the International Gay and Lesbian Archives, has regarded Hughes's alleged homosexuality as "an open secret" since the 1940s. Kepner notes that it was common in Hughes's time for gay people to "confine themselves to anonymous, emotionally hollow encounters rather than steady relationships" due to fear of being discovered or outed. To Kepner, and others who share his sentiment, Hughes was "quite possibly confused and ashamed of his sexual desires."[3]

According to Rampersad, who conducted numerous interviews with people who knew Hughes personally, he "gave his acquaintances no reason, other than his increasing age and relentless bachelorhood, to suppose that he was homosexual." Hughes had a young friend from Atlanta named Harry Murphy who would sometimes visit him in New York. To Rampersad, Murphy offered, "I never detected anything on his part that could be construed as indicative of homosexuality.... **I concluded that Lang was either a person who screened from view his personal relationships or, for whatever reason, had simply excluded from his being that part of life.**"[4] Rampersad also spent time talking to people from around Harlem who knew of or were familiar with Hughes but were not in his inner circle. To many, the fact that Hughes was "aging, unmarried, and often in the company of various handsome, sensitive, artistic young men, meant that he was homosexual.... 'Around the streets of Harlem in the '60s,' one man later insisted, 'Everyone knew that Langston Hughes was gay. We just took it for granted, as a fact. He was gay, and there was no two ways about it.'"[5]

It seems that people simply decided among themselves that Hughes was gay, having no need for confirmation from the man himself. Rampersad affirms that "Hughes's reputation as a homosexual is based almost exclusively on rumor and suspicion.... In his lifetime, he was never called upon to assert or deny that he was a homosexual, but it is clear that, whatever the truth, he did not want to be considered gay."[6] This is why his biography was so heavily critiqued by those who preferred to rest on the "open secret" of Hughes' gayness, despite the fact that he never publicly acknowledged or admitted to any rumors about his sexuality. Gay activists interpreted Rampersad's biography as a homophobic attempt to sanitize Hughes by, more or less, rescuing his memory from homosexuality.

Writings about Langston Hughes are riddled with vexations about the inability to neatly categorize him, haunted by the question of whether or not he secretly held an attraction to and desire for men. So many are frustrated with him for remaining in his closet, for not leaving sufficient breadcrumbs to lead them to an easy conclusion. Even in his death, Hughes cannot be rid of the prying eyes and prodding questions of those who feel entitled to know him more deeply than he was comfortable with allowing. "I was quite willing to reveal that Hughes was homosexual and I certainly went looking for the evidence. But I came up with nothing," Rampersad once shared in an interview about his two-volume Hughes biography. "I'm not saying he was not gay. I'm saying the evidence isn't there."[7]

Hughes, like Butler, is marked by a resistance to the prospect that he expressed no open desire to partner or marry simply because he either had no such desire or at least significantly deprioritized it in favor of his writing. Here, I implore you to consider why there has been such resistance to Rampersad's work and the idea that Hughes may have simply been asexual (or aromantic), despite how thoroughly Rampersad's biography illustrates that the "open secret" of his gayness seems to be rooted only in speculation based on his perpetual bachelorhood and the occasional exploration of queerness in his writing. Moreover, I invite you to consider why there has been such debate over his sexuality in the first place, why there is such fervor to cordon him into a clearly demarcated kind of queerness, why his ambiguity and refusal lead to such discomfort, and how often this very thing also happens with other figures.

I want us to interrogate what we demand of our queer icons—and more, what kind of performativity we demand from our own queer selves and queer kin—and how this is informed by compulsory sexuality. What are we writing onto Langston Hughes and others like him when we use them as canvases to paint our own frustrations about queer (in)visibility, performativity, and closets? What if we instead respected the poet's closet of his own making? A closet can be a cage, but it can also be a sanctum. Refusal was always his right, as it is always ours.

Nope, This Ain't It

I can change myself, but it's an effort. And it doesn't last. It's easier to do as water does: allow myself to be contained, and take on the shape of my containers.

—OCTAVIA E. BUTLER

She is remembered as a prolific writer and prophetic voice who broke barriers in science fiction through her imaginings of elaborate otherworlds which she often used to tell ugly, uncomfortable truths about our own world. Octavia E. Butler picked up the proverbial pen at a young age and began submitting manuscripts to publishing houses as early as thirteen. To her dismay, there were never any creative writing courses offered during her grade-school years, but that changed when she got to college, where she enrolled in the three courses available to her:

Creative Writing, Short Story Writing, and Writing for Publication. The instructors were baffled by Butler's fixation on sci-fi, fantasy, and grim subject matters. And so, she was met with the exasperated question, "Can't you write anything normal?" from one of her teachers. "The answer may be no," she would later say. "Or, at least, I don't want to."[8]

Butler was the first science fiction writer to receive the MacArthur Foundation Genius Grant. She also won multiple Hugo and Nebula awards, as well as a lifetime achievement in writing from the PEN American Center for her various works. Following her passing in 2006, those honoring Butler's memory began referring to her as a lesbian, even though there seemed to be no real source to justify writing lesbianism onto her. In Stephen Maglott's Ubuntu Biography Project, an ambitious endeavor to collect and catalogue biographies of Black LGBTQ+ icons and historical figures, he notes the discrepancy and lack of consensus on Butler's sexuality: "Many obituaries recognized her as 'both a Black and Lesbian science-fiction writer.' All references seem to link to an unsourced Wikipedia post. She has been described by some close friends as bisexual, as asexual, and as heterosexual. She apparently never discussed any lesbianism publicly."[9] A blog post from Ron Buckmire, who casually knew Butler when she lived in California, reads: "Black people and science fiction fans are often not thought of as having any common members, but clearly the death of the first African American female (and lesbian!) science fiction author to achieve widespread acclaim (a 1995 MacArthur Foundation 'genius' grant, Hugo and Nebula awards, etcetera) has affected many different people."[10]

Elsewhere, Butler has been described as a "famously reclusive lesbian"[11] and "a black lesbian who overcame multiple obstacles to become a best-selling author."[12] She can also be found on numerous lists of queer Black icons and is listed on them as a Black lesbian author. However, Butler offered a different narrative-of-self concerning her sexuality in a 1998 interview:

Because of the way I looked, when I was growing up, I was called various sundry unsavory names by people who thought I was gay (though at the time nobody used that word). I eventually wondered if they might not be right, so I called the Gay and Lesbian Services Center and asked if they had meetings where people could talk about such things. I wound up going down there twice, at which point I realized, **Nope,**

this ain't it. I also realized, once I thought it over, that I'm a hermit. I enjoy my own company more than I enjoy other people's—and going to parties and trying to meet Mr. or Ms. Right or whatever simply doesn't appeal to me.[13]

In another interview, she stated, "I'm Black. I'm solitary. I've always been an outsider,"[14] and in yet another, "I'm very happy alone. If I had to change myself into something else, I'd probably be unhappy."[15] People seem to have come to the conclusion that Butler was a lesbian, at least in part, because she never had any public relationships with men and never married. This refusal to allow Butler the space to be seen or understood as asexual or aromantic in the public imagination, as anything beyond an allosexual lesbian is frustrating. Especially because the narrative persists even though she never described herself as a lesbian and, in fact, confidently described herself as solitary and happy with being unpartnered. Compulsory sexuality and binary thinking have worked in tandem in the public's minds to place her into the box that makes the most sense according to the logic of a cisheteronormative society that overwhelmingly views same-gender sexuality as the binary opposite of heterosexuality. But the absence of heterosexuality—presumed or apparent—does not inherently give way to or definitively indicate a same-gender sexual attraction or desire. To write lesbianism onto her in death is to dishonor Butler's life.

Sami Schalk (she/her) is a Black queer associate professor of gender and women's studies who has had the opportunity to read through Butler's journals in the research collection of the Huntington Library, Art Museum, and Botanical Gardens in San Marino, California. "I would identify Butler as on the ace spectrum, because she definitely did not privilege sex in her life. It wasn't that she didn't have desires; there are definitely expressions of desires, but she identified as a hermit. Her writing was her love. I mean, she describes writing as sex and passion in various entries. So I think that whatever expressions of desire and passion that she had were primarily funneled into her writing," Schalk explains. "Unlike lesbian, which is something that would have been available for her to claim before her death, I don't know that asexuality would have been circulating enough for her to claim as a Black woman. So even though it's not a discourse that was circulating [much], it may have been a discourse that appealed to her or spoke to her if she had the opportunity."

Schalk also tells me that Butler, in her journals, imagines what it might be like to be a lesbian and to be questioned about it, along with a list of the disadvantages and challenges it would present. "I read all of her journals and there are these entries where she's like 'If I **were** a lesbian' or 'What are the challenges of being a lesbian?'" Schalk believes that one of the reasons Butler spent time thinking about whether or not she was lesbian is because she was constantly read as one. In one entry, Butler writes, "When loneliness comes, I think I would do a great deal to accommodate myself to the need of another person. I want another person badly enough to think about it. I'd have to bend a little, but how much? Lesbian love seems to offer so many more thorns than roses."[16]

Schalk speaks of the continual misinterpretation of Butler as a lesbian, both now and when she was still alive:

It erases a Black gender spectrum. Being a masculine woman does not automatically equal being a lesbian.... Also, the way we read masculinity is shaped by race. We read Blackness as inherently more masculine, more aggressive, because our ideas of femininity are based on white womanhood. Because she was big and because she was dark-skinned and because she didn't particularly like wearing dresses, suddenly she's a lesbian. Not being married to a man does not make you a lesbian.... I think that lack of a central or long-term partner, or the lack of desire to make that a thing she was actively pursuing, definitely aligns with my understanding of people who are aromantic. She was very much like, "I need a man to have sex, but otherwise, please go away."

In a few journal entries, Butler writes about and wrestles with her desires for men:

What do I want from him? Maybe only a little fucking—or a lot of fucking. That was all I wanted from the man in Phoenix.... I like men.... I have discovered that having sex with someone I've (A) only recently met and (B) don't like particularly except for his body, doesn't bother me unless he tries to hang on. I dislike having to shed people.... I don't know that I'll ever marry, but I would like to have a good man friend.... I do want a man (men?) for sex. Nothing else substitutes. Horniness speaks.... I may be a late bloomer, but that is no reason not to bloom at all.[17]

Butler's thought process feels familiar, reminiscent of a lot of asexual and especially aromantic journeys to understanding our relationship to sex, attraction, and desire. Schalk explains,

> Between her desires and her sexual practices, I would identify her as on a spectrum of asexuality that includes having sex, includes having **some** sexual desire, but it's not a priority and it's not a regular thing. She definitely had no sustained, serious relationships at all. These moments pop up in her journals every once in a while, but not even every year is there something about having sex or wanting to have sex. There are descriptions of writing being sex and writing being passion and desire. She writes a lot about having to "turn on your readers" and things like that. So she'll use sexual language, but mostly to talk about writing.

> I think Black queer folks want to claim people. We want to claim ancestors and to claim a legacy [but] anytime we are claiming a label for someone that they did not claim in their life, we have to think about what the larger purpose of that is. For me, it's important to ask what we get out of reading Butler through a queer or asexual framework, rather than saying definitively, "This person was xyz." What's the value in reading her through this framework instead? What do we get from it, what do we learn from it, how does it benefit people? What's the value to folks who care about Butler and her work, and also to the larger world?

Taking earnest consideration of her own words and narrative-of-self—as I believe the prescient writer to be a reliable narrator—I offer that Butler, whether asexual and aromantic or not, was someone whom we can understand as being single at heart. Schalk agrees, describing Butler as "single at heart, single in practice." Bella DePaulo has dedicated a significant amount of her sociological work to studying single people and singlism. She has identified people who seem to be naturally inclined to be happily single for most or all of their lives and has named them as "single at heart"—people who, in stark contrast to what has been socially prescribed, do not prioritize sex and romance like those who are more inclined toward and have the distinct desire to be coupled. Those who are single at heart instead prioritize and delve deeply into aspects of their lives outside of the sexual and romantic, finding profound satisfaction in remaining unpartnered and reveling in their solitary nature. This means that they have no interest in or intention of centering or restructuring their lives around sexual or romantic partnerships, because not doing so allows them to be their happiest, most prosperous, and most authentic self.

According to DePaulo's findings, the single at heart are less likely to be heterosexual, and more likely to be asexual or aromantic. She surmises, "Emotional and psychological freedom, in one of the most profound senses, means that you get to live your best life—the life you find most authentic, most meaningful, and most fulfilling. That's hard to do if the life that feels most authentic to you is at odds with the life your culture tells you that you should live." What DePaulo is describing here is, yet again, illustrative of the ways that singlism often overlaps with discrimination of and negative attitudes toward people on the asexual and aromantic spectra. She continues, "**You may think you know who you really are, but the prevailing cultural wisdom insists that people like you do not even exist.** Or, if some grudging allowance is made for your existence, then it will be deemed a lesser existence—not as good or happy or worthy or valuable as the existence of people who follow the recognized and celebrated life paths." Moreover, DePaulo notes that some defining characteristics of the single at heart are as follows:

- "They love their solitude.
- "They have a sense of personal mastery—a strong sense that they can do just about anything they set their mind to.
- "They are not all that interested in searching for long-term partnership."[18]

Butler loved to take contemplative solo walks in the early morning hours, sometimes before dawn. She also loved to travel and was known to take off on adventures on her own, once hiking nearly to the bottom of the Grand Canyon. The only reason she turned back was because she ran out of time and thought she might miss her bus. While in Peru, she climbed Huayna Picchu, one of the peaks at Machu Picchu.[19] On her lists of life goals, in which she famously predicts that she would become a renowned and best-selling author, she never mentions sexual or romantic relationships or marriage as goals.[20]

"I think that prioritization of career was very, very clear. She would constantly write out these career goals where she would say, I'm gonna do this by this time and have this much money by this point. She was very goal-driven and career-oriented," Schalk tells me. "She would work and be writing at the same time until she had enough money for at least three months, and then she would quit. Then she would write for three months or until she ran out of money, and then she would go back to a temp job.... Because what she wanted to do was write." Butler lived her life comfortable in the refusal of prescribed societal norms, of its gendered and sexual expectations. She lived authentically in that refusal. As DePaulo affirms, "People who are single at heart are less likely to live according to the prevailing cultural mandates.... They defy the ideology of marriage and coupling and the mandate of compulsory coupling.... That doesn't make life easy, but for them, it makes it authentic."[21]

Moya Bailey (she/her) serves as the digital alchemist for the Octavia E. Butler Legacy Network and is known for coining the term *misogynoir* to address the unique intersection of anti-Blackness and misogyny. Like me, she understands Butler's life as a queer project but does not agree with the naming of her as lesbian. Bailey suggests,

> I feel like people want to claim her because it would be so great if she could be a lesbian and we could claim her as a queer elder. And I think we can, even if she's not lesbian, because everything about her sexuality is queer in the sense that it does not follow a heteronormative, monogamous expectation of sexuality, and I think that letting people grapple with that is important. I think we've gotten too invested in identity in this case, as opposed to looking at behavior and how her life was very queer in terms of what people expected of Black women at the time.

To an extent, Bailey can see why Butler has been read as lesbian, and it has a lot to do with how we read and understand Black lesbianism to begin with. Bailey tells me,

> Visibly, she's giving very "Black lesbian of a certain era" in terms of her physical appearance. People don't really know how to understand that look outside of a certain sexuality, [so] people want to write a narrative about her sexuality in a way that can be limiting. [But] **one of the things about Butler is that she really defies a binary understanding of our world. People want to place her in a category, but her life defies all of that....** Whether she desired to have sex with women or

not, I still see her sex life and all of its iterations as queer, because it definitely does not fit a normative binary expectation of what sexuality is supposed to look like.

"There's something in her journals that suggests to me that she maybe had a sexual interaction with a woman, but she didn't like it. But it's really vague and unclear," Bailey says. She also encourages us to think about (un)desirability and what connections or intimacies Butler may or may not have been invited into. "There is a lot of longing for relationships with people, but also an understanding of how her dark skin, height, and voice masculinized her and made it hard for men to see her as traditionally desirable. [So] we also should think about the politics of desirability and how that impacted who she approached and who approached her." Butler's tall, dark-skinned, and masculine-presenting frame and aesthetic would have made her undesirable according to cisheteronormative and binary gender standards, leading many to assume that she must have been a lesbian because she would never have been seen as desirable by men.

Narrow ideas of sexuality can also work to obscure and diminish the nonnormative ways that erotic lives can manifest themselves. Bailey emphasizes that, for Butler, "There is a whole erotic life that she has in her writing, which I think doesn't get taken seriously as an erotic life.... Her books have sex in them, and it's really poly[amorous], queer sex. It's definitely not what falls into a heteronormative understanding of what sexuality is supposed to look like, and I think that's an important aspect of her life that people don't consider very much."

"I have been talking about Butler as on the autism spectrum. There are things she says in her work, in her journals and things that make me think that." Bailey shares,

> Of course, she was never diagnosed. In the same way that you are being careful about not labeling her as asexual, I feel very careful about not labeling her as on the [autism] spectrum, even though I see those hints and resonances in the stuff that she writes. And I think that really troubles our understanding of [her] sexuality too, because of the assumption of a neurotypical experience of sexuality. There's this neurotypical understanding of what sex and sexuality look like that her life really defies and troubles. I really appreciate holding that ambiguity.

Bailey and I are both interested in recognizing asexual and aromantic (and neurodivergent) possibilities for Butler, and others like her, and honoring what might be called an ambiguous (neuro)queerness. Bailey laments,

> The gift and curse of this moment is that people are so obsessed with identity that they want to put you into a category as opposed to letting folks say who they are. [It's] a very Western and new notion that sexuality is an identity. That's very, very recent and has a lot to do with capitalism and what is possible in the West.... I went into the archives with the goal of saying, 'Yes, Octavia is queer,' or, 'No, Octavia is straight,' [but] ultimately I think what was clear was that she defies categories and boundaries, and that trying to put an identity on her sexuality, trying to talk about her sexuality in the language of identity is not sufficient.

Though reading Butler's journals does not offer a concrete answer to the question of her sexuality—nor did I ever expect it to—it does give us a somewhat better understanding of what her desires were. It allows us entry into her inner world, but takes us only a few steps beyond the threshold. However, it does make clear that lesbianism is not an identity that Butler ever claimed for herself while she was here, and it is not an identity the world should claim for her now in her absence. When looking at a life like Butler's, Bailey says,

> The way asexuality looks for white people is different from how it looks for Black people, particularly Black women.... We need to have more models for what is possible [for Butler] beyond lesbian as an identity. We have many Black lesbians that we can claim and who I think are important parts of our legacy, but we can't participate in the same erasure we are trying to prevent when we want to claim [Butler] as a lesbian. There's another kind of erasure that happens when we call her a lesbian and we don't pay attention to the aromantic and asexual parts of her life.

Unknown and Unknowable

I believe Octavia E. Butler, Langston Hughes, and more have left impressions of asexual lives—as in, lives that can be read asexually; as in outside of, subversive of, and illegible to cisheteronormative understandings of sexuality, desire, romance, and connection. But by and large, the world has failed to consider it as a genuine possibility for them, and for many others. In them, I see asexual possibilities, even as others continue to write a different narrative on their bones.

If, according to Rampersad's biography and many people's reading of it, Hughes "put forth" the impression of "a constantly striving, almost asexual" existence, why then have we not found our way to understanding him as such, or at least the possibility of it? If Hughes was too "ambiguous" to be considered gay by those who knew him intimately and refused to indicate a sexual identity to either his peers or the public, why then has he not been allowed to rest peacefully in that ambiguity and refusal? If, according to Butler herself, she actively interrogated her desires and found that she was not a lesbian, why then have her admirers insisted on naming her as an identity that she has already refused? If Butler described herself as "solitary" and openly remarked on her aversion to seeking out romantic relationships, why then have those who remember her fondly not trusted her to be the author of her own identity?

My hope is that we will collectively do more to interrogate our preconceptions of other people's sexual identities and how compulsory sexuality implores us to project certain sexualities onto others to begin with—particularly when that projection is a response to their "failure" to meet cisheteronormative and chrononormative expectations of heterosexual relationships, gender roles, marriage, and nuclear family-making. Such projection only serves to reinscribe suffocating ideologies of binary gender and sexual performance, presentation, and expression. Beyond this hope, I carry wishful anticipation that we will begin to hold ace- and aro-spectrum queerness more dearly so that it will be more readily seen as a sincere possibility in the lives of those like Butler and Hughes, even a nebulous one.

May we move toward an understanding of ace- and aro-spectrum queerness itself as an avowal of the right to exist as enigma, as refusal—to persist in illegibility, to be unknown and unknowable. Asexuals and aromantics have so often been regarded as cryptic and inscrutable by our peers and have had many things inscribed upon us, in spite of what we have to say about ourselves. It is my belief that it would benefit us to consider what possibilities can be found in the impressions left by these writers' lives. I hope that we allow ourselves to be inspired, to embrace whatever peculiar freedom can be found in the obscurity and silence. A life that is illegible to cisheteronormative understandings of connection, intimacy, and kinship is a queer existence, and it is queer enough.

This is not a call for us to officially recognize Butler and Hughes as unequivocally asexual or aromantic figures, even as I would love to claim these two luminaries as Black ace-aro icons. It is not our place to make these declarations for the living or the departed. Rather, it is to honor the aspects of them that we can read asexually and aromantically—that is, noticeably and notably outside of normative understandings of sex, romance, and desire—because these aspects exist as part of their entire being. This is a challenge to the respective narratives that attempt to confine them both to boxes that they themselves refused in life, and a gentle push toward imagining the possibilities of a much bigger world for Butler, Hughes, and the rest of us. My intention here has only been to offer alternate readings of these beloved writers that free them from the cages they have been written into, with hopes that we will also be able to uncage others like them, including ourselves.

11

Histories

ASEXUALITY IS OFTEN LEFT out of or actively excluded from conversations about queer sexuality and experience, especially conversations about their historical presence. This erasure leaves room for people to continually dismiss asexuality as merely an "internet orientation," suggesting that it has been fabricated from thin air and only within recent years. It must be said that even if asexuality were a newly developed term or concept, it would be no less valid. It would still describe an eternal experience. Asexuals have long inhabited this world, since well before we were named as asexual. In our lifetimes, we will see queer communities coin new terminologies to name the as-yet unnamed, just as older generations have witnessed with us. We will see them form niche communities and build movements around these new terms, just as we have done, and I look forward to bearing witness to those interventions. Hopefully, they will be met with less pushback, gatekeeping, gaslighting, and exclusion than we have been met with.

The lack of preservation and teaching regarding asexual history does not mean that the history is not there. It means that it has been neglected; it has not been made cohesive. We now have the opportunity and responsibility to do our research to properly excavate and archive a history so long unacknowledged that even most asexuals are unfamiliar with it. Asexual identities—and emerging definitions of and variations on asexuality under a unified recognition of it as an othered sexuality—have been present in queer advocacy as well as discourse about sexuality, race, gender, marriage, and health for generations. People on the asexuality spectrum were always present in queer communities prior to using the term *asexual* to name a cohesive identity and form asexual communities under the moniker.

The timeline that follows is my best attempt at tracing the presence of asexuality, advocacy for it and bias against it—either in concept or in name—in texts throughout recent centuries (with the exception of frigidity, which dates back to the thirteenth century and has already been covered in chapter 6), as well as charting significant points in asexual history from this century. I am confident that for as long as people have been writing about sex and the presumed moral and psychological implications of how people engage in sex, there have also been terms and concepts to describe asexuality and asexual lives—by which I mean sexual disinterest, undesire, indifference, neutrality, apathy, and aversion, situated firmly outside normative understandings of and permissions for sexual expression. For as long as exclusive and active heterosexuality has been considered "normal" and morally right, every type of sexual existence outside it—including those who have a "self-contained sexuality"—has been considered abnormal and even immoral by those invested in maintaining the status quo. Under cisheteropatriarchal systems, all nonheterosexual sexual identities and behaviors have always been understood as being part of the same looming threat against heterosexuality and the society it upholds.

1855

- *Doctor Teller's Pocket Companion, or Marriage Guide: Being a Popular Treatise on the Anatomy and Physiology of the Genital Organs, in Both Sexes, with Their Uses and Abuses* is published by Dr. J. Teller. The guide includes thoughts on celibacy and what is referred to as "continence." It reads, "By the term continence, we mean **not only a freedom from the use of the sexual appetite, but an absolute withdrawal from all the pleasures of the consummation of the act, together with a total abstinence of solitary indulgences.**"[1] In other words: no desire for sex with others, as well as no desire to masturbate. The text continues with warnings that "continence" will resort in madness, societal downfall, and poor health:

  The productive organs have [their use] but it is not only for the propagation of the species. They give an appetite which, like hunger, must be appeased, or nature revolts, and the harmony of society falls before the unrestrained fury of maniacal solicitude. Health, the source of all earthly happiness, the greatest of all human blessings, without the possession of which this world with all its beauties, all its pleasures, would be, for all we cared, destitute of all its gratifications, tenantless, very materially rests upon a proper and moderate use of the sexual appetite. **Entire continence, one of the greatest rarities among mankind, establishes in both sexes the most miserable perversions of mind and body.** In man, from the result of perfect continence, we have manifold instances recorded of mania, melancholy, apoplexy, and various foul diseases of the skin; deafness, loss of vision, and many other evils, some greater, some less, than those just mentioned.... In the female, continence [will bring] in its train the mysteries of hysteria, and other nervous derangements, that pervade the elderly maiden branches of every family, and constitute an enemy so formidable to all domestic felicity. **Persons living a life of strict continency seldom live to an advanced age.**[2]

1869

- Austro-Hungarian journalist, memoirist, and human rights campaigner, Károly (or Karl) Mária Kertbeny, publishes pamphlets arguing against Prussian anti-sodomy laws. In these writings, Kertbeny "distinguishes between three main categories: 'monosexuals' (masturbators or onanists **who have sex only with themselves**), 'normal sexuals' (who have sex with members of the other sex), and homosexuals (who have sex with members of their own sex). He also alludes to amphisexuals or 'the doubled' *(die Doppelten)*, who have sex with people from either sex."[3]

1895

- German sexual reformist Emma Trosse publishes *Der Konträrsexualismus in Bezug auf Ehe und Frauenfrage* (Contrary-sexuality in relation to marriage and the women question), in which she argues against the prevailing idea that sexualities "contrary" to heterosexuality are unnatural, saying that "'mother nature herself' had created sexual diversity, including homosexuality and 'neutrals,' i.e. **individuals who possessed no sexual desire whatsoever."**[4]

1896

- German sexologist Magnus Hirschfeld publishes the pamphlet *Sappho und Sokrates (Sappho and Socrates),* in which he states, "There are individuals who are **without any sexual desire**" and names them as "Anästhesia sexualis."[5] He goes on to assert that this is not something that can be changed:

  It is also not possible to artificially evoke the kind of drive that is not existent or almost not noticeable. In case of a complete atrophy there is no way that it would spontaneously develop. However, if there already is a mental disposition towards it, it can be increased by the upbringing, exercise, example, seduction, and suggestion. **We can wake up sleeping drives, as long as their sprouts are big enough, but we can never create new ones.**[6]

1897

- Emma Trosse revisits her arguments against the idea that sexualities outside heterosexuality are "unnatural" with *Ein Weib? Psychologisch-biographische: Studie über eine Konträrsexuelle* (A woman? Psychological-biographical study of a contrary-sexual). In this work, she coins the term *Sinnlichkeitslosigkeit* ("asensuality" or "senseless") to refer to "people without sensuality" or those who are without sexual desire or erotic interests, who focus on leading a passionate working life instead.[7] Furthermore, "Emma Trosse confesses herself to this 'category' of the senseless."[8]

1906

- The first edition of Austro-German psychiatrist Richard Freiherr von Krafft-Ebing's *Psychopathia Sexualis: eine Klinisch-Forensische Studie* (Sexual psychopathy: a clinical-forensic study) had first been published in 1886. The twelfth and final edition, titled *Psychopathia Sexualis: With Especial Reference to the Antipathic Sexual Instinct, a Medico-Forensic Study,* published in 1906, presents four categories of "cerebral neuroses" (mental disorders), one of which he names "anesthesia" and defines as the **"absence of sexual instinct."** In this same work, he writes, "If man were deprived of sexual distinction and the nobler enjoyments arising therefrom, all poetry and probably all moral tendency would be eliminated from his life.... **Sexual feeling is really the root of all ethics."**[9]

1907

- Carl Schlegel, a German-born minister and activist living in the United States, delivers a speech calling for equality among all sexualities, saying, "Let the same laws for all the intermediate stages of sexual life: the homosexuals, heterosexuals, bisexuals, asexuals, be legal as they are now in existence for the heterosexuals."[10]
- *The Westminster Review* publishes "An Interrogatory Note on the Franchise of Women" by Unitarian minister John Lionel Tayler, in which he predicts that "masculine and asexual women" would derail the movement for women's rights (see chapter 7, "Unfit").[11]
- In "A Form of the Human Sexual Drive Not Hitherto Observed," German physician Hermann Oscar Rohleder defines "automonosexualism" as occurring when sexual arousal and satisfaction take place only through a person's engagement with their own body, or masturbation, "that is, through it alone."[12] Magnus Hirschfeld would later refer to Rohleder in his own writing, saying that Rohleder characterized automonosexuality

as "the drive being directed toward itself solely and entirely" and "the individuals by themselves and alone being the point of departure and final goal of the sex drive."[13]

1908

- *Outlines of Psychiatry* by William A. White, MD, is published as the first issue of the *Journal of Nervous and Mental Disease* Monographs Series. In the section "Anomalies of the Sexual Instinct," White identifies what he calls "Quantitative Anomalies" of sexuality to be addressed through psychiatric treatment: "These are frigidity or **lack of desire for sexual congress**—sexual anesthesia—or eroticism—sexual hyperasthesia."[14]

1914

- Magnus Hirschfeld publishes *The Homosexuality of Men and Women*, in which he briefly speculates about philosophers Immanuel Kant (lived 1724–1804) and Sören Kierkegaard (lived 1813–1855) "whom [he believes] people would have to call asexual."[15] He also writes, "among the many transvestites [men who dressed in clothing intended for women], we can distinguish among the following five groups: (1) heterosexuals, (2) homosexuals, (3) bisexuals, (4) apparent asexuals, and (5) automonosexuals."[16] The State Hospital Bulletin by the New York State Hospital Commission would also cite these categories in Volume 1 of their 1914 bulletin, adding "monosexuals" as a synonym for automonosexual.[17]

1917

- Correa Moylan Walsh publishes *Feminism*, in which he displays fear that the feminism started by "asexual women" would spread to those with "normal sexual instincts" (see chapter 7, "Unfit").[18]

1922

- *The Female-Impersonators,* written by an androgyne named Ralph Werther (who also went by Jennie June and Earl Lind), details the existence of what Werther calls "anaphrodites"—derived from the term *anaphrodisia.* According to Werther, "anaphrodites are **not suffused with adoration for any type of human.**"[19] He goes on to suggest that when Jesus speaks of "'eunuchs from their mother's womb [in Matthew 19:12],' he may of course have had in mind only anaphrodites."[20] Furthermore, Werther claims, "Prudery is one of the foremost earmarks of anaphrodites and the mildly virile,"[21] offers that "Sir Isaac Newton [lived 1643–1727] and Immanuel Kant appear to have been anaphrodites,"[22] and identifies the counterpart of "cold anaphrodites" to be "female icebergs," echoing the language around frigidity.[23]

1926

- Austrian psychoanalyst Wilhelm Stekel publishes volume 1 of *Frigidity in Woman in Relation to Her Love Life,* in which he dismissively offers, "Certain investigators still speak of **complete sexual anesthesia, or asexualism;** on closer investigation such cases prove to be largely imaginary."[24]

1936

- Writing again about transvestites in *Sexual Anomalies and Perversions: Physical and Psychological Development and Treatment,* Magnus Hirschfeld estimates that "15 percent are mostly automonosexual, but also include a small proportion of asexuals."[25]

1948

- Alfred Kinsey publishes *Sexual Behavior in the Human Male.* The "Heterosexual-Homosexual Rating Scale," now known as the Kinsey

Scale, includes the category "X" for those who report no "sociosexual contacts or reactions." The text also says, "There is another group of males ... who are **apathetic.** They never, at any time in their histories, have given evidence that they were capable of anything except low rates of activity. These are persons who would be described, figuratively, as 'low in sex drive.' Whether the factors are biologic, psychologic, or social, **it is certain that such persons exist.**" About 1.5 percent of subjects fell into this category.[26]

1953

- Alfred Kinsey publishes *Sexual Behavior in the Human Female.* The Kinsey Scale includes the category "X." The text reads, "individuals are rated as **X's** if they **do not respond erotically to either heterosexual or homosexual stimuli, and do not have overt physical contacts with individuals of either sex in which there is evidence of any response.** After early adolescence there are very few males in this classification but a goodly number of females belong in this category in every age group."[27] It also offers, "between 14 and 19 percent of the unmarried females in the sample, and 1 to 3 percent of the married females, had not made any sociosexual responses (either heterosexual or homosexual)."[28]

1965

- *Transvestia* publishes a description of what it calls the "A-sexual Range," noting that, "There are persona who simply have a very low libido—**no sex drive to speak of.**"[29]

1967

- In potentially the first mention of asexuality in U.S. policy, the Supreme Court responds to the Florida Legislative Investigative Committee's attempts to discriminate based on sexuality, declaring, "As long as Petitioner does not indulge in conduct violative of the laws of Florida, he has a constitutional right to enter a bar and associate with whom he pleases whether his associates be heterosexual, homosexual or asexual."[30]

1969

- Anton Szandor LaVey's *The Satanic Bible* states that "Satanism condones any type of sexual activity which properly [and ethically] satisfies your individual desires—be it heterosexual, homosexual, bisexual, or even asexual."[31]

1970

- An article on trans liberation in *Gay Dealer,* a Philadelphia newspaper, declares that trans liberation "includes transvestites, transsexuals, and hermaphrodites of any sexual manifestation and of all sexes—heterosexual, homosexual, bisexual, and asexual."[32]

1971

- An article seeking membership for the Gay Liberation Front is published in *The Florida Alligator.* It states that, "GLF is opened to asexuals, bisexuals, homosexuals, and confused heterosexuals."[33]
- *The Village Voice* publishes "Asexuals Have Problems Too!"—a satirical piece that mocks asexuals and the asexual experience.[34]

1972

- Lisa Orlando's "The Asexual Manifesto" is published by the New York Radical Feminists (see the Introduction).

1973

- Barnard College holds a feminist conference where, at an event called "Lesbian/Feminist Dialogue," attendees are asked to choose a label from a list of identities: "Straight, Lesbian, Gay, Butch, Femm, Asexual, Anti-sexual, ?, other, etc."[35] A photo of the board is later printed as part of the essay "Lesbian Dynamics" by Fran Pollner in *off our backs*. In another *off our backs* essay titled "Your Own Label," Frances Chapman writes, "I attended the workshop on asexuality lead by Barbara Getz. According to Barbara, **asexuality is an orientation that regards a partner as nonessential to sex, and sex as nonessential to a satisfying relationship.**"[36]

- In an issue of a self-published lesbian magazine called *Lavender Woman,* the author writes, "I want us to loosen our definition of lesbianism so that bisexuals and asexuals and newcomers can be accepted into lesbian communities without having to prove themselves worthy of trust, in bed or some other way."[37]

1977

- Myra T. Johnson publishes "Asexual and Autoerotic Women: Two Invisible Groups" in *The Sexually Oppressed* (see the Introduction and chapter 5, "Desire").

1978

- *Gay News* literary editor Alison Hennegan asserts that people have the right "not to be sexual at all." She also notes that "there's a strong case to be made for Asexual Liberation."[38]

1980

- Michael D. Storms publishes "Theories of Sexual Orientation" in the *Journal of Personality and Social Psychology,* in which he reimagines the Kinsey Scale as a two-dimensional, four-quadrant map that includes asexuality, the first scale of this type to account for asexuality.[39]

1981

- Catherine Kobaly writes to feminist newspaper *Heresies* to thank them for a recent issue centering marginalized sexualities, but adds that she had not seen herself represented as an asexual reader. She also reasons that more asexual visibility in a publication like *Heresies* would benefit asexual communities because it would make it easier for them to find each other and talk about ways to combat acephobia and internalized shame. In Kobaly's vision, "If we can attack these feelings of shame at their roots and get rid of them, then I believe we will see that there are just as many asexuals in the world as heterosexuals and homosexuals, that our lifestyle, while not our choice, is just as real and valid, and that we deserve a fair and equal representation."[40]

1983

- "Mental Health Implications of Sexual Orientation," published by Paula Nurius in *The Journal of Sex Research,* is the first study to give empirical data about asexuals and evaluates the relationship between sexual orientation and mental health, scoring participants according to sexual behavior and desire for it.[41]

1985

- In *Origins of Sexuality and Homosexuality*, John Dececco and Michael Shively write that "feelings and acts are selected and organized as a 'unity'— as a particular sexual orientation—through the cognitive process of sexual identification as bisexual, heterosexual, homosexual, or asexual."[42]

1989

- American-Canadian sexologist Ray Blanchard coins "analloeroticism"— meaning to have no sexual interest in other people—and writes about it extensively in two publications, "The Concept of Autogynephilia and the Typology of Male Gender Dysphoria" and "The Classification and Labeling of Nonhomosexual Gender Dysphorias." According to Blanchard,

  > The term *analloerotic*—from the Greek, borrowing *an-*, "lacking," and *alloerotic*, "sexual feeling or activity finding its object in another person" (*Webster's Third New International Dictionary*, 1981)—is used to designate gender dysphorics who report no erotic attraction to other persons, male or female. Two types of analloeroticism are distinguished. *Automonosexuals* are erotically aroused by the thought or image of themselves as the opposite sex but not by other persons. The label *asexual* is reserved for that subset of analloerotics who deny sexual drive or erotic interests of any kind.[43]

- The first issue of *The Alyson Almanac: A Treasury of Information for the Gay and Lesbian Community* is printed. One of the terms included in this encyclopedia of queer terminology and history is *Bambi-sexuality*, which is defined as "Physical interaction centered more about touching, kissing, and caressing than around genital sexuality."[44] The January–March 1994 edition of the *Alyson Women's Book Catalog* has a mini "Dictionary of Slang and Historical Terms" that also includes and defines Bambi-sexuality in this way.[45] Today, Bambi-sexuality is understood as a type of asexual identity.

1993

- The book *Boston Marriages: Romantic but Asexual Relationships among Contemporary Lesbians* by Esther D. Rothblum and Kathleen A. Brehony is released.[46]

1997

- Zoe O'Reilly publishes "My Life as an Amoeba" in the *StarNet Dispatches* webzine, writing, "There is one group continuously overlooked: the asexual." The personal essay would go on to spark conversation among people who identified with it. It is now regarded as the first appearance of the asexuality community online.[47]

2000

- A Yahoo group for asexuals called Haven for the Human Amoeba is created.

2001

- Asexual activist David Jay founds the Asexual Visibility and Education Network (AVEN), which would ultimately become the most prolific and well-known asexual community hub.

2002

- New York passes the "Sexual Orientation Non-Discrimination Act," in which: "SONDA defines sexual orientation as 'heterosexuality, homosexuality, bisexuality, or asexuality, whether actual or perceived.' Thus, the law affords protection where individuals are targeted either based on their actual sexual orientation, or based on what the discriminator believes their orientation to be."[48]

2004

- Psychologist Anthony F. Bogaert publishes "Asexuality: Prevalence and Associated Factors in a National Probability Sample" in the *Journal of Sex Research*. According to this paper, 1 percent of a 1994 British probability sample identified as asexual. *New Scientist* dedicates space to the exploration of asexuality in response to Bogaert's paper.[49]

2005

- AVEN community members decide on a black ring worn on the middle finger of the right hand as a symbol for the asexual community.

2006

- Anthony F. Bogaert publishes a follow-up paper, "Toward a Conceptual Understanding of Asexuality," in the *Review of General Psychology,* which seeks to better articulate and define asexuality. In it, he works to set asexuality apart from sexual conditions such as hypoactive sexual desire disorder (see chapter 5, "Desire"). He also argues that it has contributed to the negative perception of asexuals as sexually repressed.[50]

2009

- AVEN members participate in the first asexual entry into a U.S. Pride parade, walking together in San Francisco.

2010

- The asexual pride flag is introduced.
- Asexual Awareness Week, now called Ace Week, is founded by Sara Beth Brooks to both celebrate asexual spectrum pride and promote asexuality awareness.

2011

- The documentary *(A)sexual* is released.[51]

2012

- The first International Asexual Conference is held at World Pride in London.

2013

- The *Diagnostic and Statistical Manual of Mental Disorders, Fifth Edition (DSM-5)* changes the diagnosis of hypoactive sexual desire disorder to include the exception for people who self-identify as asexual (see chapter 5, "Desire").

2015

- After wrongly identifying the *A* in LGBTQIA(+) as standing for "ally," the Gay and Lesbian Alliance Against Defamation issues this apology: "Let us say without equivocation, the 'A' in LGBTQIA represents millions of Asexual, Agender, and Aromantic people, who are far too often left out of the conversation about acceptance. It was never, ever our intention to suggest otherwise, and we apologize."[52]

2017

- Simon Fraser University in Vancouver, Canada, is the first institution in the world to offer a full-length undergraduate course in asexuality studies. "Critical Nonsexualites" is taught by Ela Przybylo, author of *Asexual Erotics: Intimate Readings of Compulsory Sexuality*. Przybylo tells *The Peak* that the "core questions [in the course] were really around what is compulsory sexuality, how is it experienced by various people, and how can we take steps towards both including asexuality in feminist and queer spaces and thinking about compulsory sexuality critically." Furthermore, Przybylo affirms that having conversations focused around asexuality "helps us look critically at how so-called 'normal' ranges of sexual desire have serious effects for us all and especially for people who are deemed as having 'excessive' or 'lacking' desire."[53]

- The Ace and Aro Advocacy Project (TAAAP), originally The Asexual Awareness Project, is founded.

2019

- Washington becomes the first state in the United States to recognize Asexual Awareness Week.

2020

- The first Virtual Asexual Pride takes place, hosted by Jaymie O'Leary Doyle.

2021

- The first International Asexuality Day is held on April 6.

My hope is that others will expand on this timeline—which is certainly an incomplete one, as I am only an amateur historian. I know there is more to be found and more to be said about how asexuality has been medicalized, pathologized, infantilized, demonized, and otherwise othered throughout history, as well as how asexuals and advocates have pushed back against this othering and the mandates of compulsory sexuality. I must honor, thank, and give due credit to those who have been doing this type of research independently for many years now, cataloging what bits and pieces of asexual history they can find and sharing it through personal blogs, detailed Tumblr posts, forums, and more. If not for the efforts of those who have done this work and offered it freely, countless people, including myself, would not know anything of this history at all.

12

Possibilities

Look closely at the present you are constructing: it should look like the future you are dreaming.

—ALICE WALKER

A 2014 STUDY ATTEMPTED to analyze the relationship between asexuality, handedness, and other biological markers. It found that asexuals were approximately 2.4 to 2.5 times more likely to be left-handed (or ambidextrous) than their heterosexual counterparts.[1] The fact that left-handedness used to be punished and demonized might be unthinkable to some people today, but it is an unfortunate, albeit strange, truth. Historically, left-handedness has been associated with evil and devilry. In Christianity, the "right hand of God" is favored, as that is the side where Jesus is said to sit. The left-hand bias born from that is even present in our language: "Sinister, today meaning evil or malevolent in some way, comes from a Latin word simply meaning 'on the left side.' 'Left' being associated with evil likely comes from a majority of the population being right-handed [and] biblical texts describing God saving those on the right on Judgment day."[2] Furthermore, black magic and Satanism are often referred to as the "left-hand path," and left-handedness has even been attributed to demonic possession and resulted in accusations of witchcraft. By the twentieth century, anthropologists and psychologists had come to view left-handedness as a biological anomaly and a form of deviance that needed to be corrected.

In schools, students were reprimanded for being left-handed—often through corporal punishment (read: physical abuse)—and were forced to learn to write and perform other everyday tasks with their right hand instead. Forcible hand conversion is known to cause an array of problems for the children who experience it, including various learning and speech disorders,[3] and, of course, trauma. As left-handedness was demonized and punished less and less through-out the years, more and more people began to feel safe enough to be open about their left-handedness, especially among younger generations farther removed from more blatant and violent forms of discrimination. Since the early twen-tieth century, the percentage of left-handers in the United States has gradually risen from around 2 percent to nearly 12 percent, and most of them are younger people. Jerre Levy, a psychologist from University of Chicago, estimates that the number will eventually land at around 14 percent.[4] Today, many experts con-sider left-handedness to be a sign of creativity in an individual.[5]

Of course, it is absurd that a group of people has been discriminated against, demonized, dehumanized, and abused because of the hand they write with. Handedness is something we each have a natural inclination toward. We are either left-handed or right-handed or ambidextrous. We do not consciously decide which one will be the dominant appendage, or whether we will be able to competently use them both; we simply move and engage with our bodies in whichever way feels most natural and comfortable to us—that is, until someone tells us we are doing it wrong. Our world has a consistent history of creating excuses to ostracize those who are different from the norm, from what is con-sidered desirable by the ruling class. And since almost 90 percent of the popula-tion is right-handed,[6] the world is designed to be most comfortable and safe for right-handed people.

It's fascinating to me that there is a documented correlation between left-handedness and asexuality, since attitudes regarding them both seem to some-what mirror each other. Asexuality now has more visibility than ever and the stigma against it is being continually and loudly challenged in both digital and material spaces. Therefore, more and more people are identifying as asexual—they are learning where they fall on the spectrum, they are building commu-nity, and they are coming to understand themselves and their sexuality better. I believe that number will continue to rise as younger generations continue to unpack the societally induced shame around being uninterested in sex or being unpartnered. The more we affirm asexuality, the more asexual people will feel comfortable, safe, and valid in embracing their asexuality, and the more others will see how compulsory sexuality impacts their lives as well. As I move toward the end of this book, I must consider where we go from here. We must all consider asexual possibilities and asexual futures.

According to the "2018 Tracking Report: Lesbian, Gay, Bisexual, Transgender, and Queer Grantmaking by U.S. Foundations," out of a total of a record $209.2 million in funding, only $70 was allocated to asexual communities.[7] This was the first time any grant money had gone toward asexual outreach at all. Grant funds are used for advocacy, capacity building and training, education, research, direct service, victim support, and more—all resources that are needed in asexual communities, particularly to combat and educate on acephobic discrimination and sexual violence. Every time I witness someone argue that "asexuals steal resources" from other queer people, this report, this meager $70, is what I think of. The report illustrates the necessity of asexual advocacy and the need for others to be educated about asexuality and how compulsory sexuality begets the obstacles we consistently face. Not only will education lead to asexuality being better understood and prevent many people from spending much of their lives not understanding their own sexuality, but it will also mean that asexuals will be better protected and cared for—both within and outside of queer communities. The future we imagine must be a reality in which we collectively do more to combat the things that continually leave asexuals unprotected. To create this future, we have to consistently challenge both compulsory sexuality and white supremacist ideologies.

The truth is that much of asexual scholarship, studies, activism, and advocacy have often been reproductive of white supremacist ideals and have even worked to erase the existence of nonwhite asexual identities and possibilities—despite the fact that Anthony F. Bogaert's often-cited 2004 study on asexual prevalence, which estimated that around 1.05 percent of the population identified as asexual, found a "higher percentage (13 percent) of asexual individuals were also non-White relative to the [allo]sexual individuals (4 percent)" included in the study.[8] Since the birth of the modern asexuality movement, the most prominent and celebrated voices have been those of white asexuals; the ideas, talking points, and artifacts produced have been overwhelmingly white; and the majority of the spaces curated by those active in the movement remain safe only for white asexuals—especially when conversations never move beyond the need to be visible, because visibility is more dangerous for some than it is for others.

What Black asexuals and other asexuals of color need are acknowledgments of the racism and anti-Blackness within many asexual spaces, conversations about how we can move toward liberation from white supremacy in asexual spaces, and tangible actions taken to help make this happen.

I look forward to seeing others move beyond what I have written here, to consider how compulsory sexuality impacts other aspects of our lives and how else we can use an asexual lens to better understand the world and advocate for needed change—particularly with a racial analysis. I am inspired by Ianna Hawkins Owen, whose work was highlighted by the University at Buffalo in the Spring of 2021. In her presentation, "'No New Watchword': Asexuality, Incarceration, and Freedom," Owen brought to the fore a glimpse of the possibilities at the intersection of asexual studies and critical race theory, "about the possible synergies of asexuality and abolition—specifically, [she] wanted to think more explicitly ... about what asexual analytics can offer abolitionist thought." As Owen says, "The root of your nonsexual desire for belonging, kinship, and connection can be the starting point for understanding the stakes of prison abolition in your own life and contributing to its realization."[9] Her work reminds me that there is more for us to interrogate, more to unpack, more to theorize, more to disrupt, more to uproot, more to deconstruct, more to digest about asexuality.

I began this book by saying that I do not believe asexuality to be an orientation defined by "lack." To lack is to be without, deficient, or not have enough. Not wanting sex—either not as frequently or not at all, or not arriving at sexual engagement via clear-cut attraction the way we are told we are supposed to—is not an experience of lack, but of abundance and autonomy. Though it was necessary for me to dedicate this book to the examination of realities associated with those who rarely or never desire sex with others, I believe it is a disservice for discussions about asexual experience to focus only on the desires that are not abundantly present and leave no room to honor the desires that **are** present. Asexuals have shared with me the ways they choose to honor their nonsexual desires, and the joy they find in that intention. They speak with warmth and reverence of the space they create to allow other parts of their lives to flourish, particularly in ways that fall outside of social scripts for intimacy, kinship, and family-making.

Asexuals are actively prioritizing nonsexual forms of connection, honoring our capacity to create long-lasting bonds and express love, appreciation, and commitment in various ways. To revisit Frances Chapman's quote from her *off our backs* essay, "Asexuality is an orientation that regards a partner as nonessential to sex, and sex as nonessential to a satisfying relationship."[10] When we prioritize our desires that are present, we are choosing to hold on to the truest parts of ourselves that we have always been told should be cast off. In asexuality, there is abundance, there is room to expand, there are a multitude of possibilities for companionship, stability, and reciprocal support. There is room to let go of the myth that we are less valuable, less productive, less deserving, less human without normative sexuality.

Lisa Orlando concludes "The Asexual Manifesto" with this statement:

> As a result of examining the nature of our sexuality and reclaiming it from the sexist misconceptions surrounding it, we are able to form and maintain relationships in a way which both reflects our values and is effective in our liberation struggle. For us, asexuality is a commitment to defy and ultimately to destroy the baseless concepts, surrounding both sex and relationships, which support and perpetuate the patriarchy.[11]

It is clear to me that there continues to be a need to recognize a distinctly asexual consciousness, as well as a need to name how asexuality exists as a refusal of compulsory sexuality and prescribed cisheterosexuality. Beyond what Orlando names as a commitment to defy patriarchy, asexuality is also an opportunity to divest from the white supremacist ideologies that inform and sustain the cisheteropatriarchal system and its compulsory sexuality ethos. Colonial ideas of sex(uality) and gender performance are not innate or universal aspects of humanness and morality. They have merely been put forward as such to prop up whiteness and white values as what is "normal" and "civilized," and construct all other forms of expression as deviant and "savage," as unhuman and dysfunctional.

What we must do is abandon this singular view of "normal" sexuality, as well as the gender binary and cisheteropatriarchal gender roles that mandate sociosexual submission to men and punish those who dare to imagine lives without it. There must be a commitment to interrogating how harmful racial stereotypes and racist fetishization are used to consume racially marginalized people and reify white supremacy. And it is imperative that we divest from compulsory sexuality, from the idea that sex is universally desired, that it is the mandatory route to joy and satisfaction, intimacy and connection, emotional intelligence, maturity, sanity, morality, humanity.

Compulsory sexuality is a cage. If we cannot make our own determinations about our sexual lives because of social convention and gendered or racialized expectations of sexuality; if we cannot make our own reproductive choices because we are called on to use our bodies to produce future laborers to be exploited by racial capitalism or to counteract the mythical "white genocide"; if we cannot honor the natural ebb and flow of sexual desire because "low" desire is pathologized as an individual psychological or physiological dysfunction; if we cannot fathom untethering humanness from allosexuality because sexlessness, or near-sexlessness, makes asexuals into animal-like or mechanistic figures in the social imagination; if we cannot envisage and honor a genuine Black asexuality because Blackness and the Black body are hypersexualized, because anti-Black logics relegate the Black asexual to a space of distinct impossibility, then we are not free.

Black Asexual Insights

"Being a Black asexual makes you less seen. You have to work ten times harder than other ace activists and ace people to get recognized, and to even have a space to talk about your issues. We as Black people face things our white and even other POC ace counterparts wouldn't understand."

—*THE ASEXUAL GODDESS* (she/they), agender aceflux asexual

"There are a lot of stereotypes that we as Black people have about our sexuality. It's like we're invisibilized or we are fetishized. And I think I have experienced both, often at the same time.... I don't want to be invisible. I want to be seen, but in being seen there is this pressure for me to be someone I'm not."

—*EV'YAN WHITNEY* (they/she), nonbinary demisexual ace

"I am Black, very Black, and there is hardly any Black asexual representation. I have had to hunt near and far for just maybe three other Black asexuals. I low-key thought for a second 'Is this a white thing for me to be experiencing? Am I doing something wrong?' I had to get that out of my head quickly before it drove me crazy.

I always noticed that Black women never really had the right to their own bodies. Before I even knew what asexuality was, I thought that, as a Black woman, it was just something we had to do because we were meant to have babies.

I love being asexual because I can still be intimate with someone and not go against what my soul and mind and body desire, and that is to not have sex. There are thousands of ways to get that closeness with someone."

—*JADE* (they/them), asexual woman

"I know Black women are expected to be more sexually available, open, or adventurous than we actually might be, which has made me really cautious about who I have these conversations with. It's already challenging being someone who likes wearing feminine, curve-flattering fits and short hemlines, which men tend to take as invitations. Whether you're ace or not, you're still having to tell men, 'My outfit is not an invitation.'"

—M (she/her), biromantic asexual woman

"People I've come across have assumed I think about sex often because I present as male. So when I got into relationships, my partners assumed I'd be sexually active. Which normally led to me being guilted into sex. Since society places so much emphasis on sex, my partners assumed I wasn't attracted to them because I didn't want to have sex…. When people feel valued only for sex, it can skew their self-worth."

—MIK (he/him, ze/zir, they/them), agender asexual

"Most of my sexual experiences with cis men were nonconsensual for many reasons. Them having no respect for my asexuality was one of them…. I always knew I was having to talk myself into sexual performance with cis men…. I see how Black women are so sexualized and it's so at odds with how I feel, so it can be … a lot. It also meant that as a once closeted queer woman who dated cis men to appear heterosexual, I was in a lot of situations that ended with sexual assault. In addition to grappling with being on the asexual spectrum in an allosexual world, I'm also trying to reckon with a lot of trauma in regards to sex."

—KRYKIT (she/her), demisexual/aceflux woman

"When I got to college and met more queer people, everyone told me that my feelings weren't normal and I just wasn't attracted to men. I went through a brief period where I thought I was a lesbian because of this, but realized I feel the same indifference towards the bodies of people of all genders…. Entering Black radical spaces for the first time in my life, I felt like a lot of people linked their high sex drive, polyamory, and sexual

attraction to lots of different kinds of people to their politics, like it made them somehow more radical. I struggled a lot with feeling less free or less liberated than my other Black queer radical counterparts because I didn't enjoy sex or feel sexual attraction, and that's something I still really struggle with today. I think it's also hard because when people talk about revolutionary lifestyles and radical outlooks, conversations about moving from a scarcity mind-set to an abundance mind-set often center sex and sexual partners. I wish I saw more conversations about living abundantly that didn't involve having more than one sexual partner, or having one at all."

—G (she/her), asexual woman

"Me coming out as asexual definitely broke expectations.... Growing up in a Black family, you are often expected to find a girlfriend, get married, have kids, and live out that life.... My parents and siblings weren't pushy when it came to that cultural norm, but society and other relatives always held up that standard, even when they weren't aware of it. As a Black man, those experiences can be brutal and negative in regards to wanting to explore the spectrum of sexuality. Hopefully me being out can open more doors for fellow Black asexual men."

—MARSHALL (he/they), asexual man

"Being raised and socialized as a Black girl in the South and in the church meant that people projected a lot onto my body and my sexuality. I felt my parents and broader community had the children they were 'training up' as girls under a magnifying glass to make sure we weren't exhibiting sexual behaviors (such as clothes being 'too tight' or taking on 'fast ways' from friends). For a long time, I primarily understood my discomfort with this as tied to the misogynoir of policing Black women's sexuality. More recently, I'm understanding that another part of my discomfort with this attention growing up, or things like street harassment today, are because I typically don't enjoy being perceived as a sexual person or object of someone else's desire, and particularly as a sexual 'woman.'"

I think expanding my gender has tracked with me becoming more open and comfortable expressing my asexuality.... I'm rewriting the script in my head that says that the things that make me less like the women I admire (my asexuality, autism, queerness, etc.) are things that make me defective. I'm realizing instead that the actual defect is the gender binary! It's been freeing because it means I can take what parts of (Black) 'womanhood' serve me, and leave the parts that harm me or others, such as a certain type of 'female' sexuality."

—G, (she/they), genderflux graysexual

"A lot of the people I dated online didn't respect my asexuality. I was seen as 'the Black guy to take home' and they really only wanted to be with me because I was Black and they wanted to 'try it.' They were the most dehumanizing experiences I've ever felt."

—ANTHONY T'CHALLA (he/they), demisexual

"I hope to see society develop a wider familiarity with asexuality and a broader understanding of the diverse possibilities of ace-spec experiences of life, love, labels, presentation, representation, and demographics."

—BRANDI (she/her), gray/aegosexual woman

Afterword

A Love Letter to My Fellow Impossibles, Mythicals, Fugitives, Enigmas, and "More Than, Less Than, and Other Than" Humans

DEAR FELLOW IMPOSSIBLES, MYTHICALS, fugitives, enigmas, and the "more than, less than, and other than" humans,

I see you out here in the world, queering simply by being, and I honor you. This should be enough, and yet if it were enough, there would never have been a need for this book, and what is clear is that Sherronda J. Brown's *Refusing Compulsory Sexuality* is needed. Sometimes we impossibles, mythicals, fugitives, enigmas, and "more than, less than, and other than" humans require more words than should be enough in attempts to make legible the illegible, even if only temporarily. Even so, I celebrate our illegibilities, the worlds that we are worlding simply by existing.

In *Feminism Is for Everybody: Passionate Politics,* the beloved now ancestor bell hooks states, "To be truly visionary we have to root our imagination in our concrete reality while simultaneously imagining possibilities beyond that reality." So much of the work of our "concrete reality" is spent trying to convince a white cisheteropatriarchal imperialist world of Black people's humanness. I dare to dream about the chance to, instead, be with our humanity as a de facto premise while exploring the "more than, less than, and other than" humanness of our multitudinous possibilities.

Refusing Compulsory Sexuality leaves me simultaneously imagining the possibilities beyond our colonized reality and contending with the feigned concreteness of that reality. I am wondering, *What becomes possible when we invite*

Blackness back to the conversation that was hijacked by whiteness at varying inter-sections? What is possible within a Black (a)sexuality? What does a frame of Black-ness that is vast and abundant and refuses to be limited exclusively to the racial categorization of colonization have to say to and about asexuality? In honor of auntie bell's invitation, I passionately offer an inquiry in service of centering the vastness of Blackness as the exploration point toward an asexual framework. I am offering this inquiry from the technology that is Blackness, a place of expan-sive, freedom-loving innovation. A place where we get to explore and construct our own spaces of what I call BlackFreedomSex, the kind of sex and sexuality that all who desire to access *can* access without it hinging on whether or not we experience sexual attraction or want to share our sex with anyone else. A place that understands that to be defined by that which we don't experience in nor-mative ways obscures all of the ways we experience so much fullness, so much power, so much wholeness, so much completeness.

I ask you: Where might an asexuality in Blackness become a praxis of free-dom that is vast enough to include the pleasures and pursuits of allosexuality without having to center them or be limited by them? What curiosities emerge about asexuality when they are born of the fullness of the sensualities of Black-ness, rather than fetishization?

What is possible when we include an ethic of Black love and care in how we approach inquiry into expanded notions of eroticism and desire? What possibil-ities might unfold for us impossibles, mythicals, fugitives, enigmas, and "more than, less than, and other than" human folk when we embrace abjection as illegi-bility and the desire for such? What lessons might Blackness, as a refusal of fixed legibility, offer to a BlackFreedomSex practice within asexuality?

In "The Transformation of Silence into Language and Action," Audre Lorde asserts, "**When I** dare to be powerful—to use my strength in the service of my vision—then it becomes less and less important **whether I am afraid.**" In alchemizing her words toward a Black asexual framework, I offer this remix: "When I dare to be asexual in a freedom-seeking relationship to my Blackness, I am powerful. When I use my Black asexuality in service of my vision, my writ-ing, my creating, my existing, then it becomes less and less important whether I am afraid I will not be legible to agents limited to frameworks of compulsory sex and sexuality."

An asexual framework grounded in Blackness engages multiple realities simultaneously. It is a journey into the speculative and the knowing of the fact that there are necessary unknowables. The asexual framework through the lens of Blackness that I have put forward is a framework that is bored and ambivalent about and toward the carcerality of musings inside compulsory sexuality and the gender binary. It posits that a world of limited thinking (read: compulsory sexuality) must end in order for the full breadth of the universe of all possibilities to fully thrive, with fewer resistances for us impossibles, mythicals, fugitives, enigmas, and the "more than, less than, and other than" humans. After all, why use our energy to engage a colonized humanness so intent on killing itself in reductionism when we have things to do like world, write, make art, do dishes, steward land and communities, or do nothing at all?

I'm offering the imagination of a realm of a Black asexual possibility that can hold even the most "possibles" of the realm where we are "impossible." The realm of the asexual through Blackness is a realm of freedom full of BlackFreedomSex— the sex that shapes and is shaped by change. The asexual realm of Blackness includes a neurodivergent experience of sexuality that lends itself to simultaneities, multiplicities, and multidimensionality that is more than human in nature and thus rejects, refuses, and defies a notion of privileging sex and sexuality as a human imperative for everyone. This realm invites the possibility of a book, a conversation, a thought lineage that doesn't have to start from the tired beginning of colonized white mediocrity.

I close this letter by giving presence to those who so often are absenced in the conventional discourse around asexuality. I want to presence our pleasure-seeking, freedom-seeking, imaginative, and expansive Black asexual ancestors, transcestors, intersextors. I acknowledge the wisdom of the lands that we are individually and collectively benefitting from being in relationship to and the ancestral stewards of these lands that support us. Reading Sherronda J. Brown's *Refusing Compulsory Sexuality* has invited me to invoke my most embodied, playful, curious, audacious, impossible ancestors to guide me to a nonlinear future while contending with a colonized linear present reality. Sherronda has offered words, thoughts, and new imaginings that have encouraged me to remember and to celebrate my status as an impossible, a mythical, a fugitive, an enigma, and a "more than, less than, and other than" human.

This letter offers a shift in focus from genitally based acts of pleasure conventionally understood to be sex to a sex-positive practice space of being in our vastness and our remembering who we were before we were limited by colonial white mediocrity (shout out to Spirit McIntyre for that gem) and its compulsory sexuality in a racially capitalist endeavor. I write this letter in order to practice the freedoms that our ancestors practiced, to add, to affirm, to expand our ideas of asexuality through Blackness. May you be changed as I have been in writing to you, and may you be reminded that, in the change, we are our own decadence. May we all continue to be the product of our own generative and expansive processes. I see you; I honor you. We have always been and will always be here.

With Black Love and Care,
GRACE B FREEDOM

Notes

Introduction

1. Lisa Orlando, "The Asexual Manifesto," Asexual Caucus/New York Radical Feminists, September 1972, 2. https://tinyurl.com/23bvxxb3.
2. Myra T. Johnson, "Asexual and Autoerotic Women: Two Invisible Groups," in *The Sexually Oppressed,* edited by Jean Gochros and Harvey Gochros (New York: Association Press, 1977), 97.
3. Kristina Gupta, "Compulsory Sexuality: Evaluating an Emerging Concept," *Signs* 41:1 (2015), 132.
4. Gupta, "Compulsory Sexuality," 135.
5. Cathy J. Cohen, "Punks, Bulldaggers and Welfare Queens: The Radical Potential of Queer Politics," in *Identity/Space/Power: Lesbian, Gay, Bisexual, and Transgender Politics,* edited by Mark Blasius (Amsterdam: Gordon and Breach, 1997), 440.
6. Cohen, "Punks, Bulldaggers and Welfare Queens," 441.
7. Patricia Hill Collins, *Black Sexual Politics: African Americans, Gender, and the New Racism* (New York: Routledge, 2006), 27.
8. Ianna Hawkins Owen, "On the Racialization of Asexuality," in *Asexualities: Feminist and Queer Perspectives,* edited by K. J. Cerankowski and Megan Milks (London: Routledge, 2016), 122.
9. Richard Goldstein, "James Baldwin on Being Gay in America," *The Village Voice,* June 26, 1984. https://tinyurl.com/4y5kfmmz.
10. Owen, "On the Racialization of Asexuality," 121.
11. Roderick Ferguson, *Aberrations in Black: Toward a Queer of Color Critique* (Minneapolis: University of Minnesota Press, 2004), 174.

12. Siobhan B. Somerville, *Queering the Color Line: Race and the Invention of Homosexuality in American Culture* (Durham, NC: Duke University Press, 2000), 4.
13. Somerville, *Queering the Color Line,* 17.
14. Somerville, *Queering the Color Line,* 27.
15. Somerville, *Queering the Color Line,* 28.
16. Somerville, *Queering the Color Line,* 29.
17. Charles W. Mills, *The Racial Contract* (Ithaca, NY: Cornell University Press, 2014), 22.
18. Mills, *Racial Contract,* 57.

1. Acephobia

1. Russell T. Hurlburt, "Not Everyone Conducts Inner Speech," *Psychology Today,* October 26, 2011. https://tinyurl.com/2p99uu8j.
2. James Felton, "People Are Weirded out to Discover That Some People Don't Have an Internal Monologue," IFL Science, February 3, 2020, https://tinyurl.com/ycxu7259.
3. Russell T. Hurlburt, *Investigating Pristine Inner Experience: Moments of Truth* (New York: Cambridge University Press, 2011).
4. Bernard J. Baars, "How Brain Reveals Mind: Neural Studies Support the Fundamental Role of Conscious Experience," *Journal of Consciousness Studies* 10:9–10 (2003), 106.
5. John McWhorter, *Doing Our Own Thing* (New York: Gotham, 2003), 3.
6. Hulburt, "Not Everyone Conducts Inner Speech."
7. Charlie Bell, "Asexuality Explained: Sky Data Poll Shows Widespread Lack of Understanding." *Sky News* February 4, 2019. https://tinyurl.com/4ssbdpa4.
8. Miranda Fricker, *Epistemic Injustice: Power and the Ethics of Knowing* (New York: Oxford University Press, 2007), 1.
9. Fricker, *Epistemic Injustice,* 1.
10. Sarah Doan-Minh, "Corrective Rape: An Extreme Manifestation of Discrimination and the State's Complicity in Sexual Violence," *Hastings Women's Law Journal* 30:1 (2019), 167.

11. Caroline Bauer, Tristan Miller, Mary Ginoza, Alice Chiang, Kristin Young-blom, Ai Baba, Jessy Pinnell, et al., "The 2015 Asexual Census Summary Report," Ace Community Survey, 2017, 42. https://tinyurl.com/2p8mckhz.

12. Bauer et al., "2015 Asexual Census Summary Report," 43.

13. Robin Weis, Sig Tomaskovic-Moore, Caroline Bauer, Tristan L. Miller, Mel Adroit, Ai Baba, Tracy van der Biezen, et al., "2017 and 2018 Asexual Community Survey Summary Report," Ace Community Survey, 2020, 48.

14. Cara C. MacInnis and Gordon Hodson, "Intergroup Bias toward 'Group X': Evidence of Prejudice, Dehumanization, Avoidance, and Discrimination against Asexuals," *Group Processes & Intergroup Relations* 15:6 (2012), 731. doi:10.1177/1368430212442419.

15. MacInnis and Hodson, "Intergroup Bias toward 'Group X,'" 731.

16. Gordon Hodson, "Prejudice against 'Group X' (Asexuals)," *Psychology Today,* September 1, 2012. https://tinyurl.com/4uxrhmk7.

17. MacInnis and Hodson, "Intergroup Bias toward 'Group X,'" 733.

18. Mark R. Hoffarth, Caroline E. Drolet, Gordon Hodson, and Carolyn L. Hafer, "Development and Validation of the Attitudes toward Asexuals (ATA) Scale," *Psychology and Sexuality* 7:2 (2016). doi:10.1080/19419899 .2015.1050446.

19. Gordon Hodson, "Attitudes toward Asexuals (ATA) Prejudice Scale," *Psychology Today,* August 6, 2015. https://tinyurl.com/ywh98dhf.

20. Hodson "Attitudes toward Asexuals."

21. Hodson "Attitudes toward Asexuals."

22. UK Government Equalities Office, National LGBT Survey, 2019. https://tinyurl.com/2p8s5zff.

23. Kevin L. Nadal, Marie-Anne Issa, Jayleen Leon, Vanessa Meterko, Michelle Wideman, and Yinglee Wong, "Sexual Orientation Microaggressions: 'Death by a Thousand Cuts' for Lesbian, Gay, and Bisexual Youth," *Journal of LGBT Youth* 8:3, (July 2011), 235.

24. Tamara Deutsch, "Asexual People's Experience with Microaggressions," master's thesis, CUNY Academic Works, John Jay College of Criminal Justice, 2018, 16.

25. Nadal et al., "Sexual Orientation Microaggressions," 238.

2. Gatekeeping

1. Eric W. Dolan, "Many Heterosexuals View Bisexual Women as Promiscuous and Confused, Study Suggests," *PsyPost*, March 25, 2018. https://tinyurl.com/ak2z6h6w.

2. Mikel L. Walters, Jieru Chen, and Matthew J. Breiding, "The National Intimate Partner and Sexual Violence Survey (NISVS): 2010 Findings on Victimization by Sexual Orientation," National Center for Injury Prevention and Control, Centers for Disease Control and Prevention, 2013, 10.

3. Caroline Gorman, "Bisexual Women and Sexual Violence," Maryland Coalition Against Sexual Assault, April 10, 2020. https://tinyurl.com/2p843nar.

4. Gorman, "Bisexual Women and Sexual Violence."

5. Sam Webb, "Gay Couple Beaten Up for Refusing to Kiss for Men's Entertainment," *Metro UK*, June 7, 2019. https://tinyurl.com/3w6j6ck2.

6. Gina Martinez and Tara Law, "Two Recent Murders of Black Trans Women in Texas Reveal a Nationwide Crisis, Advocates Say," *Time*, June 5, 2019. https://tinyurl.com/2asf3hf5.

7. North Carolina Public Facilities Privacy & Security Act: An Act to Provide for Single-Sex Multiple Occupancy Bathroom and Changing Facilities in Schools and Public Agencies and to Create Statewide Consistency in Regulation of Employment and Public Accommodations, Representatives Bishop, Stam, Howard, and Steinburg, primary sponsors, passed March 23, 2016.

8. U.S. Department of Housing and Urban Development, "Making Admission or Placement Determinations Based on Sex in Facilities under Community Planning and Development Housing Programs," *Federal Register* 85:143 (2020): 44811–18.

9. Movement Advancement Project, Center for American Progress, and Youth First, "Unjust: LGBTQ Youth Incarcerated in the Juvenile Justice System," 2017 Report.

10. Nico Lang, "Trans Youth Could Face Juvenile Detention under 2021's Worst Anti-Trans Bill," *Them*, March 1, 2021. https://tinyurl.com/bdfsmevv.

11. Aubyn S. Fulton, Richard L. Gorsuch, and Elizabeth A. Maynard, "Religious Orientation, Antihomosexual Sentiment, and Fundamentalism among Christians," *Journal for the Scientific Study of Religion* 38 (1999), 19.

12. Gordon Hodson, "Prejudice against 'Group X' (Asexuals)," *Psychology Today,* September 1, 2012. https://tinyurl.com/4uxrhmk7.

13. Audre Lorde, "The Master's Tools Will Never Dismantle the Master's House," *Sister Outsider: Essays and Speeches* (Berkeley, CA: Crossing Press, 2007), 104.

14. Gloria Anzaldúa, "El Mundo Zurdo," *The Gloria Anzaldúa Reader,* edited by AnaLouise Keating (Durham, NC: Duke University Press, 2009), 49.

3. Neverland

1. Claudia M. Gold, "Understanding Childism: Are We Prejudiced against Children?" *Psychology Today,* January 12, 2012. https://tinyurl.com/azy995nn.

2. Julia Prims, "Societal Challenge and Depression, Self-Esteem and Self-Concept Clarity in Asexuals," undergraduate honors thesis, University of Colorado Boulder, Arts and Sciences Honors Program, 2012, 15.

3. Jon Fortenbury, "On 'Late'-in-Life Virginity Loss," *The Atlantic,* March 28, 2014. https://tinyurl.com/ktk2kb27.

4. Amanda N. Gesselman, Gregory D. Webster, and Justin R. Garcia, "Has Virginity Lost Its Virtue? Relationship Stigma Associated with Being a Sexually Inexperienced Adult," *The Journal of Sex Research,* 35:2 (2017), 202.

5. Elizabeth Freeman, *Time Binds: Queer Temporalities, Queer Histories* (Durham, NC: Duke University Press, 2010), 3.

6. Kiera Butler, "Why You Should Stop Eating Breakfast, Lunch, and Dinner," *Mother Jones,* March 4, 2015. https://tinyurl.com/5n74ejk5.

7. Julian B. Carter, *The Heart of Whiteness: Normal Sexuality and Race in America, 1880–1940* (Durham, NC: Duke University Press, 2007), 36.

8. Carter, *Heart of Whiteness,* 37.

9. Bella DePaulo, "Why Coupling Is No Longer Compulsory," *Psychology Today,* February 20, 2021. https://tinyurl.com/yjr3akfz.

10. Jean M. Twenge, "Possible Reasons US Adults Are Not Having Sex as Much as They Used To," JAMA Network Open, June 12, 2020. https://tinyurl.com/2p9barap.

11. Rebecca Epstein, Jamila J. Blake, and Thalia González, "Girlhood Interrupted: The Erasure of Black Girls' Childhood," Washington, DC: Georgetown Law Center on Poverty and Inequality, 2017, 1. https://tinyurl.com/ycyareah.

12. Jamila J. Blake and Rebecca Epstein, "Listening to Black Women and Girls: Lived Experiences of Adultification Bias," Washington, DC: Georgetown Law Center on Poverty and Inequality, 2019, 2. https://tinyurl.com/3t58wvsy.

13. Blake and Epstein, "Listening to Black Women and Girls," 4.

14. Jennifer Wriggins, "Rape, Racism, and the Law," *Harvard Women's Law Journal* 6 (1983), 119–20. https://tinyurl.com/yc2f7xav.

15. Wriggins, "Rape, Racism, and the Law," 121.

16. Vincent Woodward, *The Delectable Negro* (New York: New York University Press, 2014), 22.

17. Woodward, *Delectable Negro*, 22.

18. Charles W. Mills, *The Racial Contract* (Ithaca, NY: Cornell University Press, 2014), 26.

19. Mills, *Racial Contract*, 26.

20. Mills, *Racial Contract*, 27.

4. Productivity

1. Elizabeth Lopatto, "How r/WallStreetBets Gamed the Stock of GameStop," *The Verge,* January 27, 2021. https://tinyurl.com/3eyyvcky.

2. Lopatto, "How r/WallStreetBets Gamed the Stock of GameStop."

3. Scott Galloway (@profgalloway), "What Happened Here," Twitter thread, January 27, 2020. https://tinyurl.com/2tfprh4f.

4. Kate Julian, "Why Are Young People Having So Little Sex?" *The Atlantic,* December 2018. https://tinyurl.com/mrxjr6rf.

5. Jean M. Twenge, "Possible Reasons US Adults Are Not Having Sex as Much as They Used To," JAMA Network Open, June 12, 2020. https://tinyurl.com/2p9barap.

6. Julian, "Why Are Young People Having So Little Sex?"

7   Julian, "Why Are Young People Having So Little Sex?"

8. Julie Vadnal, "The Millennial Sex Recession Is Bullsh*t," *Cosmopolitan*, June 11, 2019. https://tinyurl.com/y2mvkae2.

9. Vadnal, "Millennial Sex Recession."

10. Jake Novak, "America's Sex Recession Could Lead to an Economic Depression," CNBC, October 30, 2019. https://tinyurl.com/2p8ajy29.

11. Novak, "America's Sex Recession."

12. Novak, "America's Sex Recession."

13. Elizabeth Freeman, *Time Binds: Queer Temporalities, Queer Histories* (Durham, NC: Duke University Press, 2010), 3.

14. Novak, "America's Sex Recession."

15. Dana Luciano, *Arranging Grief: Sacred Time and the Body in Nineteenth-Century America* (New York: New York University Press, 2007), 9.

16. Freeman, *Time Binds,* 4.

17. Freeman, *Time Binds,* 5.

18. Peter Coy, "Americans Aren't Making Babies, and That's Bad for the Economy," Bloomberg, July 29, 2020. https://tinyurl.com/re4bmpuf.

19. Melissa S. Kearney and Phillip Levine, "Half a Million Fewer Children? The Coming COVID Baby Bust," Brookings, June 15, 2020. https://tinyurl.com/2p9ans4u.

20. Noah Pransky, "There's No Coronavirus Baby Boom—It's More Like a Baby Bust," NBCLX, January 25, 2021. https://tinyurl.com/383x7jz2.

21. CBS News, "Experts Sound the Alarm on Declining Birth Rates among Younger Generations: 'It's a Crisis,'" CBS News, March 3, 2021. https://tinyurl.com/289fryj8.

22. Pransky, "There's No Coronavirus Baby Boom."

23. Safeeyah Kazi, "WHO Telling 'Women of Childbearing Age' Not to Drink Is Likened to *Handmaid's Tale*," *Newsweek*, June 17, 2021. https://tinyurl.com/mpjdhspv.

24. Nina Martin, "The New U.S. Maternal Mortality Rate Fails to Capture Many Deaths," ProPublica, February 13, 2020. https://tinyurl.com/yuztcxdm.

25. Terry Gross, "Pandemic Makes Evident 'Grotesque' Gender Inequality in Household Work," NPR, May 21, 2020. https://tinyurl.com/yckut4xj.

26. Yekaterina Chzhen, Anna Gromada, and Gwyther Rees, "Are the World's Richest Countries Family Friendly?: Policy in the OECD and EU," UNICEF Family-Friendly Policy Report, 2019.

27. Jocelyn Frye, "On the Frontlines at Work and at Home: The Disproportionate Economic Effects of the Coronavirus Pandemic on Women of Color," Center for American Progress, April 23, 2020. https://tinyurl.com/mr3hp79z.

28. William Johnson, Anna Milewski, Katie Martin, and Elianna Clayton, "Understanding Variation in Spending on Childbirth among the Commercially Insured," Health Care Cost Institute, May 13, 2020. https://tinyurl.com/2p8rhm4z.

29. Jennifer Rosner, "Op-Ed: Post-pandemic, Some Millennials Finally Decide to Start #adulting," *Chicago Tribune,* April 16, 2021. https://tinyurl.com/26n3fef9.

30. George Peter Murdock, *Social Structure* (New York: Macmillan, 1949), 1.

31. Roderick Ferguson, *Aberrations in Black: Toward a Queer of Color Critique* (Minneapolis: University of Minnesota Press, 2004), 188.

32. Benjamin Fearnow, "Millennials Control Just 4.2 Percent of US Wealth, 4 Times Poorer than Baby Boomers Were at Age 34," *Newsweek,* October 8, 2020. https://tinyurl.com/yc4tbaut.

33. Erik Sherman, "Median Wealth of Black and Latino Families Could Hit Zero by the Middle of the Century," *Forbes,* September 11, 2017. https://tinyurl.com/yypfasay.

34. Charles W. Mills, *The Racial Contract* (Ithaca, NY: Cornell University Press, 2014), 45.

35. Sean Illing, "Why Are Millennials Burned Out? Capitalism," *Vox,* March 16, 2019. https://tinyurl.com/2p88by8a.

36. Juliana Kaplan, "Workers Lost $3.7 Trillion in Earnings during the Pandemic. Women and Gen Z Saw the Biggest Losses," *Business Insider,* January 25, 2021. https://tinyurl.com/yck2vj39.

37. Esmé Berkhout, Nick Galasso, Max Lawson, Pablo Andrés Rivero Morales, Anjela Taneja, and Diego Alejo Vázquez Pimentel, "The Inequality Virus," Oxfam International Report, 2021, 10.

38. Illing, "Why Are Millennials Burned Out?"

5. Desire

1. Dana Densmore, "Independence from the Sexual Revolution," in *Radical Feminism*, edited by Anne Koedt, Ellen Levine, and Anita Rapone (New York: Quadrangle, 1973), 58.

2. Sari M. van Anders, Debby Herbenick, Lori A. Brotto, Emily A. Harris, and Sara B. Chadwick, "The Heteronormativity Theory of Low Sexual Desire in Women Partnered with Men," *Archives of Sexual Behavior* 2021, 2. doi:10.1007/s10508-021-02100-x.

3. Peter Ueda, Catherine H. Mercer, and Cyrus Ghaznavi, "Trends in Frequency of Sexual Activity and Number of Sexual Partners among Adults Aged 18 to 44 Years in the US, 2000–2018," JAMA Network Open, June 12, 2020. https://tinyurl.com/ycku5bx7.

4. Jennifer Yurkiw and Matthew D. Johnson, "Perceived Stress, Supportive Dyadic Coping, and Sexual Communication in Couples," *Journal of Social and Personal Relationships* 38:5 (May 2021), 1729–37. doi:10.1177/0265407521996446.

5. "Diagnostic Criteria for 302.71 Hypoactive Sexual Desire Disorder," BehaveNet, n.d. https://tinyurl.com/584m2v5z.

6. American Psychiatric Association, *Diagnostic and Statistical Manual of Mental Disorders, Fifth Edition* (Arlington, VA: American Psychiatric Association, 2013), 434.

7. *DSM-5*, 443.

8. Harry Holt and Jeffrey Tingen, "Flibanserin (Addyi) for Hypoactive Sexual Desire Disorder in Premenopausal Women," *American Family Physician Journal* 93:10 (May 15, 2016), 826–28. www.aafp.org/afp/2016/0515/p826.html.

9. Gabrielle Paiella, "Surprising Absolutely Nobody, Insurance Companies Are Not Covering 'Female Viagra,'" The Cut, June 29, 2016. https://tinyurl.com/23cn6c7d.

10. Jennifer Block and Liz Canner, "The 'Grassroots Campaign' for 'Female Viagra' Was Actually Funded by Its Manufacturer," The Cut, September 8, 2016. https://tinyurl.com/2p934vdm.

11. Steven Woloshin and Lisa M. Schwartz, "US Food and Drug Administration Approval of Flibanserin: Even the Score Does Not Add Up," *JAMA Internal Medicine* 176:4 (April 2016), 439. doi:10.1001/jamainternmed.2016.0073.

12. Block and Canner, "The 'Grassroots Campaign' for 'Female Viagra.'"

13. Hylton V. Joffe, Christina Chang, Catherine Sewell, Olivia Easley, Christine Nguyen, Somya Dunn, Kimberly Lehrfeld, et al., "FDA Approval of Flibanserin—Treating Hypoactive Sexual Desire Disorder," *The New England Journal of Medicine* 374 (January 14, 2016), 101–4. doi:10.1056/NEJMp1513686.

14. Holt and Tingen, "Flibanserin (Addyi)."

15. van Anders et al., "Heteronormativity Theory," 2.

16. Jessica Firger, "For Asexual Community, Flibanserin Is a Bitter Pill to Swallow," *Newsweek,* August 20, 2015. https://tinyurl.com/yc489htz.

17. UCLA School of Law Williams Institute, "1.7% of Sexual Minority Adults Identify as Asexual," press release, August 8, 2019. https://tinyurl.com/bdd9z5ky.

18. Keith A. Montgomery, "Sexual Desire Disorders," *Psychiatry (Edgmont)* 5:6 (June 2008), 50–55. https://tinyurl.com/2p8w7v6f.

19. Jeanderson Soares and Grayce Alencar, "Asexuality: Dysfunction or Sexual Orientation?" *Reproductive System & Sexual Disorders* 5:3 (2016), 1. doi:10.4172/2161-038X.1000185.

20. Emily Nagoski, *Come as You Are: The Surprising New Science That Will Transform Your Sex Life,* revised and updated (New York: Simon & Schuster, 2021), 232.

21. Nagoski, *Come as You Are,* 271.

22. Nagoski, *Come as You Are,* 349.

23. Nagoski, *Come as You Are,* 240.

24. David Rowland and Brittany R. Gutierrez, "Phases of the Sexual Response Cycle," *Psychology Faculty Publications* 62, (2017), 2. https://scholar.valpo.edu/psych_fac_pub/62.

25. Rowland and Gutierrez, "Phases of the Sexual Response Cycle," 2.

26. Waguih William IsHak, Albert Mikhail, S. Rod Amiri, Laura A. C. Berman, and Monisha Vasa, "Sexual Dysfunction," *Journal of Lifelong Learning in Psychiatry* III:4 (2005), 520. doi:10.1176/foc.3.4.520.

27. van Anders et al., "Heteronormativity Theory," 8.
28. van Anders et al., "Heteronormativity Theory," 4.
29. UK Government Equalities Office, "Research Report," National LGBT Survey, July 3, 2018, 83. https://tinyurl.com/2p8s5zff.
30. UK Government Equalities Office, "Research Report," 83.
31. Myra T. Johnson, "Asexual and Autoerotic Women: Two Invisible Groups," in *The Sexually Oppressed,* edited by Jean Gochros and Harvey Gochros (New York: Association Press, 1977), 99.
32. Johnson, "Asexual and Autoerotic Women," 99.
33. Johnson, "Asexual and Autoerotic Women," 99.
34. Johnson, "Asexual and Autoerotic Women," 101.
35. Johnson, "Asexual and Autoerotic Women," 99.
36. Johnson, "Asexual and Autoerotic Women," 101.
37. Johnson, "Asexual and Autoerotic Women," 102.
38. Johnson, "Asexual and Autoerotic Women," 107.

6. Frigidity

1. William Josephus Robinson, *Married Life and Happiness or, Love and Comfort in Marriage* (New York: Eugenics Publishing Co., 1922), 84.
2. Peter Cryle and Alison Moore, *Frigidity: An Intellectual History* (London: Palgrave Macmillan UK, 2011), 22.
3. Cryle and Moore, *Frigidity,* 25.
4. Cryle and Moore, *Frigidity,* 27.
5. Cryle and Moore, *Frigidity,* 29.
6. Cryle and Moore, *Frigidity,* 28.
7. Cryle and Moore, *Frigidity,* 30.
8. Cryle and Moore, *Frigidity,* 30.
9. Cryle and Moore, *Frigidity,* 30–31.
10. Cryle and Moore, *Frigidity,* 42.
11. Cryle and Moore, *Frigidity,* 61.
12. Cryle and Moore, *Frigidity,* 64.
13. Cryle and Moore, *Frigidity,* 65.
14. Cryle and Moore, *Frigidity,* 179–80.

15. Cryle and Moore, *Frigidity*, 59.

16. Cryle and Moore, *Frigidity*, 59.

17. Cryle and Moore, *Frigidity*, 58.

18. Cryle and Moore, *Frigidity*, 58.

19. Cryle and Moore, *Frigidity*, 57.

20. Emily Nagoski, *Come as You Are: The Surprising New Science That Will Transform Your Sex Life,* revised and updated (New York: Simon & Schuster, 2021), 271.

21. Nagoski, *Come as You Are*, 14.

22. Cryle and Moore, *Frigidity*, 56.

23. Cryle and Moore, *Frigidity*, 171.

24. Cryle and Moore, *Frigidity*, 171.

25. Tommy Dickinson, *"Curing Queers": Mental Nurses and Their Patients, 1935–74* (Manchester, UK: Manchester University Press, 2015), 20.

26. Cryle and Moore, *Frigidity*, 66.

27. Cryle and Moore, *Frigidity*, 116.

28. Cryle and Moore, *Frigidity*, 120.

29. Cryle and Moore, *Frigidity*, 121–22.

30. Cryle and Moore, *Frigidity*, 123.

31. Cryle and Moore, *Frigidity*, 124.

32. Cryle and Moore, *Frigidity*, 125.

33. Cryle and Moore, *Frigidity*, 126.

34. Cryle and Moore, *Frigidity*, 126.

35. Cryle and Moore, *Frigidity*, 130.

36. Cryle and Moore, *Frigidity*, 131.

37. Wilhelm Stekel, *Frigidity in Women in Relation to Her Love Life* (New York: Liveright Publishing, 1926). 31.

38. Cryle and Moore, *Frigidity*, 221.

39. Cryle and Moore, *Frigidity*, 221.

40. Cryle and Moore, *Frigidity*, 221.

41. Cryle and Moore, *Frigidity*, 221.

42. Cryle and Moore, *Frigidity*, 213.

43. Siobhan B. Somerville, *Queering the Color Line: Race and the Invention of Homosexuality in American Culture* (Durham, NC: Duke University Press, 2000), 31.

44. Cryle and Moore, *Frigidity*, 255.

45. Cryle and Moore, *Frigidity*, 254.

7. Unfit

1. Gail Bederman, *Manliness and Civilization: A Cultural History of Gender and Race in the United States, 1880–1917* (Chicago: University of Chicago Press, 1995), 23.

2. Bederman, *Manliness and Civilization*, 25.

3. Monique Wittig, *The Straight Mind and Other Essays* (Boston: Beacon Press, 1992), 55.

4. Wittig, *Straight Mind*, 54.

5. Wittig, *Straight Mind*, 57.

6. Bederman, *Manliness and Civilization*, 25.

7. Sarah Haley, *No Mercy Here: Gender, Punishment, and the Making of Jim Crow Modernity* (Chapel Hill, NC: University of North Carolina Press, 2016), 8.

8. Haley, *No Mercy Here*, 21.

9. Haley, *No Mercy Here*, 21.

10. Zakiyyah Iman Jackson, *Becoming Human: Matter and Meaning in an Antiblack World* (New York: New York University Press, 2020), 8.

11. Vikky Storm and Eme Flores, *The Gender Accelerationist Manifesto*, independently published, 2019, 11.

12. Storm and Flores, *Gender Accelerationist Manifesto*, 3.

13. Storm and Flores, *Gender Accelerationist Manifesto*, 7.

14. Wittig, *Straight Mind*, 57.

15. Wittig, *Straight Mind*, 54.

16. Donna Penn, "The Sexualized Woman: The Lesbian, the Prostitute, and the Containment of Female Sexuality in Postwar America," in *Not June Cleaver: Women and Gender in Postwar America, 1946–1960*, edited by Joanne Meyerowitz (Philadelphia: Temple University Press, 1994), 359.

17. Correa Moylan Walsh, *Feminism* (New York: Sturgis & Walton, 1917), 371.

18. Walsh, *Feminism,* 371.

19. Walsh, *Feminism,* 371–72.

20. Walsh, *Feminism,* 25.

21. John Lionel Tayler, "An Interrogatory Note on the Franchise of Women," *The Westminster Review* 167:1 (1907), 456–57.

22. Tayler, "Interrogatory Note," 457.

23. Tayler, "Interrogatory Note," 457.

24. Adrienne Rich, "Compulsory Heterosexuality and Lesbian Existence (1980)," *Journal of Women's History* 15:3 (2003), 11. doi:10.1353/jowh.2003.0079.

25. Rich, "Compulsory Heterosexuality," 13.

26. Rich, "Compulsory Heterosexuality," 13.

27. Janice Raymond, *The Transsexual Empire: The Making of the She-Male* (Boston: Beacon Press, 1979), 104.

28. Raymond, *Transsexual Empire,* 104.

29. Rich, "Compulsory Heterosexuality," 15.

30. Rich, "Compulsory Heterosexuality," 17.

31. Rich, "Compulsory Heterosexuality," 21.

32. Rich, "Compulsory Heterosexuality," 18.

33. Rich, "Compulsory Heterosexuality," 20.

34. Rich, "Compulsory Heterosexuality," 20.

35. Rich, "Compulsory Heterosexuality," 27.

36. Jackson, *Becoming Human,* 14.

8. Unhuman

1. Ian Fleming, *From Russia with Love* (1957, repr. Las Vegas, NV: Thomas & Mercer, 2012), 35.

2. Fleming, *From Russia with Love,* 12.

3. Fleming, *From Russia with Love,* 8.

4. Fleming, *From Russia with Love,* 9.

5. Ian Fleming, *Goldfinger* (1958, repr. Las Vegas, NV: Thomas & Mercer, 2012), 25.

6. Ian Fleming, *Thunderball* (1961, repr. Las Vegas, NV: Thomas & Mercer, 2012), 49.

7. *Thunderball,* motion picture, directed by Terence Young (United Artists, 1965), 1:12:36.

8. TV Tropes, s.v. "Villainous Aromantic Asexual," n.d. https://tinyurl .com/266dvy5n.

9. *Sherlock,* BBC television series, directed by Nick Hurran, 2014, season 3, episode 4, "His Last Vow."

10. Arthur Conan Doyle, *The Original Illustrated Sherlock Holmes* (Edison, NJ: Castle Books, 1976), 11. "A Scandal in Bohemia" first published 1888.

11. Nick Haslam, "Dehumanization: An Integrative Review," *Personality and Social Psychology Review* 10:3 (2006), 256. doi:10.1207/s15327957pspr1003_4.

12. Haslam, "Dehumanization," 256.

13. Cara C. MacInnis and Gordon Hodson, "Intergroup Bias toward 'Group X': Evidence of Prejudice, Dehumanization, Avoidance, and Discrimination against Asexuals," *Group Processes & Intergroup Relations* 15:6 (2012), 728. doi:10.1177/1368430212442419.

14. MacInnis and Hodson, "Intergroup Bias toward 'Group X,'" 728–29.

15. Jeanderson Soares and Grayce Alencar, "Asexuality: Dysfunction or Sexual Orientation?" *Reproductive System & Sexual Disorders* 5:3 (2016), 1. doi:10.4172/2161-038X.1000185.

16. Haslam, "Dehumanization," 256.

17. Haslam, "Dehumanization," 256.

18. *Selah and the Spades,* motion picture, directed by Tayarisha Poe (Amazon Studios, 2020), 0:19:19. https://tinyurl.com/4k74xahk.

19. *Selah and the Spades,* 1:28:43.

20. Sylvia Wynter, "No Humans Involved: An Open Letter to My Colleagues," *Forum N.H.I.: Knowledge for the 21st Century* 1:1 (1994), 42.

21. Stephen Ceasar, "LAPD Believes 'Grim Sleeper' Serial Killer Never Actually Slept," *Los Angeles Times,* May 8, 2016. https://tinyurl.com/2p9ewhcy.

22. Zachary Wigon, "The LAPD Didn't Catch an Alleged Serial Killer for 30 Years. Is It Because the Victims Were Black?" *Vanity Fair,* December 18, 2014. https://tinyurl.com/58bc7pem.

23. Encyclopaedia Britannica, s.v. "Three-fifths compromise," n.d. https://tinyurl.com/yckcntdj.

24. David Thomas Konig, "The Long Road to Dred Scott: Personhood and the Rule of Law in the Trial Court Records of St. Louis Slave Freedom Suits," *UMKC Law Review* 75:1 (2006), 55.

25. Zakiyyah Iman Jackson, *Becoming Human: Matter and Meaning in an Antiblack World* (New York: New York University Press, 2020), 5.

26. Frantz Fanon, *Black Skin, White Masks* (London: Pluto Press, 1986), 165.

27. Fanon, *Black Skin,* 169–70.

28. Jackson, *Becoming Human,* 9–10.

29. Jackson, *Becoming Human,* 4.

9. Utility

1. Noelle Perdue, "How Porn's Racist Metadata Hurts Adult Performers of Color," *Wired,* April 28, 2021. https://tinyurl.com/yckpvumt.

2. Mireille Miller-Young and Xavier Livermon, "Black Stud, White Desire: Black Masculinity in Cuckold Pornography and Sex Work," *Black Sexual Economies: Race and Sex in a Culture of Capital,* edited by Adrienne D. Davis and The BSE Collective (Urbana, IL: University of Illinois Press, 2019), 79.

3. Gail Dines and Carolyn M. West, "White Girl Moans Black Lives Matter," Slate, July 9, 2020. https://tinyurl.com/5n8de9rx.

4. Miller-Young and Livermon, "Black Stud," 77.

5. William Lee Howard, "The Negro as a Distinct Ethnic Factor in Civilization," *Medicine IX* (1903), 424–25.

6. Jennifer Wriggins, "Rape, Racism, and the Law," *Rape and Society, Harvard Women's Law Journal* 6 (1983), 108. https://tinyurl.com/yc2f7xav.

7. Miller-Young and Livermon, "Black Stud," 79.

8. Miller-Young and Livermon, "Black Stud," 80.

9. Pornhub, "Pornhub Stands in Solidarity against Racism and Social Injustice," Twitter, May 30, 2020. https://tinyurl.com/msj8v7mk.

10. Dines and West, "White Girl Moans."

11. Kenya Evelyn, "How Black Voters Lifted Georgia Democrats to Senate Runoff Victories," *The Guardian*, January 7, 2021. https://tinyurl.com/4e2c5e4y.

12. Ianna Hawkins Owen, "On the Racialization of Asexuality," in *Asexualities: Feminist and Queer Perspectives*, edited by K. J. Cerankowski and Megan Milks (London: Routledge, 2016), 122.

13. Owen, "On the Racialization of Asexuality," 121.

14. Owen, "On the Racialization of Asexuality," 122.

15. Owen, "On the Racialization of Asexuality," 122.

16. Owen, "On the Racialization of Asexuality," 121.

17. Charles W. Mills, *The Racial Contract* (Ithaca, NY: Cornell University Press, 2014), 27.

18. Owen, "On the Racialization of Asexuality," 121.

19. Owen, "On the Racialization of Asexuality," 121–22.

20. Owen, "On the Racialization of Asexuality," 124.

21. Owen, "On the Racialization of Asexuality," 124–25.

22. Owen, "On the Racialization of Asexuality," 123.

23. Owen, "On the Racialization of Asexuality," 123.

24. Nicole Carr, "Misreading Mammy: Towards a Sexual Revolution of Contemporary/Third Wave Black Feminisms," PhD dissertation, University of Miami, 2016, 21.

25. Carr, "Misreading Mammy," 4.

26. Carr, "Misreading Mammy," 46.

27. Carr, "Misreading Mammy," 28.

28. Carr, "Misreading Mammy," 33.

29. Carr, "Misreading Mammy," 6.

30. Carr, "Misreading Mammy," 7.

31. Carr, "Misreading Mammy," 7.

32. Carr, "Misreading Mammy," 11.

33. Carr, "Misreading Mammy," 48.

34. Carr, "Misreading Mammy," 33.

35. Carr, "Misreading Mammy," 34.

10. Refusal

1. Arnold Rampersad, *The Life of Langston Hughes, Volume II: 1941–1967, I Dream a World,* 2nd ed. (New York: Oxford University Press, 2002), 335–36.

2. Hilton Als, "The Elusive Langston Hughes," *The New Yorker,* February 16, 2015. https://tinyurl.com/yxazvyek.

3. Scott Harris, "Battle Lines: Use of Hughes Poem on Gay History Poster Ignites Furor," *Los Angeles Times,* June 13, 1991. https://tinyurl.com/c5xwk7aj.

4. Rampersad, *Life of Langston Hughes,* 149.

5. Rampersad, *Life of Langston Hughes,* 335.

6. Rampersad, *Life of Langston Hughes,* 337.

7. Harris, "Battle Lines."

8. David Streitfeld, "A Life Apart," *The Washington Post,* July 9, 1995. https://tinyurl.com/27y3tem7.

9. Stephen Maglott, "Octavia Butler," National Black Justice Coalition, 2017. https://tinyurl.com/y8kanapk.

10. Ron Buckmire, "'Kindred' Spirit Remembered," *Buckmire Blog,* February 28, 2006. https://tinyurl.com/2p9n5b5w.

11. Kodwo Eshun, "Octavia Butler Obituary," *The Guardian,* March 15, 2006. https://tinyurl.com/bdf6m2um.

12. Terrance Heath, "This Black Lesbian Became a Giant in Her Field No Matter What Her Critics Threw at Her," LGBTQ Nation, February 20, 2019. https://tinyurl.com/5x64h83t.

13. Larry McCaffery and Jim McMenamin, *Conversations with Octavia Butler,* edited by Consuela Francis (Jackson, MS: University Press of Mississippi, 2010), 14.

14. Joshunda Sanders, "Interview with Octavia Butler," *In Motion Magazine,* March 14, 2004. https://tinyurl.com/zuezsym9.

15. Streitfeld, "A Life Apart."

16. Octavia E. Butler, "Octavia E. Butler Papers (1969–1974)," San Marino, CA: Huntington Library, 928.

17. Octavia E. Butler, "Octavia E. Butler Papers (1978–1979)," San Marino, CA: Huntington Library, 3218.

18. Bella DePaulo, "Single at Heart: The World's Most Joyful and Unapologetic Single People," Medium, December 17, 2020. https://tinyurl.com/yc5t3ady.
19. Sanders, "Interview with Octavia Butler."
20. Lincoln Michel, "Read Octavia E. Butler's Inspiring Message to Herself," Electric Lit, February 2, 2016. https://tinyurl.com/4csx8k7r.
21. Bella DePaulo, "Why Coupling Is No Longer Compulsory," *Psychology Today,* February 20, 2021. https://tinyurl.com/yjr3akfz.

11. Histories

1. James Teller, *Doctor Teller's Pocket Companion, or Marriage Guide* (Albany, NY: published for the author, 1855), 5.
2. Teller, *Doctor Teller's Pocket Companion,* 5–6.
3. Robert Deam Tobin, *Peripheral Desires: The German Discovery of Sex* (Philadelphia: University of Pennsylvania Press, 2015), 122.
4. Ralph M. Leck, *Vita Sexualis: Karl Ulrichs and the Origins of Sexual Science* (Chicago: University of Illinois Press, 2016), 71.
5. Magnus Hirschfeld, *Sappho und Sokrates* (Magdeburg, Germany: M. Sophr, 1896), 6.
6. Hirschfeld, *Sappho und Sokrates,* 18.
7. Christiane Leidinger, "Emma Trosse (1863–1949), verheiratete Külz," *District of Ahrweiler Yearbook* (Monschau, Germany: Monschau Weiss-Druck, 2012), 197.
8. Christiane, Leidinger, "Transgressions—Forays through the Life and Work of Emma Trosse (1863–1949)," *Invertito,* May 7, 2013. https://tinyurl.com/43br7h6h.
9. Richard Freiherr von Krafft-Ebing, *Psychopathia Sexualis: With Especial Reference to the Antipathic Sexual Instinct, a Medico-Forensic Study* (New York: Rebman, 1906), 1–2.
10. Jonathan Ned Katz, "Carl Schlegel: The First U.S. Gay Activist, 1906–1907," Out History, June 1, 2019. https://tinyurl.com/h6j5upuv.
11. John Lionel Tayler, "An Interrogatory Note on the Franchise of Women," *The Westminster Review* 167:1 (1907), 475.

12. Ulrike May, *Freud at Work: On the History of Psychoanalytic Theory and Practice, with an Analysis of Freud's Patient Record Books* (London: Routledge, 2018), 21.

13. Magnus Hirschfeld, *The Homosexuality of Men and Women,* translated by Michael A. Lombardi-Nash (Amherst, NY: Prometheus Books, 2000), 285.

14. William A. White, *Outlines of Psychiatry* (New York: Journal of Nervous and Mental Disease Publishing Co., 1908), 220.

15. Hirschfeld, *Homosexuality of Men and Women,* 739.

16. Hirschfeld, *Homosexuality of Men and Women,* 285.

17. New York State Hospital Commission, *State Hospital Bulletin* VII:1 (1914), 344.

18. Correa Moylan Walsh, *Feminism* (New York: Sturgis & Walton, 1917), 371.

19. Ralph Werther, *The Female-Impersonators* (New York: Medico-Legal Journal, 1922), 14.

20. Werther, *Female-Impersonators,* 15.

21. Werther, *Female-Impersonators,* 149.

22. Werther, *Female-Impersonators,* 14.

23. Werther, *Female-Impersonators,* 46.

24. Wilhelm Stekel, *Frigidity in Woman in Relation to Her Love Life* (New York: Boni and Liveright, 1926), 64.

25. Magnus Hirschfeld, *Sexual Anomalies and Perversions: Physical and Psychological Development and Treatment* (London: Francis Aldor, 1966), 197.

26. Alfred Kinsey, *Sexual Behavior in the Human Male* (Philadelphia: W. B. Saunders, 1948), 658.

27. Alfred Kinsey, *Sexual Behavior in the Human Female* (Philadelphia: W. B. Saunders, 1953), 472.

28. Kinsey, *Sexual Behavior in the Human Female,* 474.

29. Michael Waters, "Finding Asexuality in the Archives," Slate, March 6, 2020 https://tinyurl.com/3kmp789s.

30. Supreme Court of the United States, *Richard A. Inman* v. *City of Miami Writ of Certiorari,* 1967, 9.

31. Anton Szandor LaVey, *The Satanic Bible* (New York: Avon Books, 1969), 70.

32. Waters, "Finding Asexuality in the Archives."

33. Mike Cahlin, "Gay Front Seeks Campus Recognition," *The Independent Florida Alligator,* January 13, 1971.

34. Tony Ortega, "Asexuals Have Problems Too!" *The Village Voice,* November 22, 2010. https://tinyurl.com/3yaj3r7k.

35. Susan Rennie, "Late Copy," *off our backs* 3:6 (1973), 7.

36. Frances Chapman, "Your Own Label," *off our backs* 3:5 (1973), 6.

37. Julie Kliegman, "How Zines Paved the Way for Asexual Recognition," Them, November 6, 2019. www.them.us/story/asexual-zines.

38. Waters, "Finding Asexuality in the Archives."

39. Michael D. Storms, "Theories of Sexual Orientation," *Journal of Personality and Social Psychology* 38:5 (1980), 783–92. doi:10.1037/0022-3514.38.5.783.

40. Catherine Kobaly, "Letter to *Heresies,*" *Heresies,* 4:1 (1981), 94.

41. Paula Nurius, "Mental Health Implications of Sexual Orientation," *Journal of Sex Research* 19:2 (May 1983), 119–36. doi:10.1080/00224498309551174.

42. John Dececco and Michael Shively, *Origins of Sexuality and Homosexuality* (New York: Routledge, 1985), 87.

43. Ray Blanchard, "The Classification and Labeling of Nonhomosexual Gender Dysphorias," *Archives of Sexual Behavior* 18:4 (1989), 316–17. doi:10.1007/BF01541951. See also Ray Blanchard, "The Concept of Autogynephilia and the Typology of Male Gender Dysphoria," *Journal of Nervous and Mental Disease* 177:10 (October 1989), 616–23. doi:10.1097/00005053-198910000-00004.

44. *The Alyson Almanac: A Treasury of Information for the Gay and Lesbian Community* (Boston: Alyson, 1989), 89.

45. "A Dictionary of Slang and Historical Terms," *Alyson Women's Book Catalog,* January–March 1994, 11. https://tinyurl.com/ycknn9xh.

46. Esther D. Rothblum and Kathleen A. Brehony, *Boston Marriages: Romantic but Asexual Relationships among Contemporary Lesbians* (Amherst, MA: University of Massachusetts Press, 1993).

47. Zoe O'Reilly, "My Life as an Amoeba," *StarNet Dispatches,* May 30, 1997. https://tinyurl.com/3m26wp24.

48. New York Attorney General, "The Sexual Orientation Non-discrimination Act, 'SONDA,'" 2002. https://tinyurl.com/mpedfcju.

49. Anthony F. Bogaert, "Asexuality: Prevalence and Associated Factors in a National Probability Sample," *Journal of Sex Research* 41:3 (2004), 279. doi:10.1080/00224490409552235.

50. Anthony F. Bogaert, "Toward a Conceptual Understanding of Asexuality," *Review of General Psychology* 10:3 (2006), 241. doi:10.1037/1089-2680 .10.3.241.

51. Angela Tucker, director, *(A)sexual,* 2011.

52. GLAAD, "A Is for Asexual, Agender, Aromantic," GLAAD, February 11, 2015. https://tinyurl.com/2p8drf62.

53. Henry Tran, "SFU Becomes First University to Offer Asexuality Studies," *The Peak,* February 6, 2018. https://tinyurl.com/2d4zh6mh. See also Ela Przybylo, *Asexual Erotics: Intimate Readings of Compulsory Sexuality* (Columbus, OH: Ohio State University Press, 2019).

12. Possibilities

1. Morag A. Yule, Lori A. Brotto, and Boris B. Gorzalka, "Biological Markers of Asexuality: Handedness, Birth Order, and Finger Length Ratios in Self-Identified Asexual Men and Women," *Archives of Sexual Behavior* 43:2 (2014), 299. doi:10.1007/s10508-013-0175-0.

2. Merriam-Webster, "The Left Hand of (Supposed) Darkness," n.d. https://tinyurl.com/2p8fu4tv.

3. Wendell Johnson and Lucile Duke, "Changes in Handedness Associated with Onset or Disappearance of Stuttering," *The Journal of Experimental Education* 4:2 (2015), 112. doi:10.1080/00220973.1935.11010003.

4. Lisa Tracy, "On the Other Hand, Consider Who's Left," *Washington Post,* August 13, 1979. https://tinyurl.com/yckt63kh.

5. Sebastian Ocklenburg, "Are Left-Handers More Artistic than Right-Handers?" *Psychology Today,* June 10, 2019. https://tinyurl.com/2p857xw5.

6. Sara M. Scharoun and Pamela J. Bryden, "Hand Preference, Performance Abilities, and Hand Selection in Children," *Frontiers in Psychology* 5:82 (2014). doi:10.3389/fpsyg.2014.00082.

7. Lyle Matthew Kan and Andrew Wallace, "2018 Tracking Report: Lesbian, Gay, Bisexual, Transgender, and Queer Grantmaking by U.S. Foundations," Funders for LGBTQ Issues, March 30, 2020, 10.

8. Anthony F. Bogaert, "Asexuality: Prevalence and Associated Factors in a National Probability Sample," *Journal of Sex Research* 41:3 (2004), 279. doi:10.1080/00224490409552235.

9. Lily Smith, "UB Hosts a Presentation about the Combination of Asexual Studies and Critical Race Theory," [University at Buffalo, NY] *The Spectrum,* April 15, 2021. https://tinyurl.com/2jbf97ct.

10. Frances Chapman, "Your Own Label," *off our backs* 3:5 (1973), 6.

11. Lisa Orlando, "The Asexual Manifesto," Asexual Caucus/New York Radical Feminists, September 1972, 8. https://tinyurl.com/23bvxxb3.

Index

A

(A)sexual, 165

"A Form of the Human Sexual Drive Not Hitherto Observed" (Rohleder), 155

"A Scandal in Bohemia" (Doyle), 112

Aberrations in Black (Ferguson), 64

Aberrations in Black: Toward a Queer of Color Critique (Ferguson), 13

ableism, 81

Abrams, Stacey, 129

abstinence, queerphobia amidst, 33

abundance, 171, 175

abuse, 34, 80

Ace and Aro Advocacy Project (TAAAP), 166

ace people/asexual spectrum
    as "abnormal," 6
    affirmation of, 6–7
    anti-Black attitudes and, 13
    author's experience as, 43
    bias against, 25–26
    comfortable expression by, 176
    compound factors, 81–82
    concern trolling of, 80
    conversion therapy for, 78
    corrective rape of, 23
    defined, 2, 5
    dehumanization of, 112–113, 114
    demonization of, 69
    denial of, 23
    in the *DSM*, 70
    education on, 82
    as "emotionless," 25, 115–117
    "fixing" female, 80–81
    freedom to choose, 136
    as "frigid," 83, 92
    handedness and, 167, 168
    health warnings about, 152–153
    healthism/ableism and, 81
    historical references, 151–166
    invalidating queerness of, 29
    invisibility of, 6
    as "late bloomers," 25, 43–45, 49
    lens on cisheteropatriarchy, 10
    and the lesbian experience, 99, 105, 106
    liberation for, 150, 160, 171
    as "liminal," 45, 46
    microaggressions against, 27
    moral aversion to, 1
    myth of "insufficient" trauma for, 33
    as non "productive," 66
    Octavia Butler, 141–142, 144, 148, 150
    online appearance of, 163
    online dating by, 176
    pride flag, 164
    as queer, 4, 35–41
    right to exist, 149
    self-definition by, 6
    sex myths and, 3
    sexual autonomy for, 24, 32–33
    social denial of, 7–8
    as a spectrum, 5
    study of, 19
    trauma hierarchy myth and, 34–35
    understanding, 8, 176

ace people/asexual spectrum *(continued)*
  utility of, xi
  validity of, xii
  variety of experience for, 4–5
  as villains in fiction, 109–112, 114–117
  visibility of, 168
  white, 169
  willful misinterpretation of, 131
  women, 78–79
  See also Black asexuals
Ace Week, 164
acephobia
  and complicity in violence, 25
  and corrective rape, 22
  as dehumanizing, 25
  as epistemic injustice, 21
  and exclusion from queerness, 35–38
  fear inherent in, 24
  healthism as, 81
  misogyny as root of, 107
  roots of, 21–22
  singlism and, 26
  study of, 25, 26, 28
  trauma hierarchy myth and, 35
  white supremacy and, 13
activism, sexual/political factors of,
  128–130
Addyi/flibanserin, 70, 71, 72
adulthood
  for Black children, 50
  compulsory coupling and, 48
  heteronormative view of, 47, 49
  post-COVID "adulting," 63
  sex and entrance into, 46
adultification
  of Black girls, 22, 49–50
  of Black people, 52
aggression, lateral, 38
allosexuals/allosexuality
  ace experience as outside, 4
  defined, 2
  forced conversion to, 74–75
  humanity as defined by, 121–122
  impulse to "fix" aces, 22

  need for term, 20
  prejudice against asexuality, 20, 21
  sexual history review by, 24–25
Als, Hilton, 138
*The Alyson Almanac: A Treasury of
  Information for the Gay and Lesbian
  Community*, 162
"Americans Aren't Making Babies, and
  That's Bad for the Economy," 61
"An Interrogatory Note on the Franchise
  of Women" (Tayler), 101, 155
"analloeroticism," 162
anaphrodisia. *See* "frigidity"
"anaphrodites," 157
"anästhesia sexualis," 154
ancestors, invoking, 179
"animals"/animalism
  asexuals as, 25, 113
  Black people presumed as, 52, 106,
    118–120
  and the Black phallus, 125
  as dehumanizing, 112
"Anomalies of the Sexual Instinct"
  (White), 156
anti-Black attitudes
  and anxiety about deviance, 13
  attempted absolution from, 130
  Black asexuals vs., 16
  contradictions of, 52–53
  culture of, 9–10
  in the LAPD, 117
  misogynoir, 22, 107, 145, 146, 175
  myths informing, 2
  sexual stereotypes, 12, 120
  world stratification via, 15
Anzaldúa, Gloria, 39
aromantic people
  depicted as emotionless, 115–117
  Octavia Butler as, 141–142
  overlap with asexuality, 6
  as villains in fiction, 109–112
arousal, 85–86
  See also desire
"asensuality," 154

"Asexual and Autoerotic Women: Two Invisible Groups" (Johnson), 6, 78, 160

Asexual Awareness Week, 166

Asexual Community Census, 23

Asexual Goddess, 173

"The Asexual Manifesto" (Orlando), 5, 159, 171

Asexual Visibility and Education Network (AVEN), 163, 164

asexual women
    in the heteronormative system, 104
    as "masculine," 102
    threat to white men, 100–101

asexuality. *See* ace people/asexual spectrum

"Asexuality: Dysfunction or Sexual Orientation?," 75, 113

"Asexuality: Prevalence and Associated Factors in a National Probability Sample" (Bogaert), 164

"Asexuals Have Problems Too!" (*The Village Voice*), 159

The Atlantic, 57, 58

atony, 89

Attitudes Towards Asexuals (ATA), 26, 33

autoeroticism, 79

"automonosexualism," 155

autonomy, sexual
    allosexual misunderstanding of, 24
    for Black people, 52
    consent and, 7
    infantilization as denial of, 43–44
    vs. social expectation, 23, 136

aversions, personal, 1

B

Baars, Bernard, 17–18

Baartman, Sarah, 132

Bailey, Moya, 146

Baldwin, James, 13

Bambi-sexuality, 162

Barral, Georges, 86–87

Bathroom Bill of 2016, 32

Becoming Human: Matter and Meaning in an Antiblack World (Jackson), 98, 118

Bederman, Gail, 95, 97

behavior, social ideas as regulating, 7

bias/discrimination
    against ace people, 9, 26–28
    adultification of Black girls, 50
    epistemic injustice, 21
    intertwining, 34, 38–39
    against left-handedness, 167–168
    microaggressions as, 27–28
    misunderstanding and, 21
    against older virgins, 44
    singlism, 26
    trauma hierarchy myth and, 34–35

biological disposition, 114

biphobia, 38

birth rates, declining, 61

The Birth of a Nation (Griffith), 126

Black asexuals
    in the collective, xii
    dehumanization of, 120–121
    experience of pleasure for, 19
    freedom call to, 177–180
    historical narrative against, 12
    impossibility of, 53
    invisibility of, 173
    lack of representation for, 173
    liberation from white supremacy, 169–170
    marginalization of, 13
    stereotypes as uprooted by, 16
    as threat to white supremacy, 121
    and "utility," 11
    visibility of, 180

Black girls
    adultification of, 49–50
    rape of, 50–51
    in the South, 175

Black liberation, 124

Black Lives Matter porn, 128

Black men
    Black phallus fantasy, 123, 125–126
    social expectations of, 175

Black people
   bodies of, 15, 132
   childhood as denied to, 49–50, 51
   criminalized sex of, 119
   dehumanization of, 12, 118
   effect of COVID-19 on, 63
   family structure, 64
   financial issues, 64–65
   free (a)sexual life of, 177–180
   infantilization of, 51–52
   mortality and childbirth, 62
   myths about, 2
   objectification of Black bodies, 15
   presumed "savage" sexuality of, 10
   queer, 14, 15
   sex as weapon against, 11
   white consumption of, 130
   white hunger/desire for, 51–53
Black Sexual Politics: African Americans,
   Gender, and the New Racism
   (Collins), 10
Black sexuality
   cultural icons, 137–138
   and denial of consent, 11
   hypersexuality myth, 11, 13
   nonheteronormative, 13–14
   outside of colonial ideology, 12
   the phallus in, 125–126
   pornographic fixation on, 123–124
   and radical politics, 174–175
   as "savage," 10, 12
   white supremacist narrative of,
      11–12
   white supremacy as supported by, 133
Black Skin, White Masks (Fanon), 120
Black women
   abuse by white women, 133–135
   erasing sexuality of, 134–135
   gender binary and, 98–99, 107, 176
   incongruent narratives about, 132
   "masculinity" of, 143
   queer, 14–15
   sexual dichotomy about, 131
   trans, 32

BlackFreedomSex, 178, 179
Blackness
   asexuality and, xii, 11, 178
   and negation of consent, 11
   and self-determination, xii
   sexuality and, 11
Blanchard, Ray, 162
Blofeld, Ernst Stavro, 110
Bloomberg, 61
"bloomer," "late," 43, 45, 48
Bogaert, Anthony F., 164, 169
Bond series, 109–110
Boston Marriages: Romantic but Asexual
   Relationships among Contemporary
   Lesbians (Brehony and Rothblum), 163
boundaries
   gatekeeping and power, 37–38
   no-sex, 23–24
Brandi, 176
Brehony, Kathleen A., 163
Bréviaire de l'amour expérimental
   (Guyot), 86
Brookings, 61
Brooks, Sara Beth, 164
Brown, LaTosha, 129
Brown, Sherronda J., 16, 177, 179
Buckmire, Ron, 141
Bunt, Irma, 110
Butler, Octavia E., 137, 140, 141–149

C

Capitalism and Slavery (Williams), 46
capitalist system
   chronobiopolitics, 60
   chrononormativity and, 46–47
   compulsory sexuality and, 56–57, 59
   family expectation and, 61, 64
   labor exploitation, 65–66
   living conditions under, 62
   and lowered desire, 69–70
   and "productivity," 66–67
   shifting to life beyond, 180
Carr, Nicole, 133, 134
Carroll, Abigail, 46

Carter, Julian B., 46, 47
Cartwright, Samuel A., 51
Catholic Church, 84
celebrating the "impossibles," 177–180
Center for Healing Racial Trauma, 19
change, 19, 179, 180
Chapman, Frances, 171
chastity, 50–51
"childishness"
    lack of sex and, 43–44
    of nonwhite people, 47, 51–52
chronobiopolitics, 60, 66
chrononormativity
    and the Black experience, 51
    chronobiopolitics and, 60
    defined, 45
    economics of sex, 60
    as heteronormative, 47, 49
    Western expectation of, 47
"cis," need for term, 20
cisheteronormativity
    acephobia and, 28
    compulsory sexuality and, 9
    microaggressions and, 27
    orgasm gap and, 87
    as presumed ace experience, 35
    queerphobia and, 33
    violent projection of, 35–37
    virginity loss and, 45
cisheteropatriarchy
    ace as challenge to, 41
    "adulthood" as defined by, 49
    asexual lens on, 10
    black buck fantasy, 124–125
    Black life beyond white, 177–178
    childbirth and, 63
    chrononormative lens of, 47–48
    compulsory sexuality and, 9
    desire expectations under, 76
    disengaging with, 179
    failure to project, 149
    "frigidity" as affront to, 90
    lesbian response to, 105
    liberation from, 13, 171

"low" women's desire and, 77
    in the medical system, 77
    as product of whiteness, 15
    "productive" adulthood under, 66
    queerphobia and, 33, 97
    sexual pathologizing by, 93
    social coercion by, 105
    trauma hierarchy myth and, 34
    as white, 119
    white women's complicity with,
        133–135
    "woman"/"man" roles in, 95–97, 99
"civilization," 95, 97, 132
clitoral engagement, 87
closet, as a sanctum, 140
CNBC, 59, 60
Cohen, Cathy J., 9, 10, 62
Cohen, Philip, 61
Collection exclusive d'hygiène et de
    médecine (Riolan), 88
Collins, Patricia Hill, 10
colonial legacy/thought
    acephobia and, 28
    asexuality beyond, 178
    vs. Black queerness, 14, 15
    Black women and, 98–99
    excavating Black sexuality from, 12
    family mandates, 64
    free Black life beyond, 179
    heteronormative, 46–47
    liberation from, 171
    NHI (no humans involved), 118
    normative chronology, 46
    and sex as "human," 119
Come as You Are: The Surprising New
    Science That Will Transform Your Sex
    Life (Nagoski), 76
community
    ace/lesbian kinship, 107
    enemy of the queer, 39
    growth of ace, 168
    online ace, 163
    queer, 39, 40–41
compliance, heteronormative, 36

compulsory coupling, 48, 146
compulsory heterosexuality
 ace's inability to comply with, 35–36
 messages to women, 103
 questioning, 105
 social ramifications of, 104
"Compulsory Heterosexuality and
 Lesbian Existence" (Rich), 103
compulsory romance, 6
compulsory sexuality
 allosexual rethinking of, 24–25
 capitalism and, 57
 under cisheteropatriarchy, 93
 defined, 5, 7
 desire as "innate" in, 69, 121
 disengaging with, 179
 effect on marginalized people, 10
 ideas about queer relations, 30–31
 liberation from, 169, 172, 177–178
 pronatalism and, 62
 reproduction and, 67
 understanding, 74
 violence and, 8–9, 22
"Compulsory Sexuality: Evaluating an
 Emerging Concept" (Gupta), 7
concern trolling, 80, 81
consensual sex, 3
consent
 allosexual rethinking of, 24
 compulsory sexuality and, 9
 as denied to Black people, 11–12
 and "fixing" ace people, 23
 sexual autonomy and, 7
context-dependent desire, 76
continence, 152
control
 and "correcting" sex response, 83
 via sexual violence, 11
 white sexual, 121–122
 of women in the hetero system,
  97, 103
conversion therapy, 78, 80
Coronavirus Baby Bust, 61–62, 70
corrective rape, 22–23

Cosmo, 58
COVID-19 pandemic, 59, 61–62, 65
creativity, Black, 178
"Critical Nonsexualites," 165
Cryle, Peter, 84, 89, 90, 92
cuckolding, 124, 126, 127
@cyberlesbian, 105

D

de la Prade, Charles Dufaure, 86–87
*De sancto matrimonii sacramento dis
 putationum* (Sánchez), 84
death threats, 37
Dececco, John, 162
dehumanization
 of ace people in fiction, 111
 acephobia as, 25, 33, 120
 adultification of Black youth as, 50
 of the Black body, 15
 of Black people, 12, 118
 infantilization as, 43–44
 of Mammy, 135
 in online dating, 176
 opposing forms of, 120, 121–122
 two types of, 112
 via Black sexual stereotypes, 125
*The Delectable Negro: Human
 Consumption and Homoeroticism
 within U.S. Slave Culture* (Woodard),
 51, 52
Dell, Floyd, 47
demonization, of left-handedness, 167
Densmore, Dana, 68
DePaulo, Bella, 48, 144, 145
*Der Konträrsexualismus in Bezug auf Ehe
 und Frauenfrage* (Trosse), 153
desirability politics, 57
desire
 among nonwhite people, 91
 asexual, 170–171
 and Black consent, 12
 for Black flesh, 51–53
 distress about lack of, 72–73
 "frigidity" as malfunction of, 90

male vs. female, 85
medication for, 70–71, 92
myths about, 2–3
presumed inevitability of, 2, 69, 75
technology vs. human, 59
varying types of, 76
See also "low" desire
Dexter, 111
Dictionnaire des sciences médicales, 85
Dictionnaire encyclopédique des sciences médicales (Fonssagrives), 86
diet culture, 2
discomfort/disapproval, 28
discrimination. *See* bias/discrimination
disorder
    asexual/autoerotic as presumed, 79
    "frigidity" as, 87
    lack of spontaneous desire as, 76
    "low" desire is not, 82
    non "vanilla" sex as, 88
    sexual desire disorder, 70, 72, 75
    as a social construct, 74
    white patriarchy as defining, 73
Doctor Teller's Pocket Companion, or Marriage Guide: Being a Popular Treatise on the Anatomy and Physiology of the Genital Organs, in Both Sexes, with Their Uses and Abuses (Teller), 152–153
Doyle, Arthur Conan, 111
drug users, 118
DSM-5, 165
DSM-IV-TR, 70, 75

E

eating habits, 46
education
    on asexuality, 151, 169–170
    change of worldview via, 18–19
    on differing desire, 82
Ein Weib? Psychologisch-biographische: Studie über eine Konträrsexuelle (Trosse), 154
"El Mundo Zurdo" (Anzaldúa), 39

Ellis, Havelock, 15, 91
emancipation, 14
emotions
    ace people as "emotionless," 25, 112, 115–117
    freedom and singleness, 145
    strategic, 116
empathy, 19
entitlement to sex, 8–9
environmental factors, sex and, 3
epistemic injustice, 21
eugenicists, 14
exoticization, 28
experience, personal, 18
Eynon, Dr., 89

F

family
    as "adulthood," 63
    Black, 64
    definition of "nuclear," 63–64
    economics and, 60–61
    "ideal," 48
Fanon, Frantz, 120
fantasy, racial, 123–124
FDA, 71
fear, 24, 178
The Female-Impersonators (Werther), 157
female sexual interest/arousal disorder (FSAD), 70, 77, 83, 92
femininity
    as awakened by virility, 89–90
    Black women and, 98–99
    in queer relations, 30
feminism
    "frigidity" as evidence of, 90–91
    "masculine" women as threat to, 102
    non-reproductive doom of, 100
    threat to white men, 100–101
Feminism (Walsh), 100, 156
Feminism Is for Everybody: Passionate Politics (hooks), 177
Ferguson, Roderick, 13, 64

fetishization
    of the Black phallus, 125–126
    of lesbians, 31
    of queer people, 32
    of race and sexual politics, 129
fiction
    awakening by "virility" in, 89
    Bond series, 109–112
    Butler, Octavia E., 147
    Selah and the Spades, 114–117
"fixing" ace people, 80–82
Fleming, Ian, 109
Floyd, George, 127
fluctuation/variability, 4–5
Fonssagrives, Jean-Baptiste, 86
food, sex and, 1
Franklin, Lonnie, 117–118
Freedmen's Bureau, 14
freedom
    BlackFreedomSex, 178, 179
    Ianna Hawkins Owen on, 170
    practicing ancestral, 180
    sexual, 79–80
    See also liberation
Freedom, Grace B., 180
Freeman, Elizabeth, 45, 60, 61, 66
Freud, Sigmund, 87
Fricker, Miranda, 21
"friend zone," 22
"frigidity"
    as affront to gender binary, 91
    asexuality as, 92
    as civil threat, 91
    history of, 83–92
    as insufficient female pleasure, 86–87
    males as "awakening," 89–90
    medical treatment for, 88
    as psychological issue, 85
frigidity, 82
Frigidity: An Intellectual History (Cryle and Moore), 84
Frigidity in Women in Relation to Her Love Life (Stekel), 90, 157
From Russia with Love (Fleming), 109

G

G, testimonials of, 175, 176
GameStop debacle, 55–57
Garnier, Pierre, 85, 88
gatekeeping, 37–38
Gay and Lesbian Alliance Against Defamation, 165
Gay Dealer, 159
Gay Liberation Front, 159
gender accelerationism, 99
The Gender Accelerationist Manifesto, 99
gender binary
    ace/lesbian resistance to, 107
    Black women and, 98–99
    defying, 146–147
    doomed challenges to, 100
    "frigidity" and, 90–91, 92
    lateral aggression and, 38
    performance roles, 95–97, 101
    policing borders of, 95
    and reproductive labor, 99
    sexuality and, 86
    sexualized pressure of, 175
    transgressing the, 100–103
    as white invention, 97
gender identity
    among nonwhite people, 97–99
    and bathroom use, 32
    expanding, 176
    genital difference, 14–15
    lateral aggression and, 38
    as nonsexual, 97
    in queer relations, 30
    sexual scripts informing, 10
    traditional role endorsement, 27
gender non-conforming people
    corrective rape of, 22–23
    pregnancy issues, 62–63
    social oppression of, 9
    See also queer people/queerness
gender wage gap, 64
General Social Survey, 57

genitalia
    questions about trans, 31–32
    utility of female, 85–86
Get Out, 126
Getz, Barbara, 160
"Girlhood Interrupted: The Erasure of
    Black Girls' Childhood" (Georgetown
    Law), 50
Goldfinger (Fleming), 110
Goldfinger, Auric, 110
Gordon, Lewis, 15
grant money for LGBTQIA+ people, 169
Gregory IX, Pope, 84
Griffith, D. W., 126
Grim Sleeper, 117–118
growth, 19
Gupta, Kristina, 7
Guyot, Jules, 86

H

Haley, Sarah, 98
Hargons, Candice N., 19
Harlem Renaissance, 138
harassment, 28, 104
Harris, Malcolm, 65
Haslam, Nick, 112, 114
The Hateful Eight, 126
health care system
    conversion therapy in, 78, 88
    gender-affirming, 32
    misogyny in, 73, 77
    relationship of asexuals to, 74–75
    warnings about asexuality, 152–153
healthism, 81
*The Heart of Whiteness: Normal Sexuality
    and Race in America* (Carter), 46
"helping" asexual women, 79–80
Hennegan, Alison, 160
Heresies, 161
heteronormativity
    and ace villains, 111
    and Black repression, 13–14
    compulsory sexuality and, 9
    in queer relations, 30

"The Heteronormativity Theory of Low
    Sexual Desire in Women Partnered
    with Men," 69
"The Heteronormativity Theory of Low
    Sexual Desire in Women Partnered
    with Men," 72, 77
heterosexuality
    capitalist basis for, 46–47
    compulsory, 103, 104
    "correction" toward, 79–80, 88
    demonizing pleasure beyond, 87–88
    "low" women's desire and, 77–78
    performing, 77–78, 95–96
    as presumed asexual default, 35–36
    as socially compulsory, 49
    "woman"/"man" roles in, 95–97, 99
    women's subpar experience with, 87
hierarchy of trauma, 33–39
Hirschfeld, Magnus, 154, 155, 156, 157
history of asexuality, 151–166
    See also "frigidity"
Hodson, Gordon, 25, 26, 28, 33, 38, 112
Holmes, Sherlock, 111
The Homosexuality of Men and Women
    (Hirschfeld), 156
hooks, bell, 29, 177
Howard, Dr. William Lee, 125
Hughes, Langston, 137–138, 139,
    149, 150
human needs model, 113–114
humanness, 112, 114
hunger, for Black flesh, 51–53
Hurlburt, Russell T., 17
hypersexualization
    asexuality and, 132
    of Black girls, 22
    of Jezebel, 136
    myth of Black, 11, 13, 106, 120
    myth of lesbian, 31
    myth of nonwhite, 91
    of queerness, 31
hypoactive sexual desire disorder
    (HSDD), 70, 77, 83, 92
hysteria, 86

I

identity
   ace as queer, 30
   allosexual, 20
   ambiguous, 147–148
   challenges to ace, 44
   and label for asexuality, 151
   need to name, 20
   removing trauma from queer, 34
   and right for self-definition, 6
   servitude of, xi
   sexual, 119
   variable sexual, 19
   See also gender identity
imagining new realities, 177–180
impossibility
   of asexual women, 79
   asexuality as presumed, 21, 37
   as beyond your experience,
      18–19
   of the Black asexual, 53, 121
impossibles, love letter to, 177–180
impotence, 85
impulse control, 2
incels, 8–9, 57
inclusivity of queerness, 10
Indigenous peoples
   eating habits of, 46
   of North Carolina, 16
infantilization, 25, 43–44, 51
Informulary, 71
injustice, epistemic, 21
Institute for Policy Studies, 65
internal monologues, 17
International Asexual Conference, 165
International Gay and Lesbian
   Archives, 138
intersex people, 38, 179
invalidation, 29
invisibility
   of ace people, 6, 29–30, 36, 148
   of asexual women, 79
   of Black asexuals, 173

lesbian, 103
violence and, 29

J

Jackson, Zakiyyah Iman, 98, 106, 118,
   120–121
Jade, 173
Jay, David, 163
Jezebel, 11–12, 16, 131, 132
Johnson, Myra T., 6, 78, 79, 160
Johnson. Virginia E., 76
Joran, Théodore, 89
joy, asexual, 170

K

Kaplan, Helen Singer, 76
Kepner, Jim, 138
Kertbeny, Károly (or Karl) Mária, 153
*Kids These Days: Human Capital
   and the Making of Millennials*
   (Harris), 65
King, Rodney, 117
Kinsey, Alfred, 157–158
Kinsey Scale, 157–158, 161
KKK, 119
Klebb, Rosa, 109
knowing
   conflict and, xii
   embracing unknowables, 179
   epistemic injustice, 21
Kobaly, Catherine, 161
Krykit, 174
Kujichagulia, xii

L

LA riots, 117
lateral aggression, 38
Lavender Woman, 160
LaVey, Anton Szandor, 158
Le Mensonge du féminisme (Joran), 89
learning new ideas, 18–19
left-handedness, 167–168
"Lesbian Dynamics" (Pollner), 160
Lesbian Masterdoc, 105, 106

lesbians
  and ace experience, 99, 105, 106
  Black, 146
  "curing," 110
  as default category, 148
  hypersexuality myth, 31
  institutional invalidation of, 103
  as not "women," 96, 100
  Octavia Butler as presumed, 141–143
  threat to status quo, 101
lesbophobia, 107
Levy, Jerre, 168
liberation
  from compulsory sexuality, 172
  vs. hierarchical oppression, 38
  from sexual control, 121–122
  from white heteropatriarchy, 172
  white response to Black, 124
  from white supremacy, 169–170
  See also freedom
libido pill, 70–71
The Life of Langston Hughes, Volume II
  (Rampersad), 138
"Listening to Black Women and Girls:
  Lived Experiences of Adultification
  Bias" (Georgetown Law), 50
Lorde, Audre, 17, 39, 178
Los Angeles Police Department
  (LAPD), 117, 118
Love, Hess, xiii
love letter to the "impossibles," 177–180
"low" desire
  conversion therapy for, 78
  as a "disorder," 69, 74
  distress about, 72–73
  as "frigidity," 83–86, 92
  gender and, 77
  healing of distress about, 74
  historical references to, 151–166
  is not a disorder, 82
  pathologizing, 83
  pressure to get beyond, 74–75
  reasons for, in hetero women, 77
  socioeconomic factors, 69–70

  in women, 70–72
  See also "frigidity"
Luciano, Dana, 60
lynching, 125–126

M

MacInnis, Cara C., 25, 26, 28, 33, 38, 112
Maglott, Stephen, 141
male supremacy, 22
Mammy
  apparent asexuality of, 132, 136
  latent sexuality of, 135
  stereotype of, 16, 131, 134
  white women's exploitation of, 133,
    134–135
Mandingo, 16, 125, 126, 127
*Manliness and Civilization: A Cultural
  History of Gender and Race in the
  United States* (Bederman), 95
marginalized groups
  Black asexuals, 13
  compound factors, 26
  dehumanization of, 25–26, 120
  effect of compulsory sexuality on,
    9–10
  financial, 64–65
  studies of, 19
marriage
  annulled for "frigidity," 84, 85
  declines in, 59, 60
  "ideal," 48
*Married Life and Happiness or, Love and
  Comfort in Marriage* (Robinson), 83
Marshall, 175
masculinity, in queer relations, 30
Maslow, Abraham, 113
Masters, William H., 76
"The Master's Tools Will Never
  Dismantle the Master's House"
  (Lorde), 39
Masterson, Jill, 110
masturbation
  historical references, 155
  as immature, 80

maturity
    aces as "immature," 25, 43–44
    heterosexual behavior as, 80
    sex as marker of, 45
Maxxie, 115, 116
McIntyre, Spirit, 180
McWhorter, John, 18
mealtimes, 46
medical industry. *See* health care system
medication for desire, 70–71, 92
medicine, necessary, xii–xiii
men
    "frigidity" as corrected by, 89–90
    hypoactive sexual desire in, 70
    interracial porn for, 124
    "manly," 101–102
    as penetrator/dominator, 99
    sex as owed to, 9, 103, 104
    social power of white, 100–101, 104
    socially conditioned response to, 105
    women's "responsibility" to, 57
    See also cisheteropatriarchy
"Mental Health Implications of Sexual
    Orientation" (Nurius), 161
mental health issues
    "frigidity" as, 85
    microaggressions and, 27–28
Mercuriale, Girolamo, 85
microaggressions, 27
Mik, 174
millennials, exploitation of, 65–66
Mills, Charles W., 15, 52, 65, 131
misogynoir, 22, 107, 145, 146, 175
misogyny
    acephobic violence and, 22
    in medicine, 73
    misogynoir, 22, 107, 145, 175
    racial issues, 107
"Misreading Mammy: Towards a Sexual
    Revolution of Contemporary/Third
    Wave Black Feminisms" (Carr), 133

money
    Black family finances, 64–65
    exploitation of millennials, 65–66
    gender wage gap, 64–65
    parental leave, 63
    reproduction and, 61–62
    sex and, 56–57, 66
    sex deficits and, 59, 60
monosexuals, 153
Moore, Alison, 84, 89, 90, 92
morality
    about food, 1–2
    of sex as "human," 119
Morgan, Dexter, 111
Morris, Wendy, 48
Morrison, Toni, 1
murder, 117
Murdock, George, 63
Murphy, Harry, 139
"My Life as an Amoeba" (O'Reilly), 163
myths
    about Black people, 2, 106
    about lack of sex, 87
    about sex and desire, 2–3
    chrononormativity, 47
    "frigidity" awakened by "virility,"
        89–90
    gender and queer relations, 30
    of "insufficient" asexual trauma, 33
    Mammy, 133–134
    racist pornographic, 123–124
    of "savage" Black sexuality, 10, 11–12

N

Nagoski, Emily, 76
narratives, "frigidity," 89–90
National LGBT Survey, 27, 78
"The Negro as a Distinct Ethnic Factor in
    Civilization" (Howard), 125
negrophobia, 119
"neutrals," 154

new ideas, 18–19
NHI (no humans involved), 117, 118
No Mercy Here: Gender, Punishment, and the Making of Jim Crow Modernity (Haley), 98
"'No New Watchword': Asexuality, Incarceration, and Freedom" (Owen), 170
nonmonogamy, 47
nonnormative sexuality, "threat" of, 101–102, 152
nonwhite people
    as "children," 47
    "frigidity" among, 91
    and the gender binary, 95, 97–99
    Indigenous peoples, 16, 46
    sexualization of, 124
    See also Black people
"normal"
    Black asexuals as failing, 121
    white cisheteropatriarchy as defining, 73
normative chronology. *See* chrononormativity
"normative" sexuality
    abandoning singular view of, 171
    ace experience as outside, 40
    ace lens on, 77–78
    aces as transgressive to, 4, 28, 40
    author's use of term, 6
    control via, 121–122
    "correction" toward, 80–81
    desire as innate to, 75–76
    medical industry ideas about, 78
    myths about, 2–3
    Octavia Butler as defying, 146–147
    performing, 86, 95–97
    personal experience as, 19
    power and, 99
    questioning, 106
    See also cisheteronormativity

norms, presumed, 17–18
North Carolina HB2 Bathroom Bill of 2016, 32
Nurius, Paula, 161

O

Ojwang, Melanie, 115
On Her Majesty's Secret Service (Fleming), 110
"On the Racialization of Asexuality" (Owen), 11, 130
online dating, 176
oppression
    interlocking web of, 22
    and policing of borders, 37–38
    via the status quo, 100
O'Reilly, Zoe, 163
orgasm gap, 87
Origins of Sexuality and Homosexuality (Dececco and Shively), 162
Orlando, Lisa, 5, 159, 171
oversexualization, 31, 32
Owen, Ianna Hawkins, 11, 13, 130, 131, 170

P

Paloma, 115, 116
parental leave, 63
pathologization, sexual
    heteropatriarchal, 93
    historical, of ace people, 151–159
    lack of female orgasm, 87
    LGBTQIA+ microaggressions, 28
    of "low" female desire, 79, 82
    of nonreproductive behavior, 92
    of "perversions," 88
    of women, 84
patriarchal domesticity, 64
patriarchy. *See* cisheteropatriarchy
Peele, Jordan, 126

penises
Black people as, 120
Black phallus fantasy, 123, 125–126
sex as "receipt" of, 85
Penn, Donna, 100
phallocentricity, 58, 87
phobias, 24, 38
"pink Viagra," 71–72
policing borders, 37–38, 95
politics
in acephobia, 27
chronobiopolitics, 60
desirability politics, 57
exclusion vs. community, 39
race and sexual politics, 129
radicalism and sexuality, 174–175
Pollner, Fran, 160
population management, 60
porn
Black Lives Matter, 128
Black male fantasies in, 124, 125–126
increased access to, 59
lesbian, 31
power and hetero, 106
racist, 123–124
Pornhub, 123, 127, 128
"Possible Reasons US Adults Are Not
Having Sex as Much as They Used To"
(Twenge), 48
pregnancy
among nonwhite or queer people,
62–63
pronatalism, 62
unplanned, 61
prejudice. *See* discrimination
pride flag, 164
privilege, of normative sexuality, 3
productivity
life timeline of, 61
sex as, 66
pronatalism, 62
Prosperity Now, 65
Przybylo, Ela, 165–166
psychological disorders, 75, 156

*Psychopathia Sexualis: With Especial
Reference to the Antipathic Sexual
Instinct, a Medico-Forensic Study* (von
Krafft-Ebing), 155
psychopathic characters, 111
punishment, 50
"Punks, Bulldaggers and Welfare
Queens: The Radical Potential of
Queer Politics" (Cohen), 9
purity culture
and erasing Black women's sexuality,
134–135
and rape of Black girls, 50–51
sex as presumed in, 2, 119
whiteness and, 124

Q

Quaestiones medico legales (Zacchia), 85
queer exclusionists, 35–36
queer people/queerness
ace exclusion from, 30, 35–38
ambiguous, 147–148
asexuality as, 10, 29, 39–41, 103
beyond trauma, 34
biographies of, 141
Black "savagery" and, 15
celebrating, 179
community of, 39, 40–41
and compulsory heterosexuality, 49
corrective rape of, 22–23
defined, 29
dehumanization of, 25–26
"deviant" genitalia and, 14
grant money for, 169
and hierarchy of trauma, 34
historical references to, 151–166
interrogating icons, 140
kinship among, 107
of Langston Hughes, 138
life timeline of, 47–49
love letter to, 177–180
mental health issues, 27–28
as multidimensional, 40–41
as not "adult," 47

oversexualization of, 31
repression of Black, 13–14
sociosexual liberation via, 96–97
spirituality of, xi–xii
and temporal expectation, 45
white vs. Black, 13, 14, 15–16
queer sex
gender myths about, 30
supporting autonomy of, 32–33
voyeuristic inquiries about, 31
Queering the Color Line: Race and the Invention of Homosexuality in American Culture (Somerville), 14
queerphobia, 33

R

race suicide, 91
Racial Contract, 52, 53
The Racial Contract (Mills), 15, 52, 65, 131
racism
contradictions of, 52–53
corrective rape and, 23
as fuel for acephobia, 22
and the gender binary, 95
as heteronormative, 47
medical, 62
in popular culture, 124
on Pornhub, 128
racialization of bodies, 14
racist violence, 10
as sexual, 121–126
sexual scripts informing, 10
radical politics, 174–175
Rampersad, Arnold, 138, 139, 149
rape
and focus on the Black phallus, 125–126
of Mammy, 134
statutory, 50–51
See also sexual violence
rape culture
acephobia's roots in, 22
allosexual complicity in, 25

compulsory sexuality and, 8–9
Raymond, Janice, 103
reality, envisioning a new, 177–180
reconstruction, 119
Reddit, 55–57
rejecting new ideas, 18–19
relationships
aromantic people and, 6
asexual, 170–171
compulsory coupling, 48
decline in young adult, 60
gender in queer, 30
myths about sex in, 3
rape within, 23
sex lens on, 32
reproduction
compulsory sexuality and, 67
Coronavirus Baby Bust, 61–62, 70
division of labor, 99
and doom of feminist ideals, 100
pathologizing absence of, 92
research, sex, 19
response cycle, sexual, 76
Rich, Adrienne, 103, 105
Riolan, Dr., 88
rites of passage, 47
Robinson, Dr. William Josephus, 83, 91
Rohleder, Hermann Oscar, 155
romantic partners
"frigidity" as dissolved by male, 89–90
presumption of sexual interest, 174
rape by, 23
Rothblum, Esther D., 163
Roubaud, Félix, 87
r/WallStreetBets, 55, 56, 57

S

Sánchez, Tomás, 84
Sappho und Sokrates (Sappho and Socrates) (Hirschfeld), 154
The Satanic Bible (LaVey), 159
satanism, 159

"savage" sexuality
  myth of Black, 10, 11–12
  overtaking of white culture by, 91
  queerness and Black, 15
savior complex, 22
Schalk, Sami, 142, 143, 144, 146
Schlegel, Carl, 155
Schwartz, Lisa M., 71
Selah and the Spades, 114, 120
self-determination, xii
selling short, 55
sensuality, asexual, xii
service, identity as, xi
sex
  ace boundaries around, 23–24
  as activist tool, 130
  as "adulthood," 63
  for the asexual person, 5–6
  asexuals as urged toward, 74–75
  capitalist system and, 56–57
  changing definitions of, 58–59
  during COVID-19 pandemic, 61–62
  criminalization of Black, 119
  eroticism of black/white, 126
  historical definitions of, 85
  as "human," 118
  as lens on queerness, 30, 33
  penetrative penis-vagina, 87, 88
  as presumed core of life, 43
  "productive," 66
  queer, 30, 31, 32–33
  as a "right" owed, 22
  sexual response cycle, 76
  social expectation of, 8–10, 23
  virginity loss, 44
  as weapon against Black people, 11
  youthful postponement of, 48,
    57–59
sex education, 19
sex recession, 57–59, 60, 70
sex work, 56, 118
sexual aversion disorder (SAD), 75
Sexual Behavior in the Human Female
  (Kinsey), 158
Sexual Behavior in the Human Male
  (Kinsey), 157
sexual dysfunction
  contemporary understanding of, 84
  diagnoses of, 70
  "frigidity," 92
  medication for, 72
  physiological vs. psychological, 85
  as a social construct, 74
  women as responsible for men's, 84
"sexual revolution" of the 1970s, 79
sexual violence
  against ace people, 8
  complicity in cycle of, 25
  control and abuse via, 11
  dehumanization and, 26
  by incels, 9
  oversexualization of queers and, 31
  savior complex in, 22
  slavery and, 11–12, 50
  against women, 8
  See also rape
sexuality
  challenging worldview about, 18–19
  and gender binary roles, 86
  gender identity and, 97
  in human needs model, 113–114
  intersection of Blackness with, xii, 11
  of Langston Hughes, 137–140
  myths about, 2–3, 106
  non-normative relationship to, 2
  performing hetero, 77–78, 95–96
  as presumed innate, 75, 113
  purity culture and, 2
  "savage," 10
  as white supremacist utility, 130–131
shame, 2, 138
Sherlock, 112
Shively, Michael, 162
shorting stock, 55
Simon Fraser University, 165
single people, 145
"Singles in Society and in Science"
  (Bella and Morris), 48

singlism
and compulsory coupling, 48
discriminatory, 26
happiness and purpose of, 144–145
Sky Data, 20
slavery, chattel
justification of sexual violence and, 11–12
legacy of, 51
post-emancipation heteronormativity, 14
racial wage gap, 65
sexual "uncivility" and justification for, 132–133
sexual violence in, 50
white women's complicity with, 133–135
social dominance orientation, 26, 27
social expectation
ace as outside, 40
acephobia and, 27
of Black females, failing, 106–107
of Black men, 175
chrononormativity, 45–46, 47
of cisheteronormative compliance, 36
compulsory sexuality as, 8–9
"frigidity" vs., 91
for hetero women, 77, 87
to maintain status quo, 100–101
"man"/"woman" roles in, 96–97, 101–102
nonnormative sexuality vs., 152
of normative sexuality, 105
of pre-marriage sex, 45
of sex as a "right" owed, 22, 23
sex/coupling timeline, 48–49
socialization, 104–107
sociopaths, 112
Somerville, Siobhan B., 14
SONDA (Sexual Orientation Non-Discrimination Act), 163
spectrum of asexuality, 5
spirituality of queerness, xi–xii
spontaneous desire, 76

Sprout Pharmaceuticals, 71, 72
status quo, 100
Stekel, Wilhelm, 90, 91, 157
stereotypes, sexual
of "animalistic" Black people, 120
and Black consent, 11
of Black girls, 50
interrogating racist, 171–172
Jezebel, 11–12, 131
Mammy, 16, 131
stigma, virgin, 44
Storms, Michael D., 161
"straight passing," 35, 36
"The Straight Mind" (Wittig), 96
Summers, Selah, 114

T

Tales of the Grim Sleeper, 118
Tardieu, Auguste Ambroise, 89
Tayler, John Lionel, 101, 103
T'Challa, Anthony, 176
technology, 59
Teller, Dr. J., 152
terminology for asexuality, 151, 152
terrorism, white, 119
"Theories of Sexual Orientation" (Storms), 161
threats, 28, 100–103
Three Squares: The Invention of the American Meal (Carroll), 46
Thunderball (Fleming), 110
Time Binds: Queer Temporalities, Queer Histories (Freeman), 45
"Toward a Conceptual Understanding of Asexuality" (Bogaert), 164
trans people
acknowledging the wisdom of, 179
article on liberation of, 159
discrimination against, 32, 103
pregnancy issues, 62–63
voyeuristic inquiries about, 31–32
The Transsexual Empire: The Making of the She-Male (Raymond), 103
transgression, gender, 100–103

transphobia, 38
"The Transformation of Silence into
    Language and Action" (Lorde), 178
Transvestia, 158
trauma
    COVID-19 pandemic, 63
    presumed hierarchy of, 33–39
    queer identity beyond, 41
    reckoning with sexual, 174
Trosse, Emma, 153, 154
Troutman, Tea, 119, 120
truths, presumed, 18
Twenge, Jean M., 48
"2018 Tracking Report: Lesbian,
    Gay, Bisexual, Transgender,
    and Queer Grantmaking by
    U.S. Foundations," 169

U

understanding
    allosexual misunderstanding, 21
    Black asexuality, xi–xii
    compulsory sexuality, 74
    of relationship via sex, 32
    "usefulness" of sexuality, xi–xii
United States
    individualistic society, 65
    living conditions in, 62
    parental leave, 63
    population levels, 61
unwanted sex, 3
U.S. Supreme Court, 158
utility
    asexuality and, xi–xii
    of female genitalia, 85–86
    reproductive, 67
    sex as, 10–11
    of sex as "human," 119
    of sex for white supremacy, 123
    sexual-political, 129

V

"vanilla" sex, 88
victimization, of women, 8

The Village Voice, 13
Villainous Aromantic Asexual trope, 111
violence
    acephobic, 21–22
    against Black people, 118
    against Black trans women, 32
    dismissal of, 117–118
    gender as product of, 98
    identity beyond, 41
    lynching, 125–126
    of white women against
        Mammy, 133
Virey, Julien-Joseph, 85
virginity
    loss, 44
    rape and, 50–51
virility, 89, 98
Virtual Asexual Pride, 166
voice, inner, 17–18
"Voice Memos for the Void," 115
von Krafft-Ebing, Richard Freiherr, 155
von Schrenck-Notzing, Albert, 88

W

Walker, Alice, 167
Wall Street, 55–57
Walsh, Correa Moylan, 100, 103, 156
Washington, Chris, 126
Werther, Ralph, 157
White, MD, William A., 155
white people
    complicity of white women, 134
    desire for Black flesh, 51–53
    "frigidity" as problem of, 91
    queer, vs. Black queers, 15–16
    sexual/political control by, 129
    willful misunderstanding, 52–53
white supremacy
    as anti-asexual, 13
    asexual/feminist threat to, 100–101
    Black asexuals and, 16, 121, 136
    Black sexuality as supporting, 133
    chrononormativity and, 51
    and consumption of Blacks, 130

culture of, 9–10
exclusivity to reassert, 15–16
in film, 126
gender binary and, 95
as heteronormative, 46–47
intentional misrepresentation
    of, 131
and legacy of slavery, 51–52
liberation from, 13, 28, 169–170, 171
and Mammy's dehumanization, 135
myths of Black libido, 11–12
NHI as end point of, 118
objectification of Black bodies, 15
and the promotion of childbirth, 62
reactionary rhetoric, 124
as a sexual fantasy, 123–124
utilizing sex for, 10–11, 130–131
white terrorism, 119
whiteness
    and asexual-as-ideal, 132
    as "civilized," 95
    and cuckold fantasy, 124
    as exclusive space, 16
    gender binary as invention of, 97
    negrophobia and, 119
    as "normal," 51
    queer, 13
Whitney, Ev'Yan, 74, 80, 81–82, 173
WHO Global Alcohol Action Plan, 2022-
    2030, 62
Williams, Eric, 46
Williams Institute, 73
Wittig, Monique, 96, 97, 99
Woloshin, Steve, 71
"womanhood," 97

women
    asexual, 78–79, 102
    "civilized," 95
    defined, 8
    "frigidity" in, 83–90, 92
    harassment of, 104
    lesbians as not, 96, 100
    low sexual desire in, 70–72, 77
    orgasm gap for, 87
    role in the gender binary, 95–97
    sex as expected of, 73, 103
    social conditioning of, 105–106
    sociosexual control of, 83, 93, 99
    stereotypes of Black, 11–12
    "threat" of Black man to white,
        125–126
    victimization of, 8
    white, vs. Mammy, 134–135
    "womanly," 101–102, 107
Woodard, Vince, 51
workers, exploitation of, 65–66, 67
worldview-challenging information,
    18–19
Wynter, Sylvia, 117

Y

young people
    current financial statistics, 65
    postponement of sex by, 57–59
"Your Own Label" (Getz), 160
Youth Risk Behavior Survey, 57

Z

Zacchia, Paolo, 85

About the Author

SHERRONDA J. BROWN is a Southern-grown essayist, editor, and storyteller with a focus on media analysis and cultural critique. They have devoted much of their work to writing and thinking about asexuality, hoping to push conversations beyond what is familiar and comfortable in order to make new interventions about a topic and identity that has been long misunderstood.

About North Atlantic Books

North Atlantic Books (NAB) is an independent, nonprofit publisher committed to a bold exploration of the relationships between mind, body, spirit, and nature. Founded in 1974, NAB aims to nurture a holistic view of the arts, sciences, humanities, and healing. To make a donation or to learn more about our books, authors, events, and newsletter, please visit www.northatlanticbooks.com.